I0762364

The Art of Simz

3dtotalPublishing

3dtotal Publishing

Correspondence: publishing@3dtotal.com
Website: 3dtotal.com

First published in the United Kingdom, 2023, by 3dtotal Publishing.

Address: 3dtotal.com Ltd,
29 Foregate Street, Worcester
WR1 1DS, United Kingdom.

Hard cover ISBN: 978-1-912843-72-5

Printed and bound in China by
C&C Offset Printing Co., Ltd

Visit 3dtotalpublishing.com for a complete list of available book titles.

Managing Director: Tom Greenway
Studio Manager: Simon Morse
Lead Designer: Joseph Cartwright
Lead Editor: Samantha Rigby
Editorial Project Manager: Rhiannon Joseph

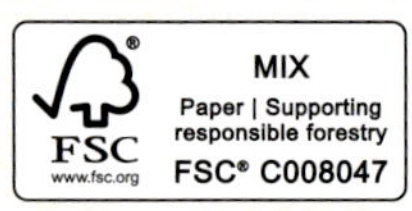

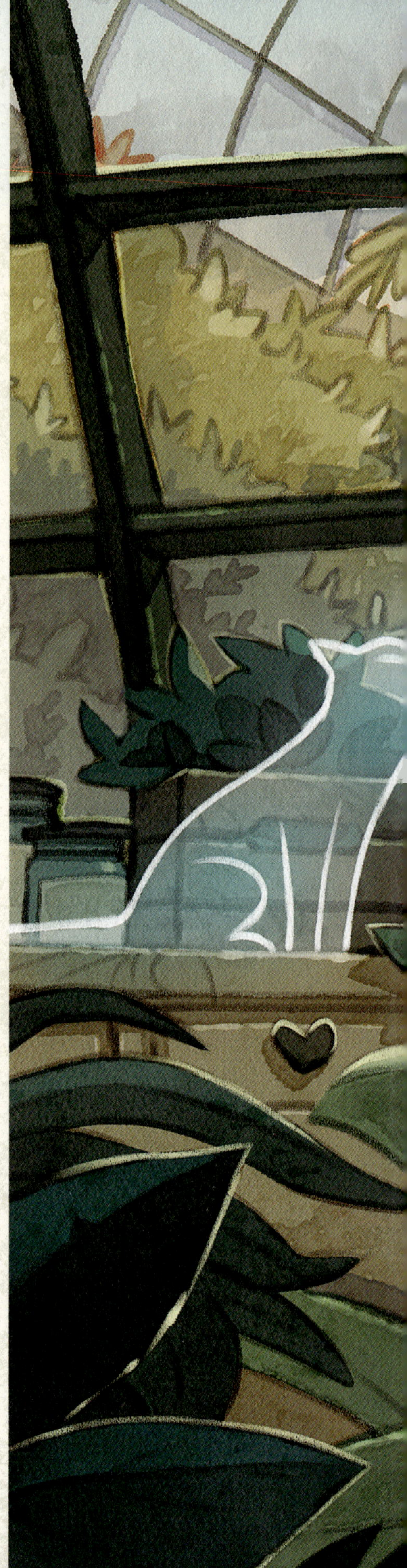

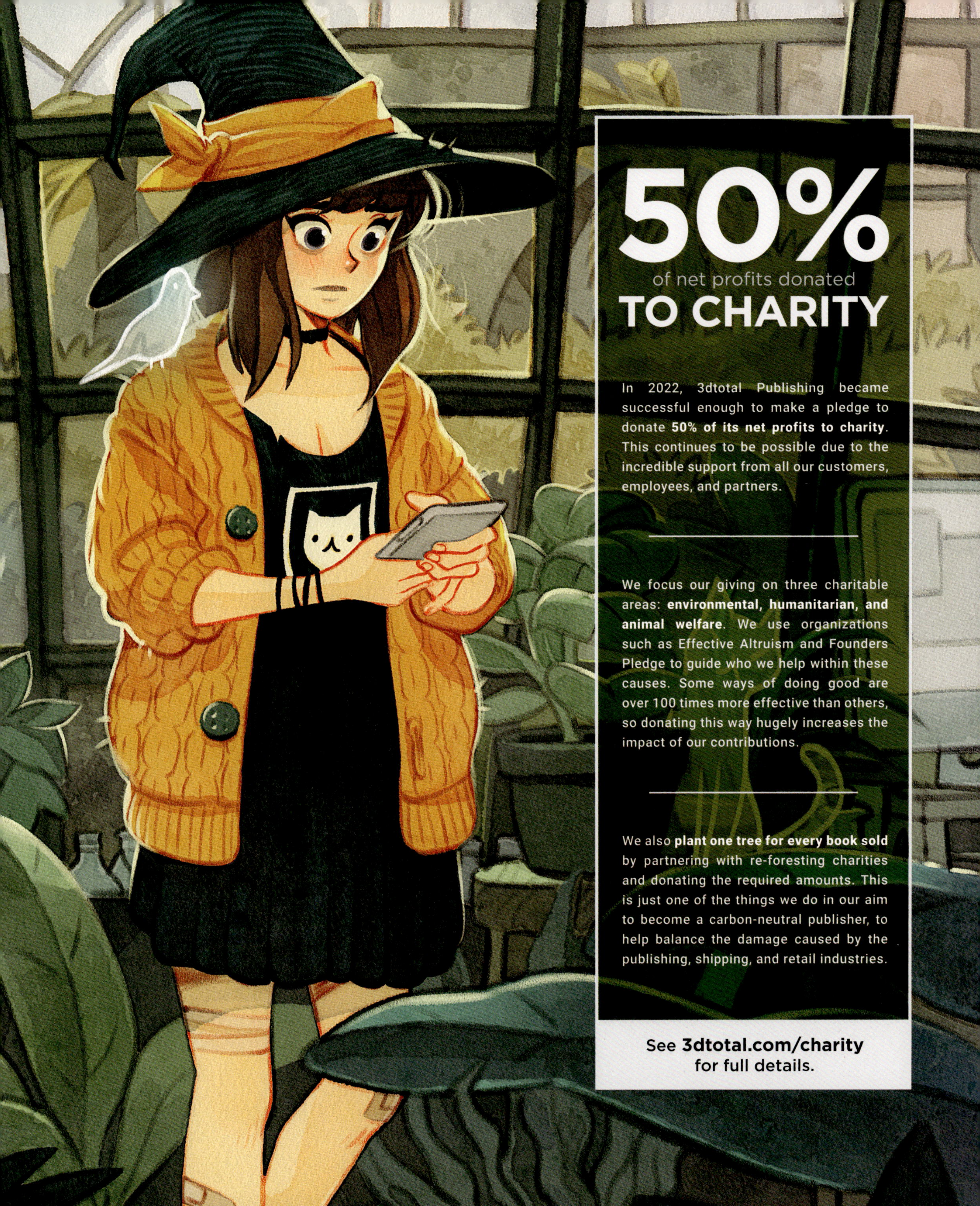
50%
of net profits donated
TO CHARITY
In 2022, 3dtotal Publishing became successful enough to make a pledge to donate 50% of its net profits to charity. This continues to be possible due to the incredible support from all our customers, employees, and partners.
We focus our giving on three charitable areas: environmental, humanitarian, and animal welfare. We use organizations such as Effective Altruism and Founders Pledge to guide who we help within these causes. Some ways of doing good are over 100 times more effective than others, so donating this way hugely increases the impact of our contributions.
We also plant one tree for every book sold by partnering with re-foresting charities and donating the required amounts. This is just one of the things we do in our aim to become a carbon-neutral publisher, to help balance the damage caused by the publishing, shipping, and retail industries.
See 3dtotal.com/charity
for full details.

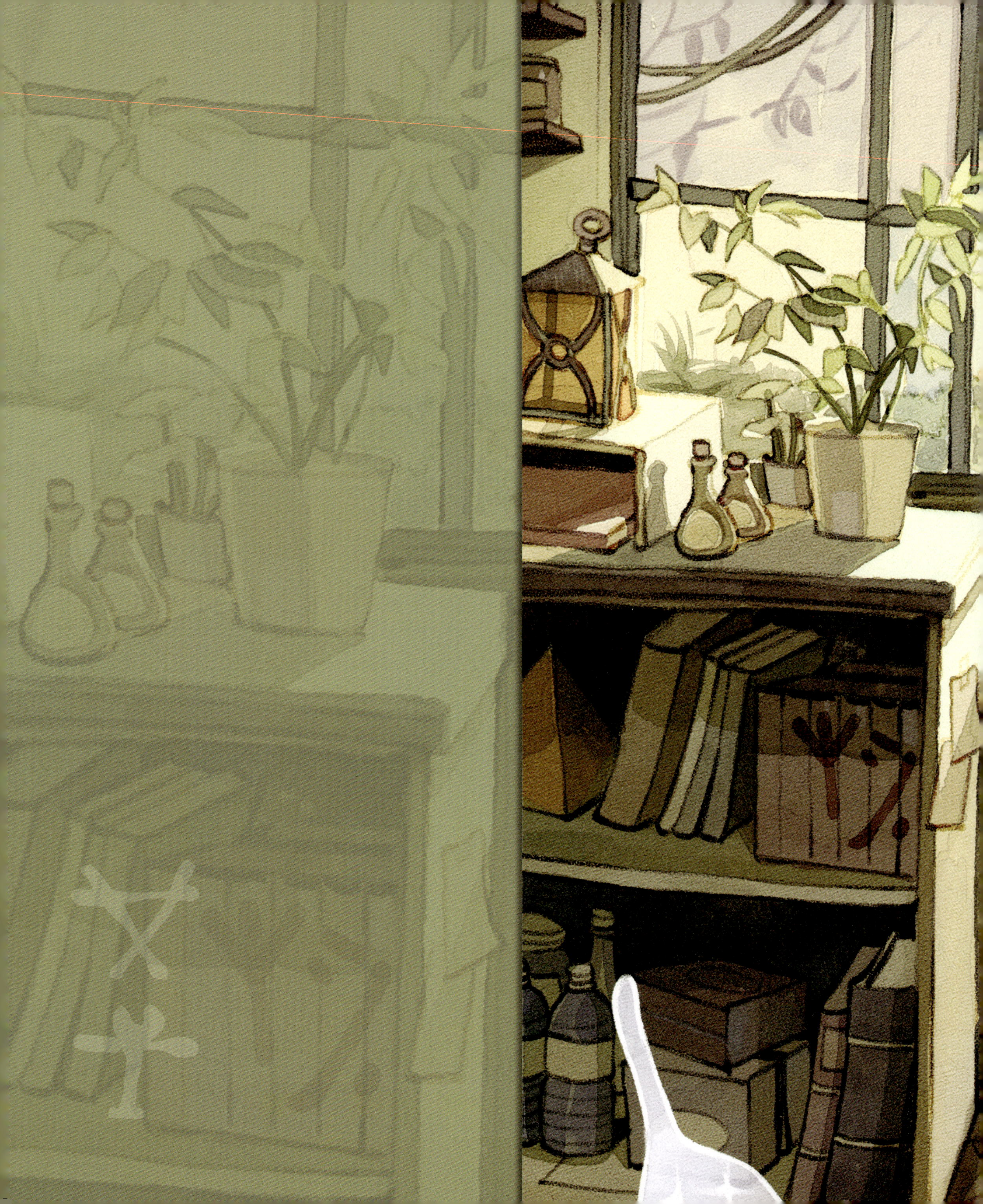

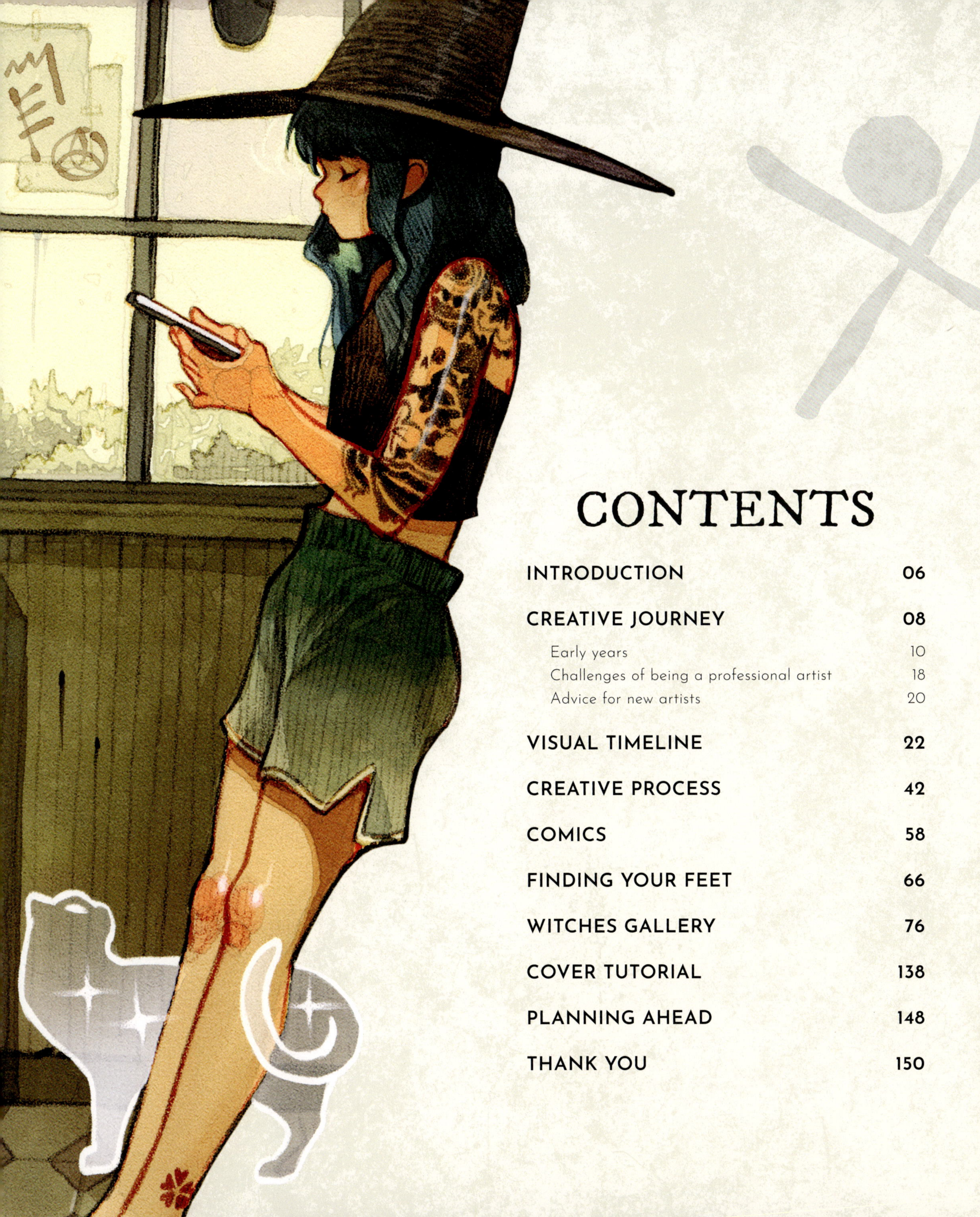

CONTENTS

INTRODUCTION

As a full-time artist, I'm asked many questions about my profession:

'How did you get to this point in your career?'

'When did you go freelance? What's it like?'

My favourite one is, 'Why did you become an artist in the first place?' because the answer is simple: I wanted to share my experiences, and what better way is there to immortalize ideas and inspire others than through an art book?

I've made it my mission to show that, despite the size of a project or quality of an artwork, the most important thing for an artist to consider is their approach. Of course, aesthetics, style, and technical ability are all important aspects, but in the grander scheme, it's really about how much heart, time, and consistency you're willing to dedicate to your craft. For me, that makes the difference between the amateur and professional.

Inside this book, you'll discover the lessons and obstacles I've faced on my career path, figure out how to find your own creative style, and learn all about the tools and techniques I regularly use to create my modern witches and their spectral cat companions.

Although it's my intention for you to feel inspired as you flip through these pages, I hope most of all you feel relief. We've all faced challenges that have made it seem like we're not good enough to continue, but the important thing is to keep going. Whether in big or small amounts, you'll start drawing again, and start believing in your dreams again. Believe me – I've been there! So, if you're just starting out, or you're going through a moment of uncertainty, I hope this book validates your ideas and gives you that boost of inspiration to continue on your journey.

Thank you for coming along on mine!

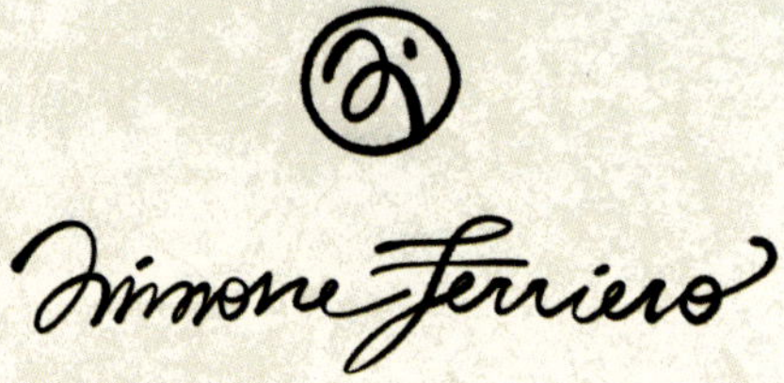

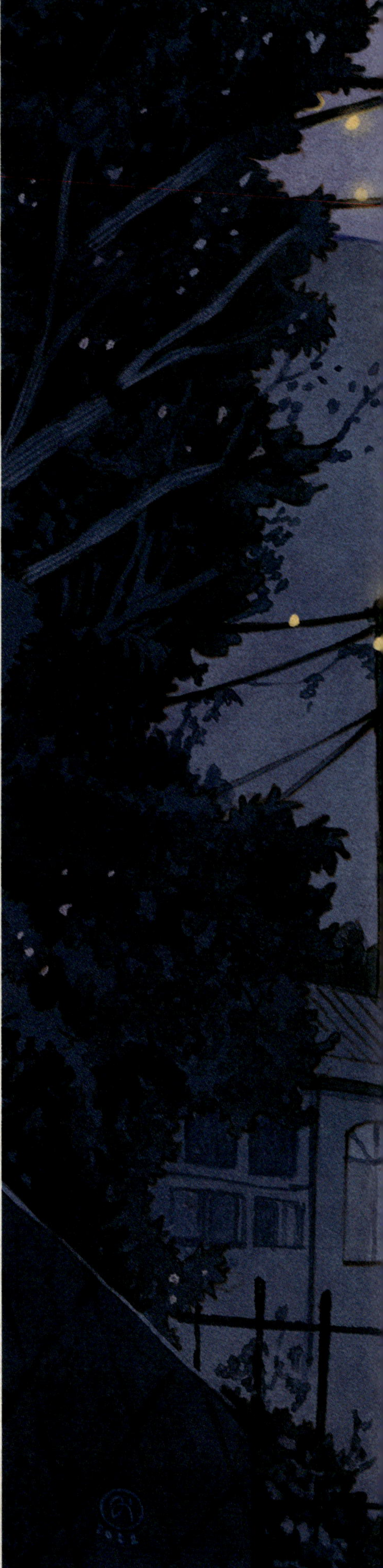

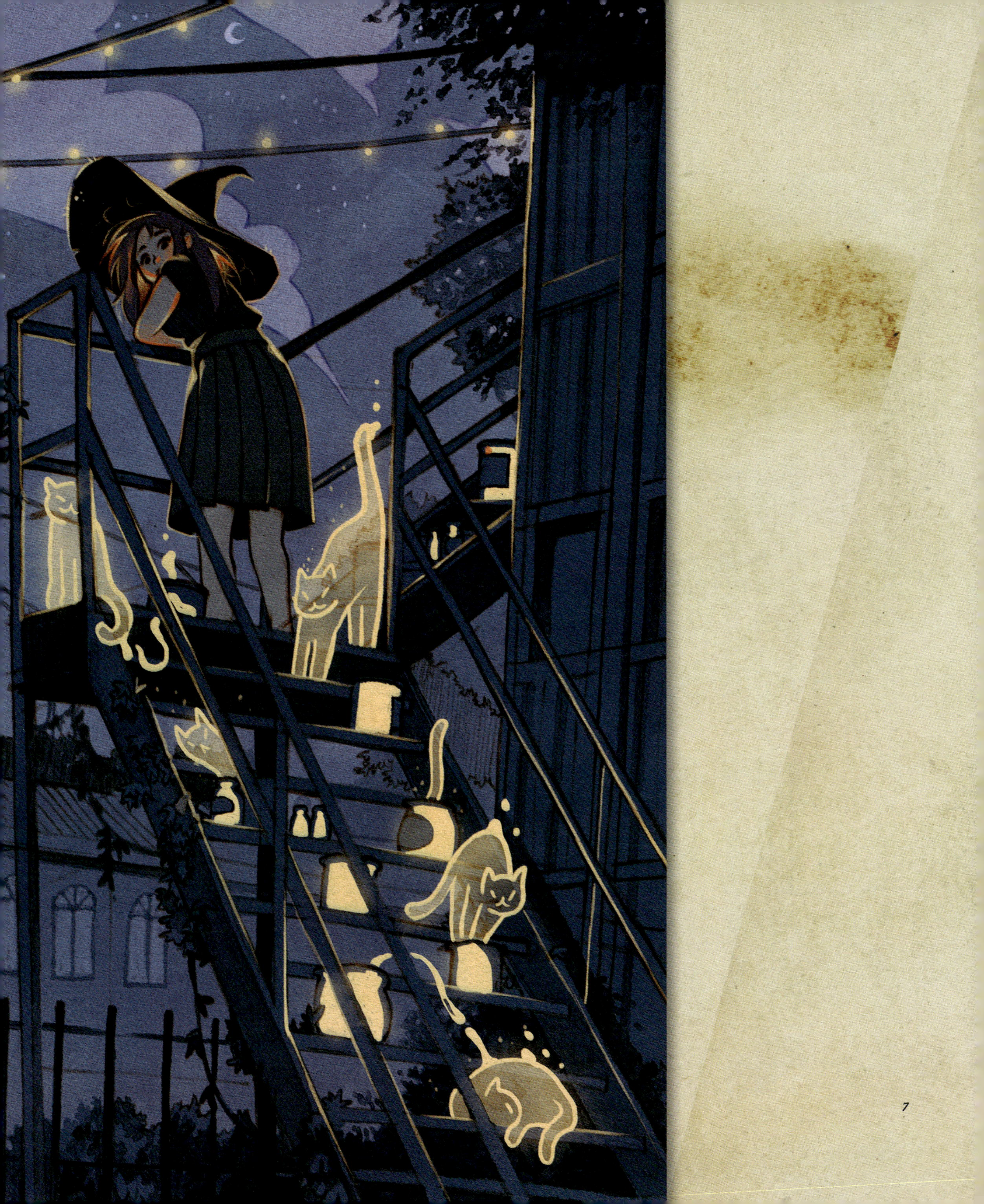

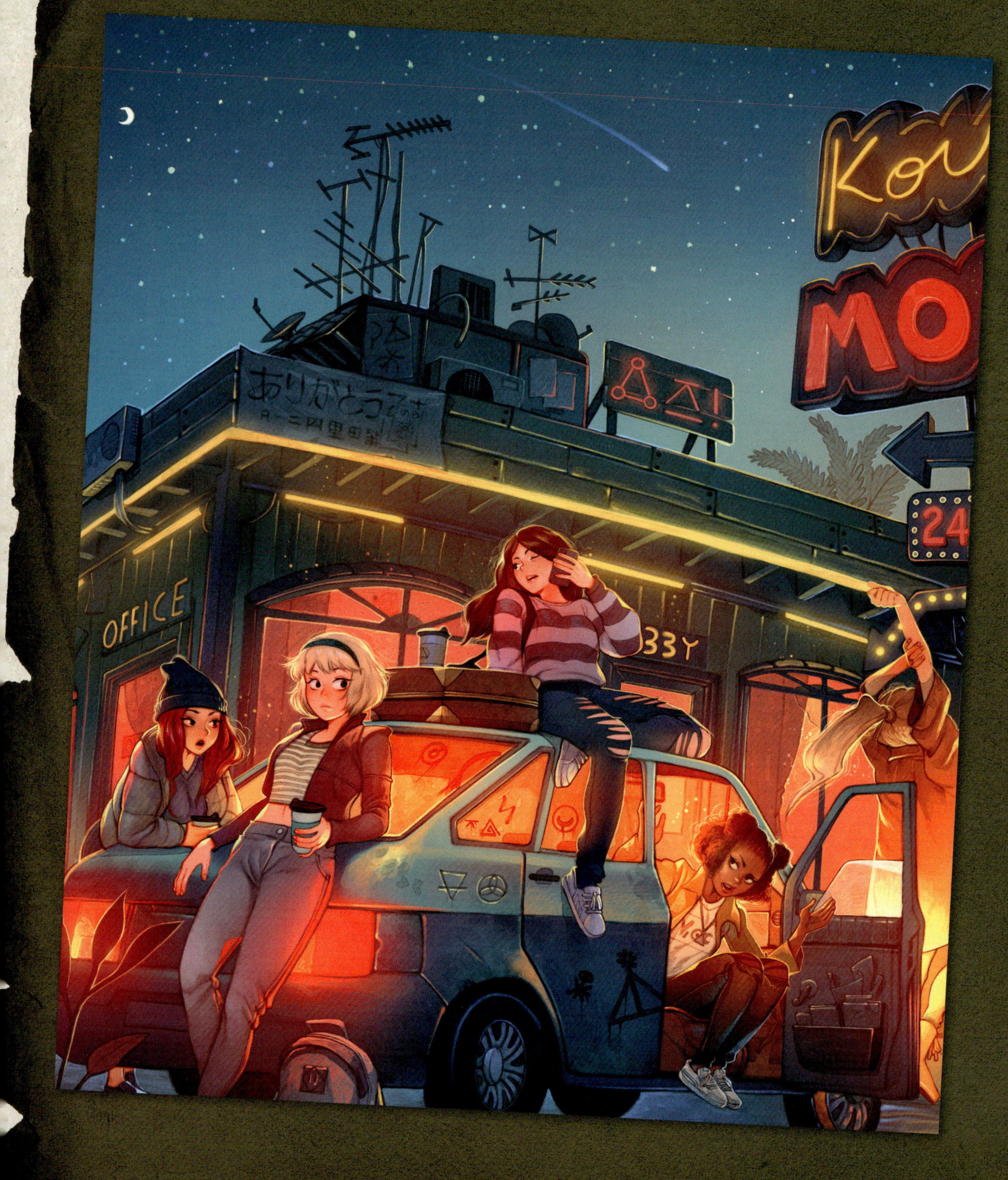
Ko
MO
24
ありがとう
OFFICE

CREATIVE JOURNEY

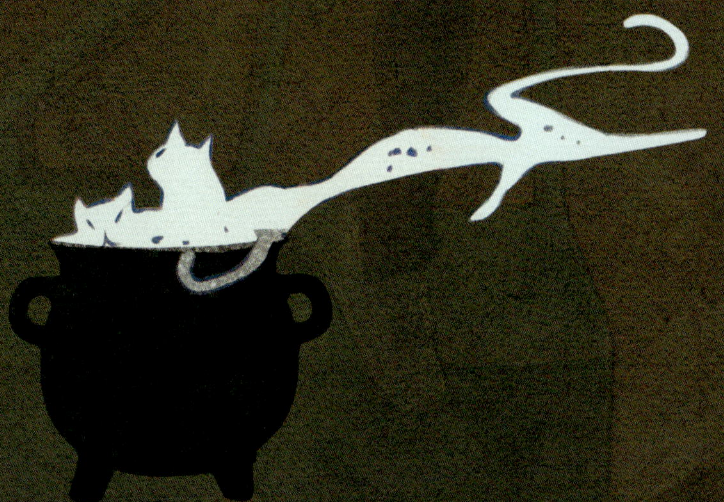

EARLY YEARS

Childhood

Looking back to the beginning, my art journey started thanks to my dad's pens and pencils. He's an architect, and though he doesn't draw illustrations, he had all the tools I needed to embark on what would become a lifelong passion.

After realizing that I was borrowing his materials, my dad influenced me to keep going. He was very encouraging, but also made sure to point out the things I needed to work on. Those criticisms motivated me to strengthen my skills and build a stronger attention to detail – something I'm grateful for to this day.

In childhood, I was often seen as the artsy guy. That's something that's always stuck with me. I made people happy with my drawings, and I still remember the joy on my friends' faces as they looked at my work. That's what it's all about, right? Creating something that makes people feel good. That's the reason I did it then, and why I still do it now. I love seeing people inspired.

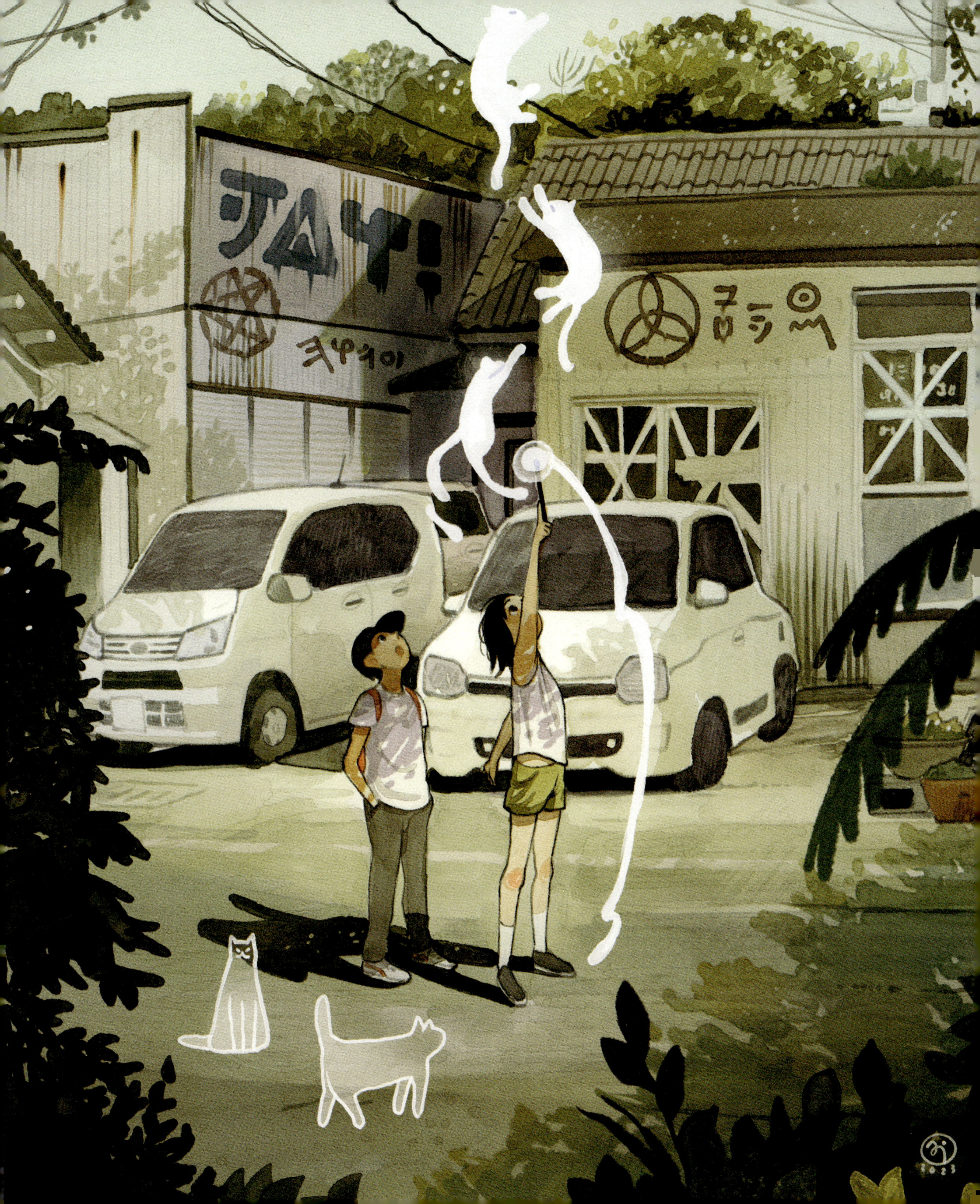

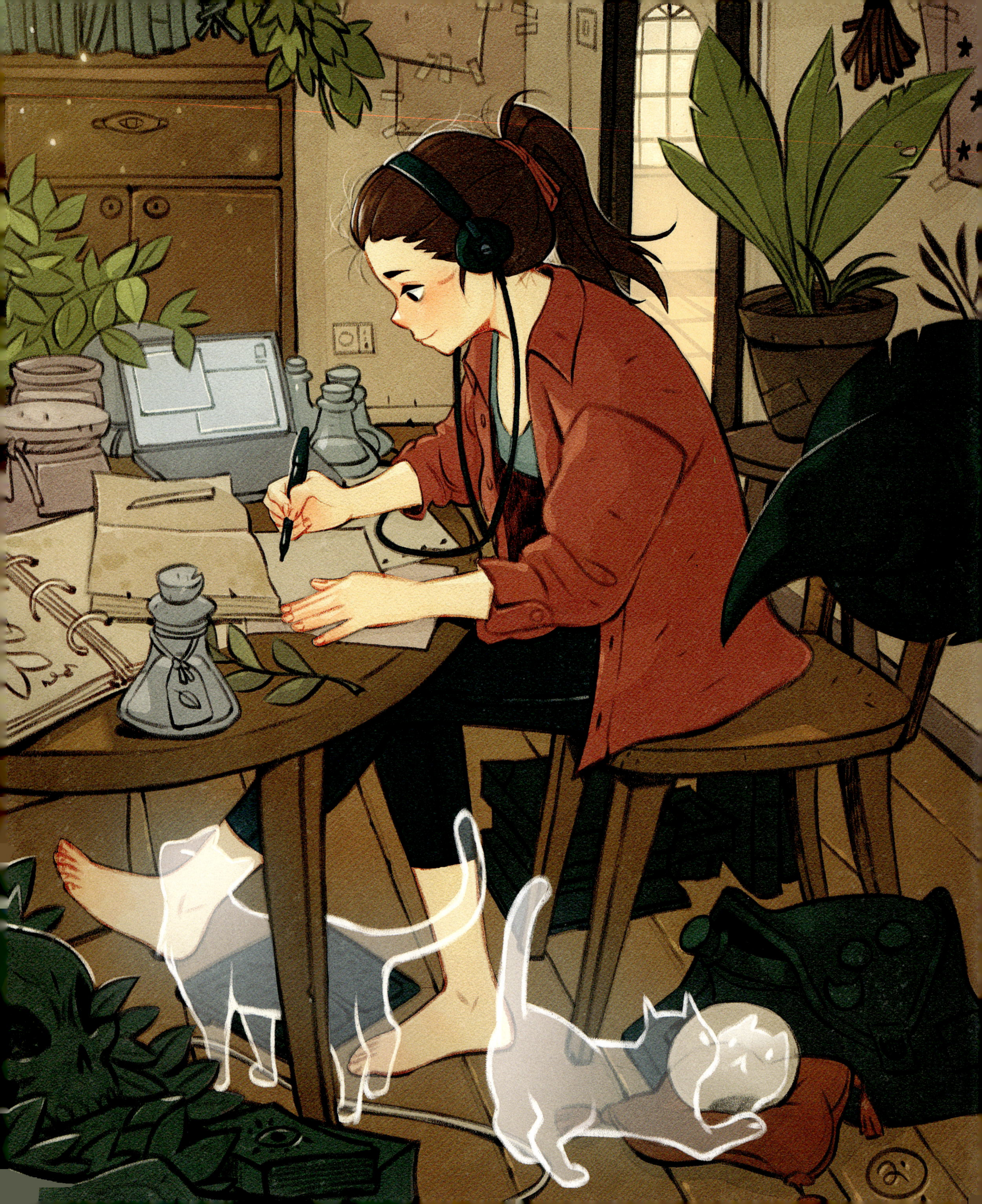

Education

Despite my passion for illustrating, I went on to study engineering. Though it was difficult and I didn't particularly enjoy it, I studied it for three whole years before my life changed direction. One day, I had this very complicated calculus exam where I had to complete a written portion, then explain my answers to the professor. I'd doodled something small on the back of the paper before handing it in, and quickly forgot about it. When it was my turn to meet with the professor, he flipped over the paper in front of him, considered the doodle, and asked bluntly, 'Why do you want to be an engineer? There's already so many out there. Shouldn't you pursue art instead?'

That was a crucial turning point for me, as I was already on the fence. My parents weren't thrilled about the idea of art school, but I wasn't the science-y guy – I was the artsy guy. Even during important exams, I was drawing, so I thought, 'You know what? I'm going to try it.'

I was nineteen when I made the decision to go to art school, and I've never had any regrets. I chose to study New Media Art at Accademia di Belle Arti di Napoli, which surprisingly wasn't oriented towards illustration. It was very technical, including classes on photography and 3D art (which I studied), but also provided traditional classes like the history of art and sociology. The lessons were very unconventional and creative; students from all years would attend the same lessons and learn from each other, and I found it really inspiring.

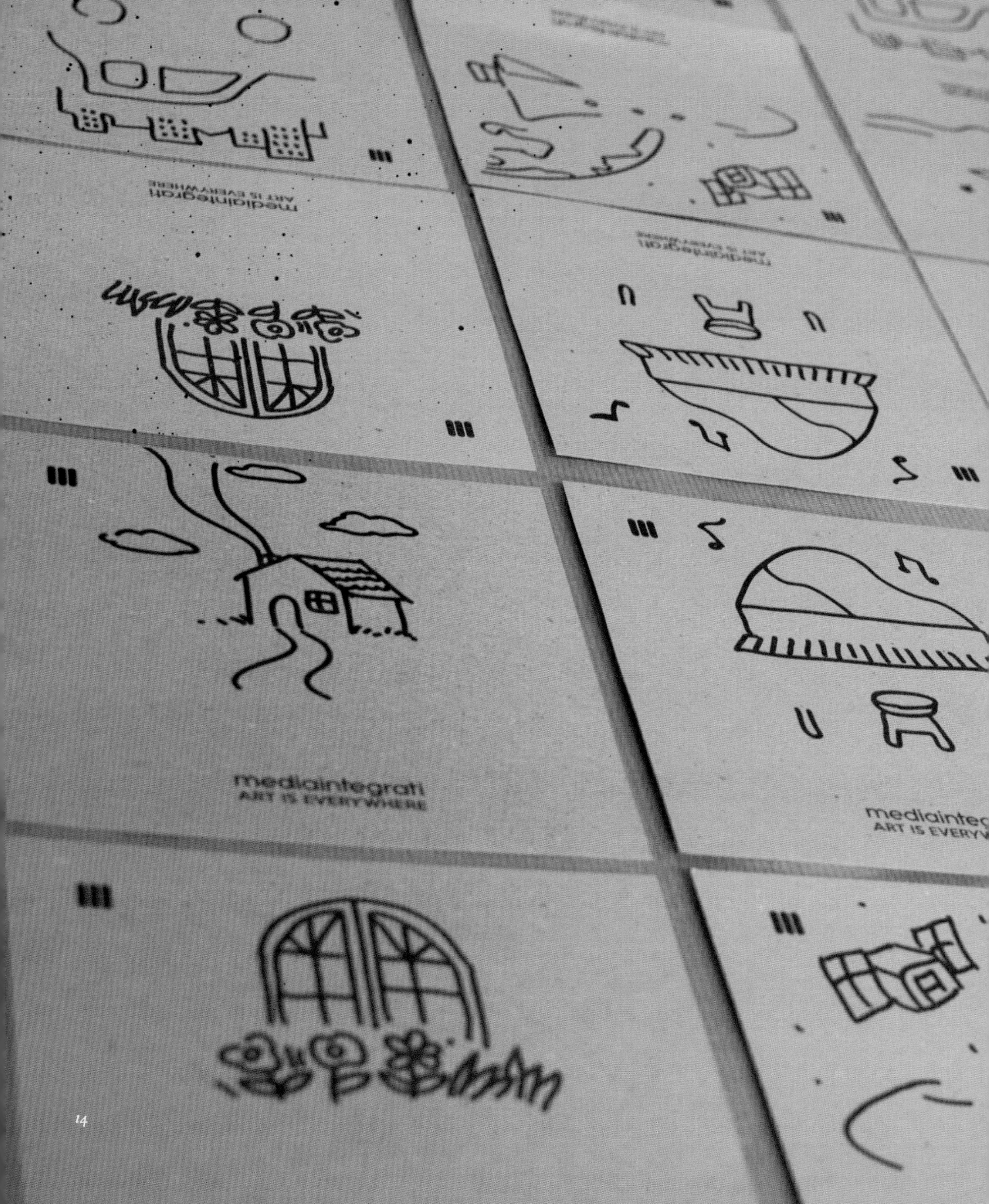
mediaintegrati
ART IS EVERYWHERE

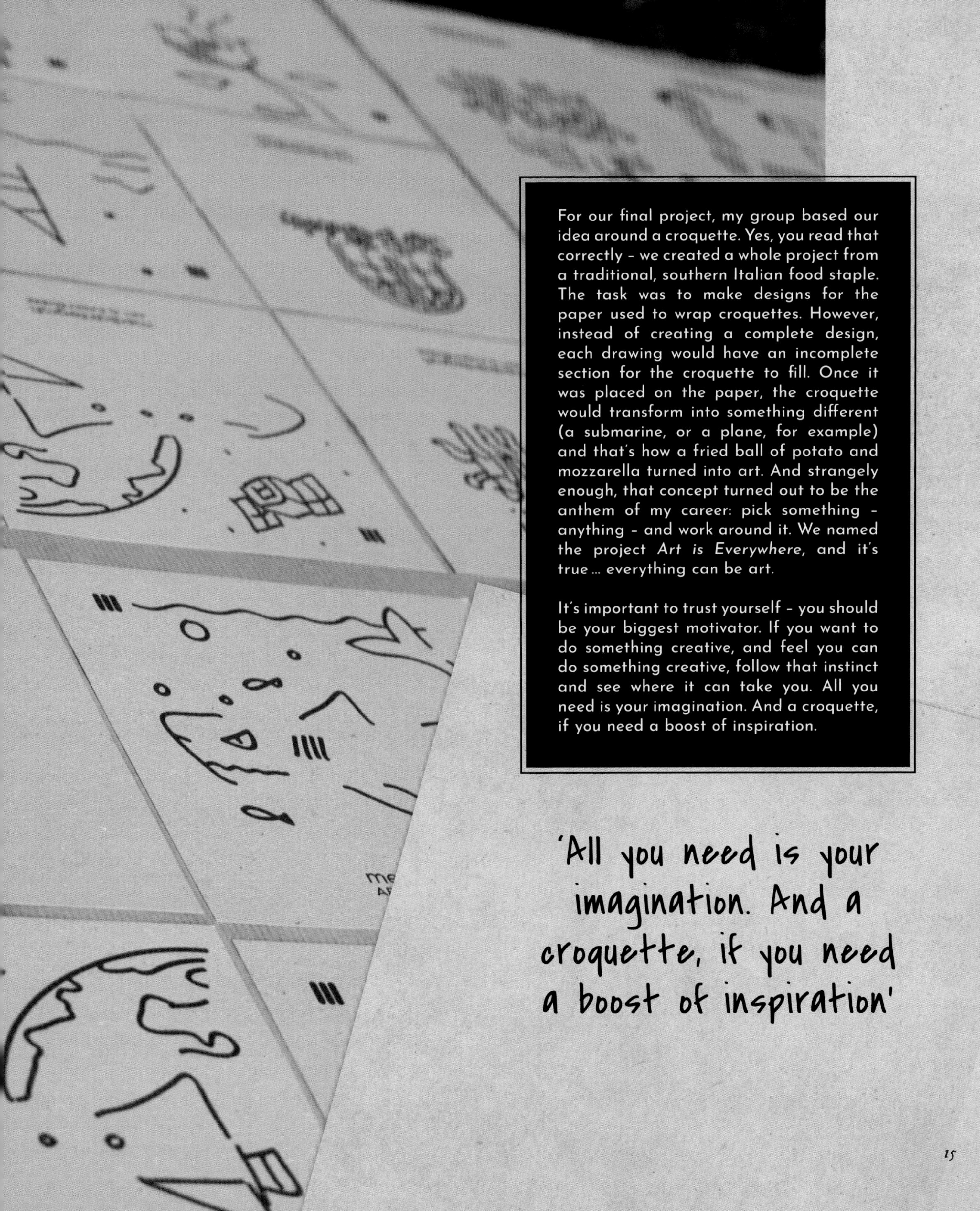

For our final project, my group based our idea around a croquette. Yes, you read that correctly – we created a whole project from a traditional, southern Italian food staple. The task was to make designs for the paper used to wrap croquettes. However, instead of creating a complete design, each drawing would have an incomplete section for the croquette to fill. Once it was placed on the paper, the croquette would transform into something different (a submarine, or a plane, for example) and that's how a fried ball of potato and mozzarella turned into art. And strangely enough, that concept turned out to be the anthem of my career: pick something – anything – and work around it. We named the project *Art is Everywhere*, and it's true … everything can be art.

It's important to trust yourself – you should be your biggest motivator. If you want to do something creative, and feel you can do something creative, follow that instinct and see where it can take you. All you need is your imagination. And a croquette, if you need a boost of inspiration.

'All you need is your imagination. And a croquette, if you need a boost of inspiration'

Professional steps & milestones

One of my first gigs was as a graphic designer for a video-game start-up in Italy. It sounded cool, so I tried it, but soon found that a corporate career wasn't on the cards for me. I'd gone from an incredibly liberal, open-minded environment to a strict, creatively stifling office, and so I took another leap of faith and fired myself.

With the help of my parents, I became a freelancer and started accepting commissions, but I still felt that it was very controlling and left little room for personal projects. I didn't want to use it as an excuse for not creating my own art. That's why I decided to dedicate one hundred per cent of my time to growing my social-media presence, with the hope I could reach larger audiences, express my authentic self, and inspire others with art.

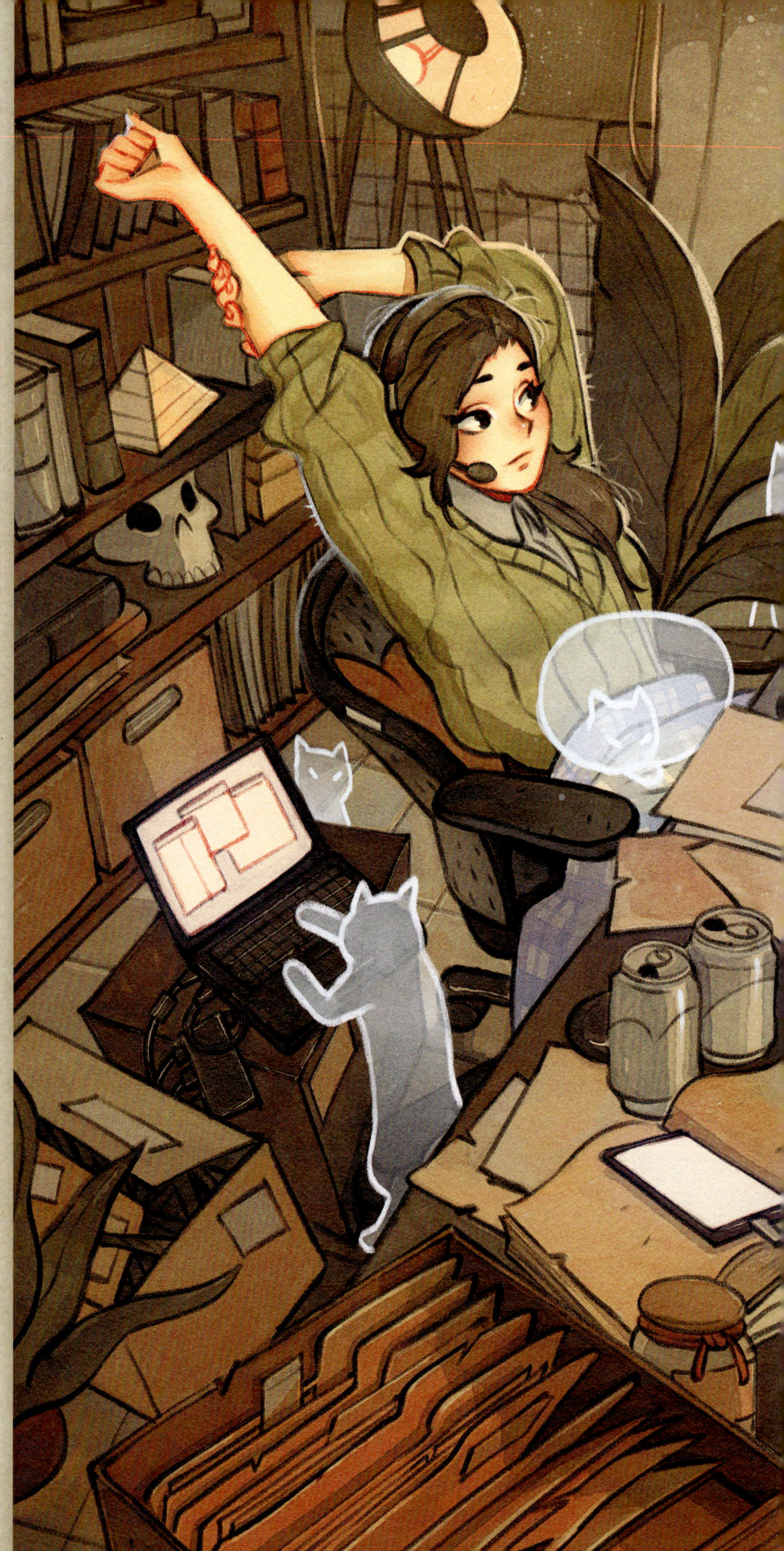

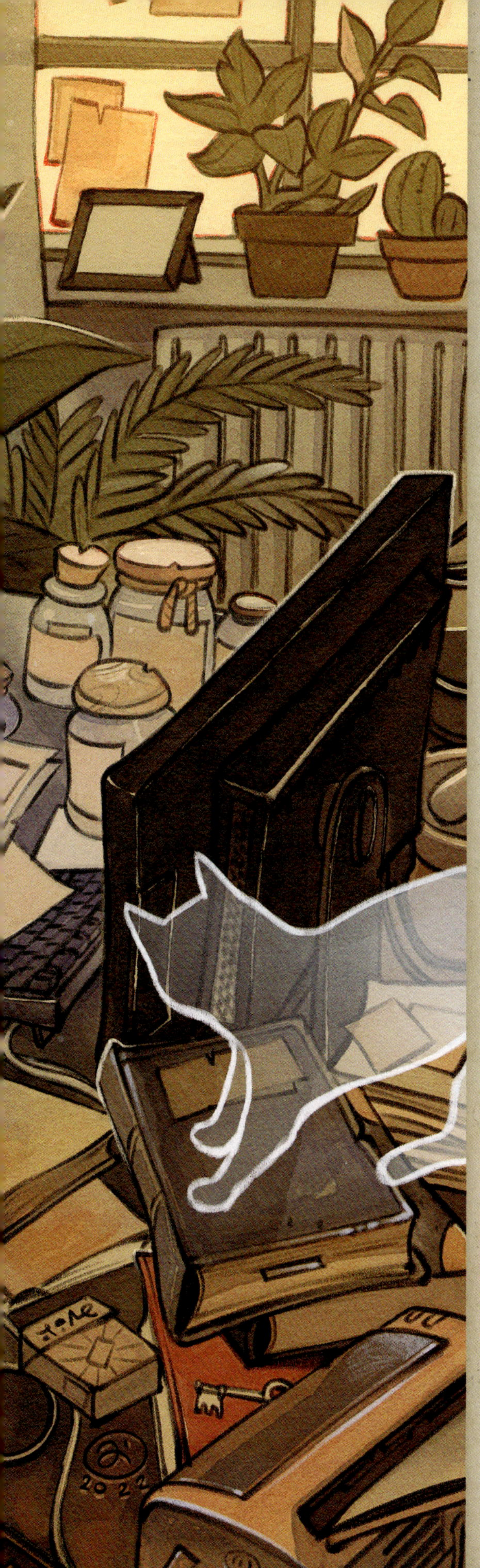

It's a very complicated career to pull off, and you need to be creative, have good ideas, and be ready to ask for a lot of help. A pinch of luck is also useful. There is so much uncertainty when you decide to go out on your own. It's the biggest bet I've ever made, and I've been stubborn, lucky, and maybe even a little naive. But having a supportive family and community has made all the difference.

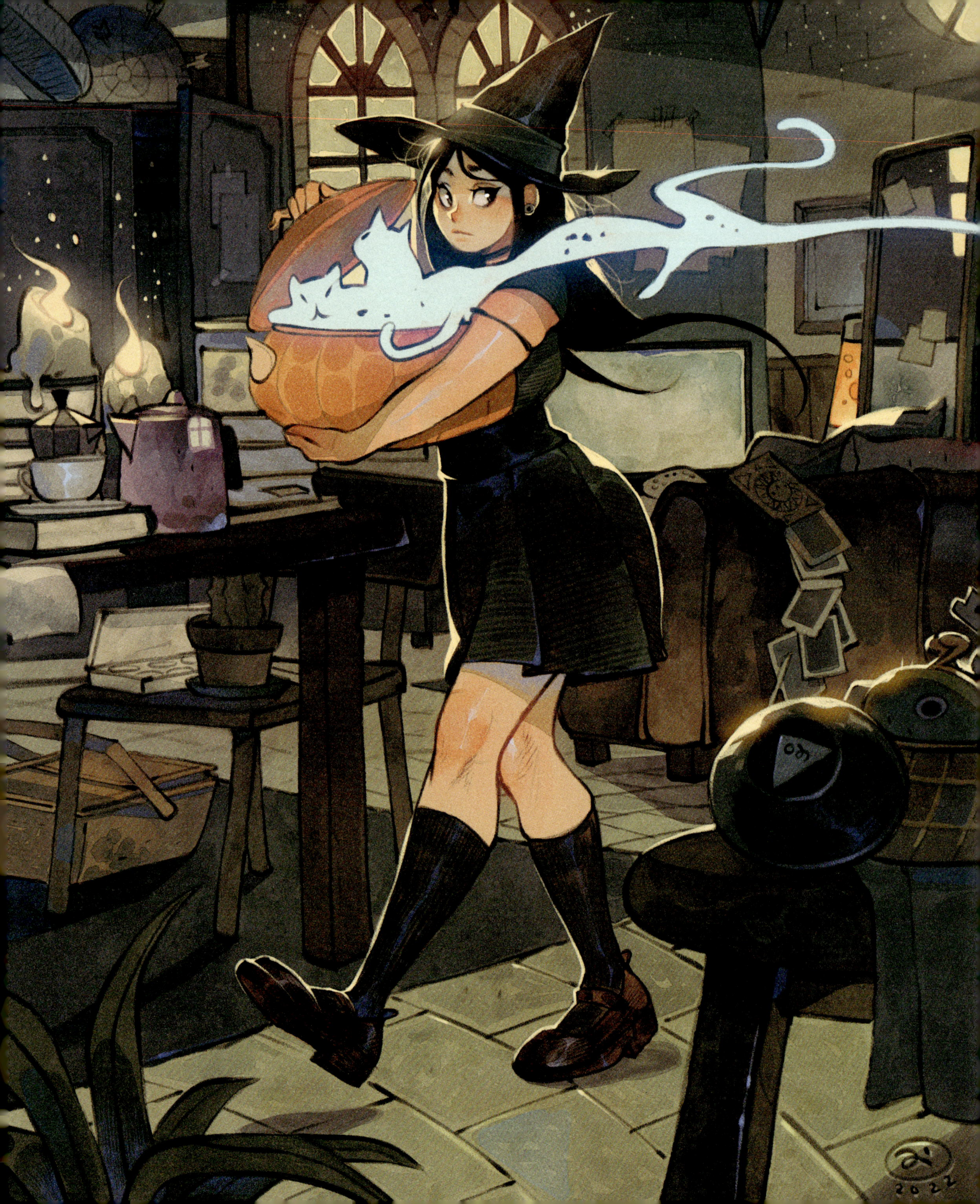

CHALLENGES OF BEING A PROFESSIONAL ARTIST

Self-doubt

I thought about giving up plenty of times. People actually pushed me towards it, and it's surprising how triggering it can be. Many expect to see instant results, and there's this stigma that comes with taking time to develop as an artist. I was only twenty-six, but some of those around me thought I was a drop-out who didn't want to work. Thankfully, I didn't succumb to the negativity. I was my first and biggest fan, so I just continued believing in myself. That meant I had to push away unsupportive voices, and keep the supportive ones close.

You'll always have these thoughts in this field, because there's no certainty or stability. You have to make hard choices every single day. What's my next project? Is it worth continuing? Am I good enough? Am I good enough to make it twice? Social media can also feed the doubt, especially if you don't have many followers or much interaction. Naivety definitely saw me through those moments, alongside the supporters who have stuck by me since the beginning. The live-streaming service Twitch has also helped me persevere, especially during times where I thought about throwing in the stylus.

Artist's block & burnout

Though many artists experience this affliction, I don't seem to suffer as much. I've always managed to keep working. Sure, I've been stuck on styles or mindsets that didn't allow me to fully express my vision, but I never stopped creating. I've always been the kid with the pencil and sketchbook. For me, drawing is like clockwork.

If I'm working on a big project that is testing me, it's usually because it's not letting me communicate what I want. After I finish it (which I normally do), I go back to the basics and draw what I love: objects around me. Drawing unforced things is how I recharge.

Impressions

I feel like my current work represents me and my growth as an artist, but I sometimes feel it can be little misinterpreted. Specifically, on my most recent project, there are some people who seem to think I'm into witchcraft. I love the witch aesthetic, and witch culture, but just to clarify: I'm not a witch myself! To help with my work, I bought many books and learned about the various symbols and histories associated with Wicca and witchcraft, and it's no different to any other artist. If they have a project about birds, they'll study birds.

There are many things I like about my style and subject matter, and I'm proud of the way it represents me aesthetically, but there's always room to open the door a little further. There's always an opportunity to learn and grow.

ADVICE FOR NEW ARTISTS

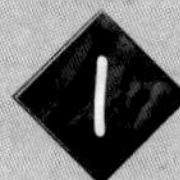

Believe in yourself as much as possible. If you don't, no one is going to help you. One evening while streaming on Twitch, I felt super negative because I had a minimal number of viewers. Noticing my frustration, another artist said, 'You are too self-aware, Simone. You have people who are watching you right now, enjoying what you're doing. If you focus on the negatives, you'll lose charisma.'

Both charisma and personality show up in your art and help define your career. People appreciate confident creators. Choosing pessimism and doubt only closes doors. There's no certain way to do things – do them your own way, explore your own personality, find your voice. Then there will be an audience for you.

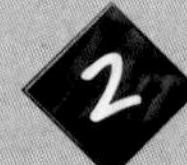

Don't let trends change your personality. You're vulnerable when you're first starting out, so make sure to put your own spin on things and keep true to your gut. Often, the things you think are flaws wind up being what you're known for later down the line. And they won't be considered flaws then, trust me. I used to think that in order to be a successful artist, you had to be the best. It's less black and white than that.

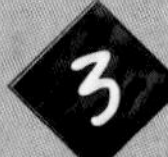

Foster a healthy relationship with criticism. I once listened to an interview with YouTuber PewDiePie, where he spoke about the importance of weeding out trolls from what would otherwise be healthy, constructive criticisms. People are quick to critique in the early stages, when you're not yet able to bend style to your will. But among the vitriol, there will be a comment that will help you improve, even if you don't like it at first.

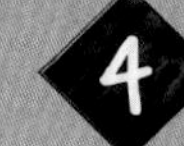

Don't start tomorrow, or next week, or next year. Start your art journey now! If I could go back in time, I would've begun mine earlier because market platforms like Instagram and Twitter were already pretty saturated.

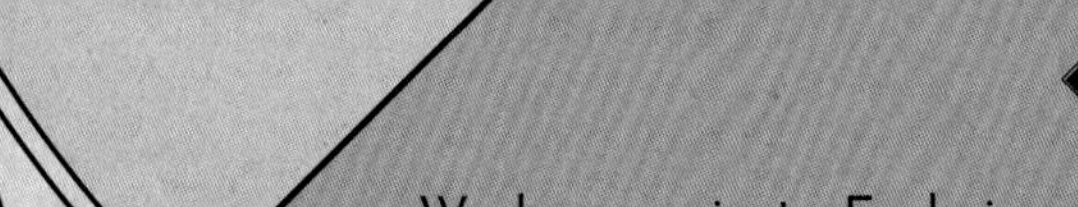

Work on projects. Early in my career, I posted a lot on social media, but I wasn't working on anything specific. My pages looked like research because they lacked personality. So, when you're ready and your own artistic personality has developed, stay consistent and be intentional about your creative choices.

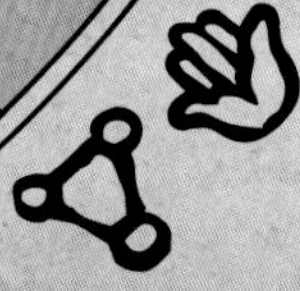

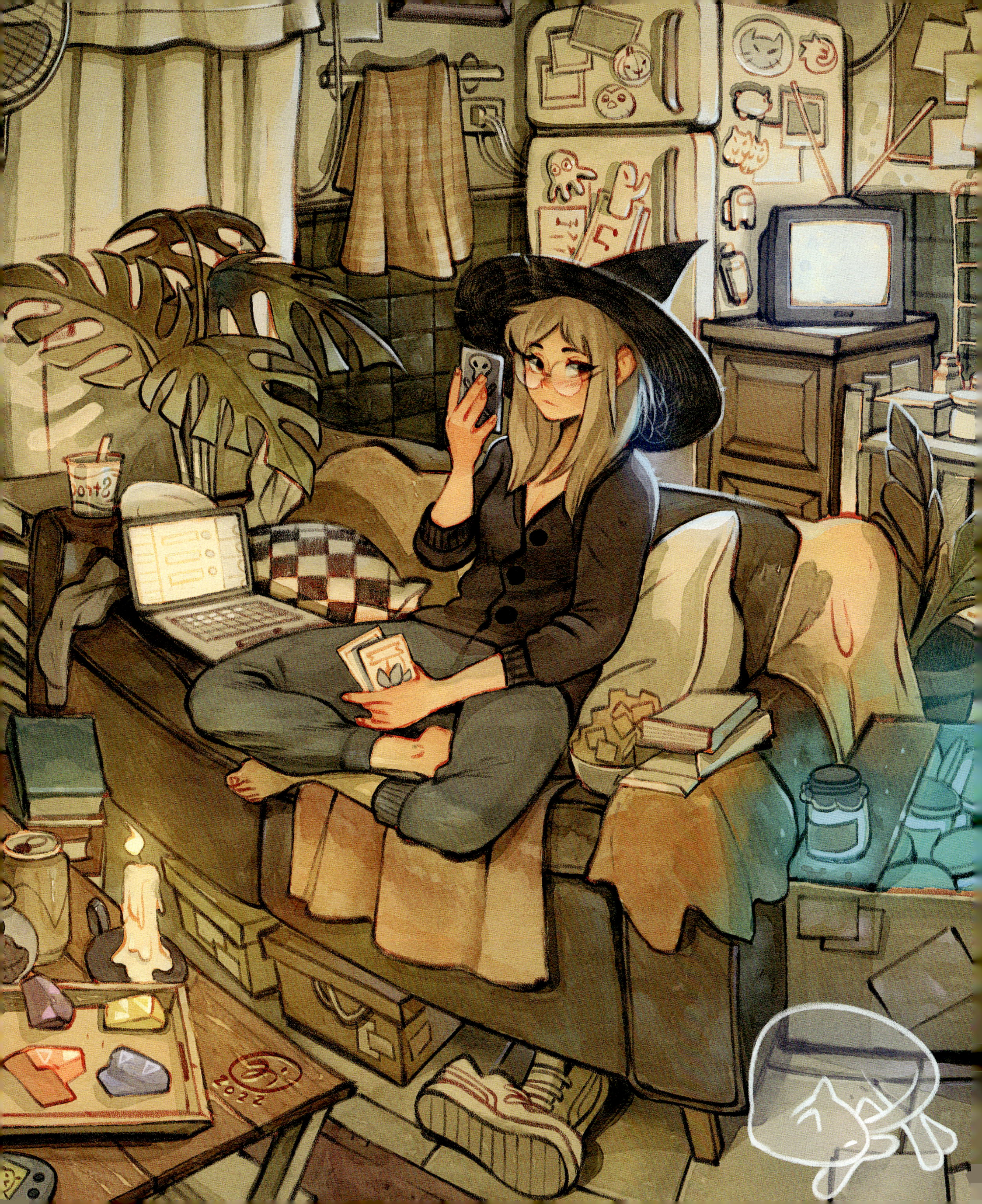
2022

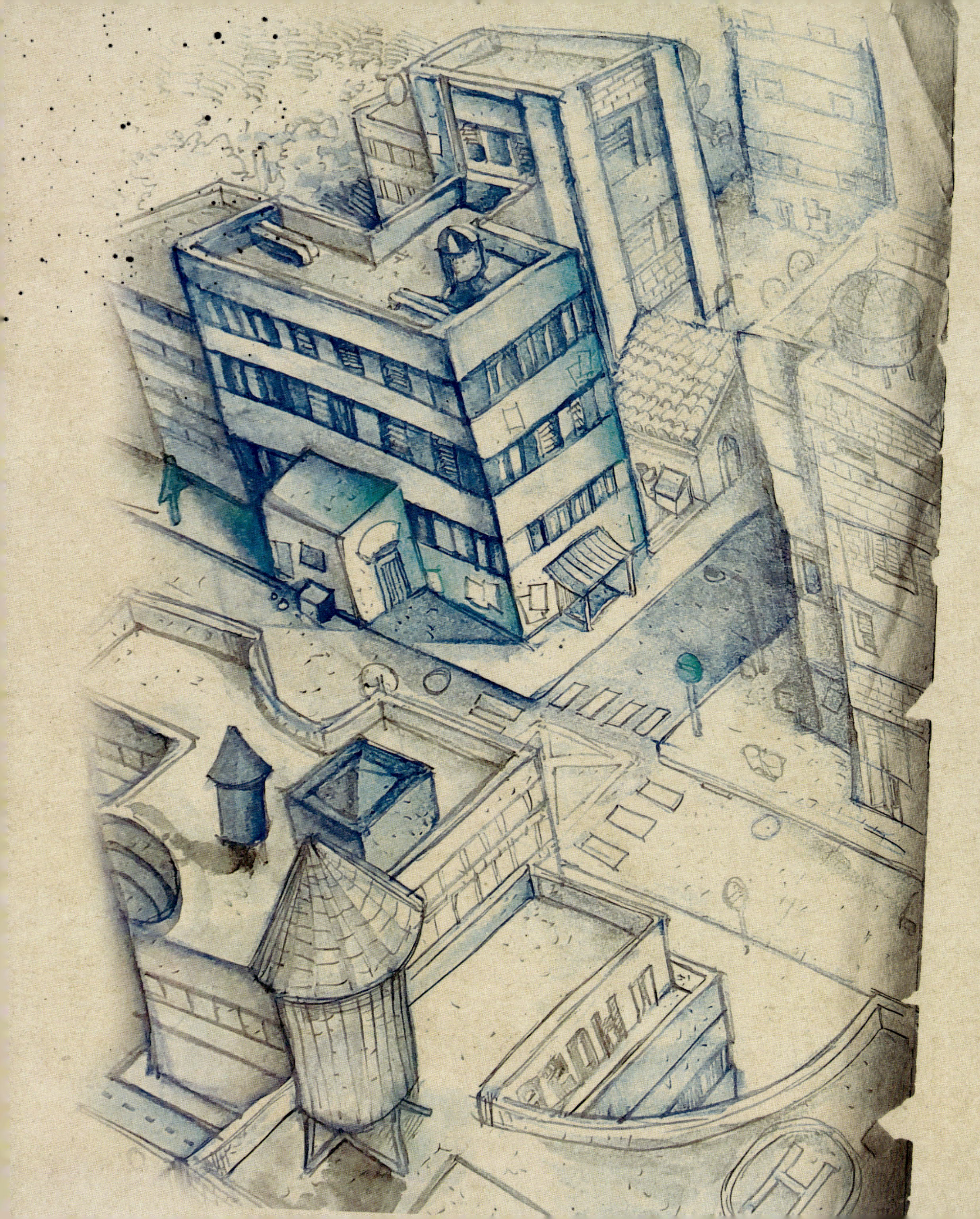

VISUAL TIMELINE

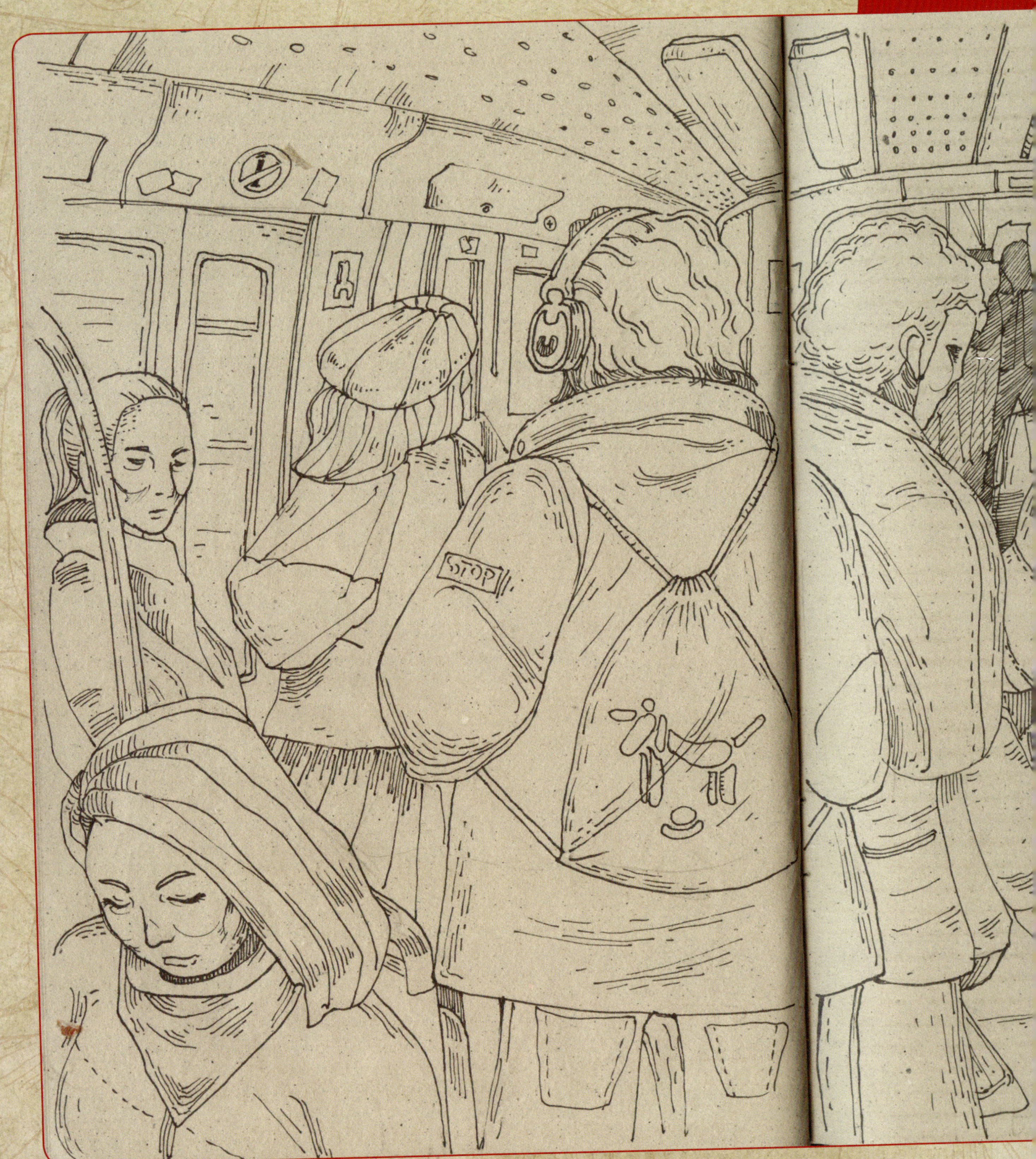
STOP

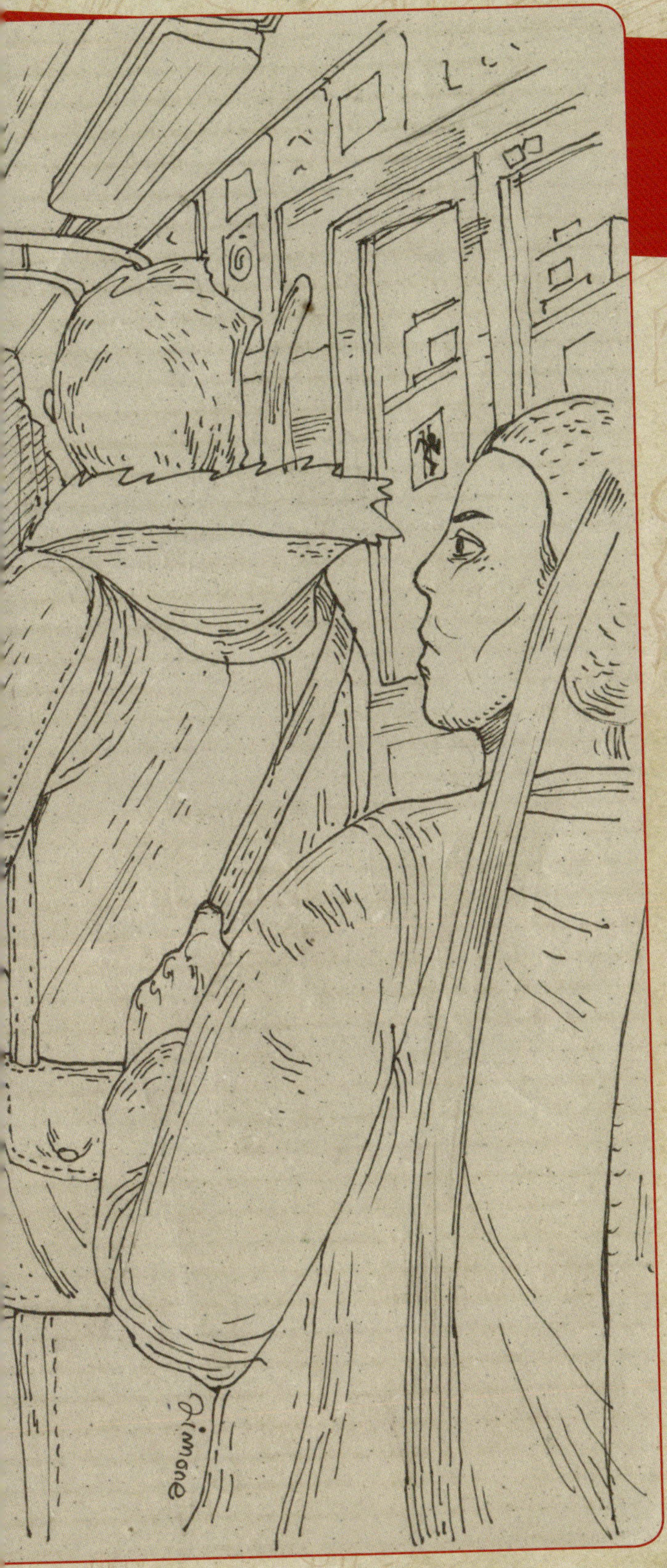

Drawing where I can, and when I can, has been an important part of my journey – especially when it involves real life. I really recommend trying this out if you're looking to improve.

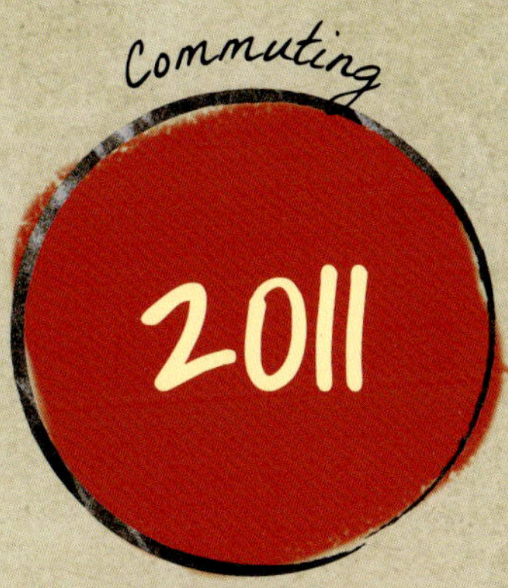

This picture was made during one of my commutes to college. I was on the train, observing my surroundings with a pen in hand. It's definitely not what I would call 'good', but it shows perspective, improvisation, and dedication to practice.

You learn how to be fast by simplifying the world around you.

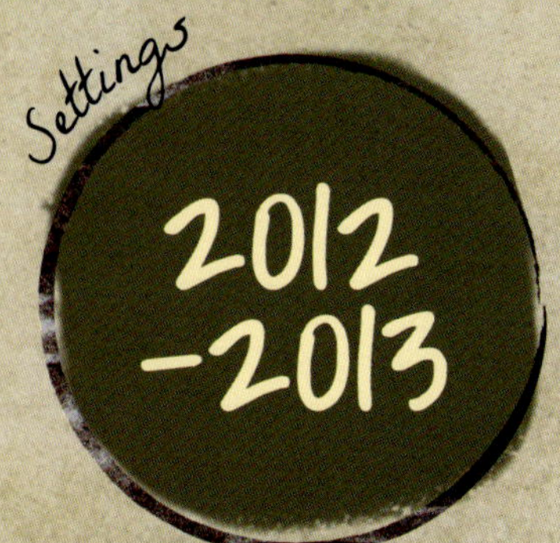

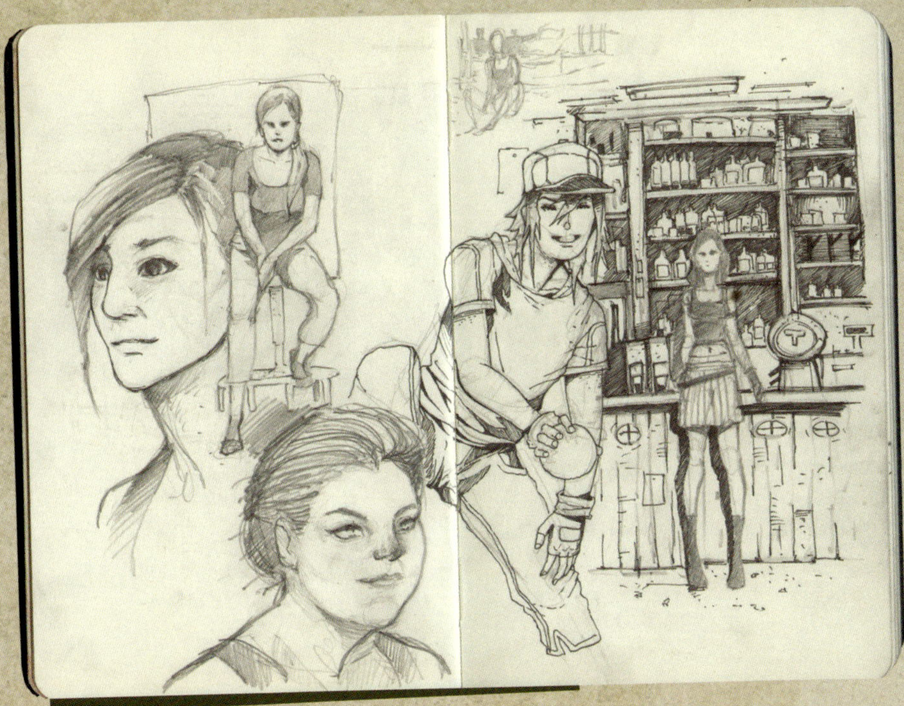

I particularly like the image of the girl on the right. There's a really nice contrast between the details in the background and the character in the front, and it's a style I still apply to this day. This was one of the first times I approached an environment-focused piece. I like how the blurry character is in front of the darker ink.

Parisian Portraits

2012 -2013

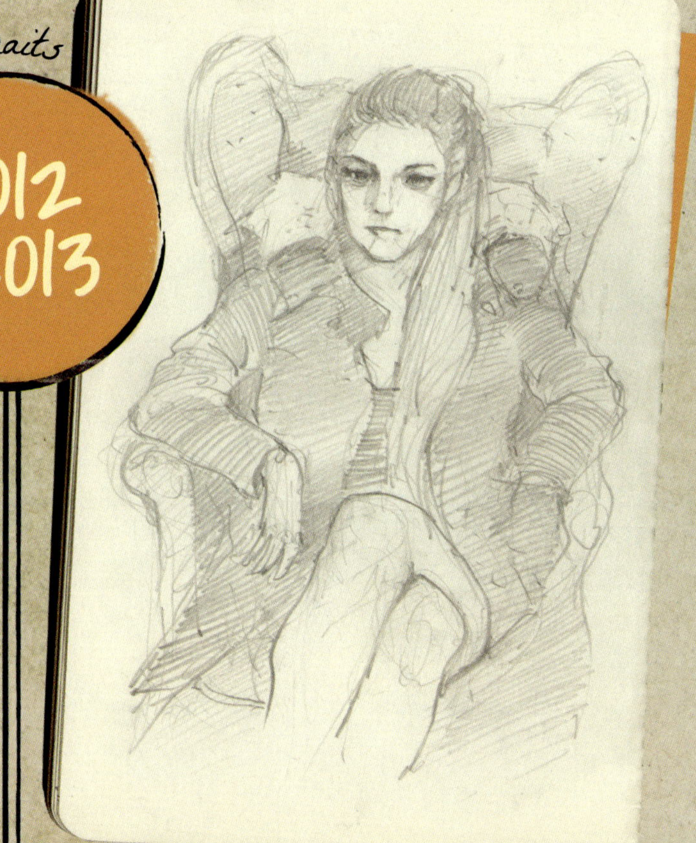

This was a live portrait during one of my trips to Paris. Always having a sketchbook with me has been a huge part of my journey because I learned how to draw quickly, how to draw real-life scenes, and how to draw with others around me.

It's something that has helped me with streaming and starting a career as an online content creator. You're under judgement constantly, so if streaming is something you're looking to pursue, it's important to learn how to deal with it as early on as possible.

The woman in this image was at the same party as me. She waited patiently for me to finish, so there was extra pressure to draw really fast. All of these scrapbook pictures are done with only a limited amount of time.

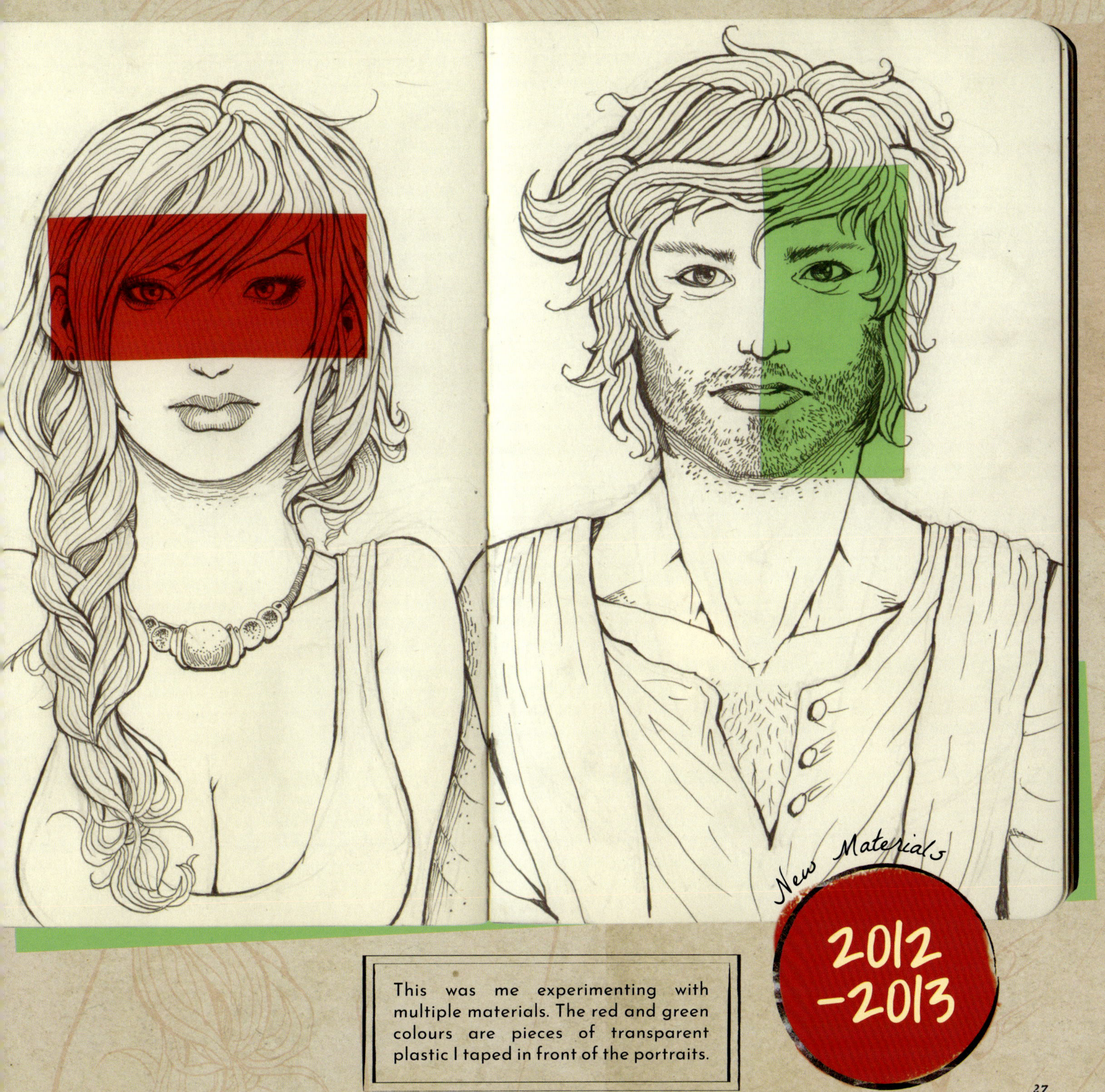

2012
-2013

This was me experimenting with multiple materials. The red and green colours are pieces of transparent plastic I taped in front of the portraits.

Pushing Boundaries

2012 -2013

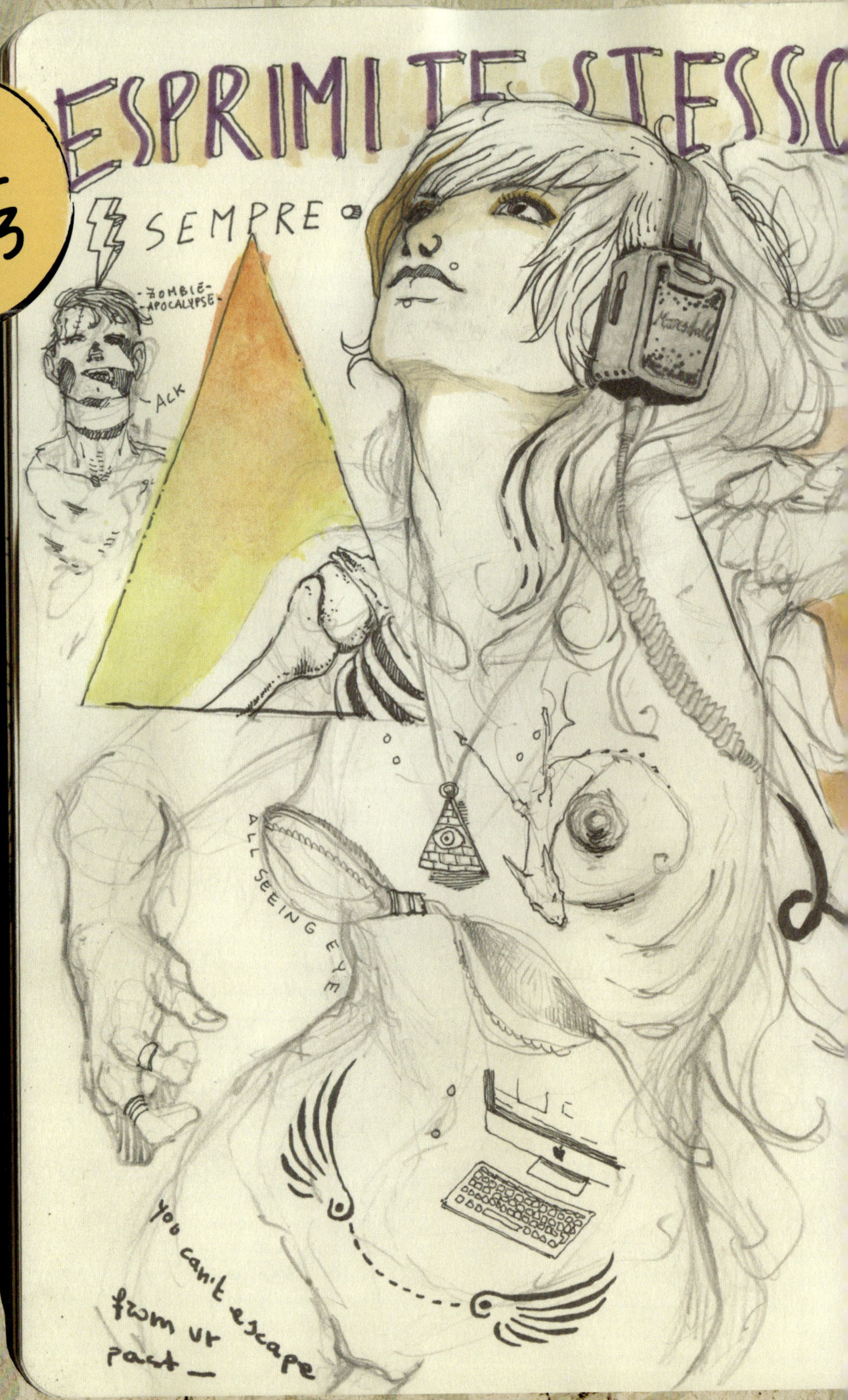

ESPRIMI TE STESSO

SEMPRE

ZOMBIE APOCALYPSE

ACK

ALL SEEING EYE

you can't escape from ur past

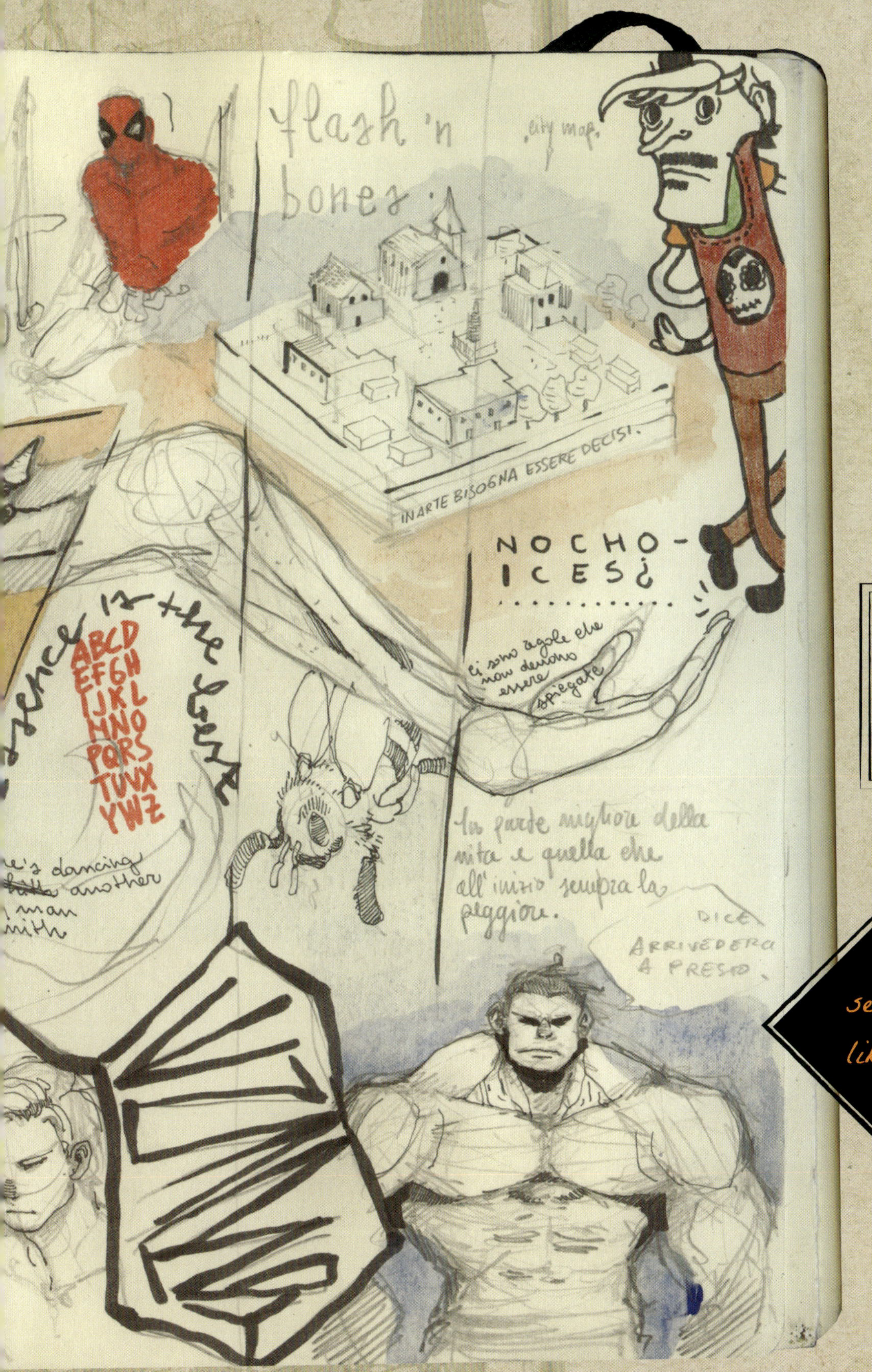

This is a selection of my scrapbook aesthetic from 2012 and 2013. It shows my exercises, bone and anatomy studies, and notes of my mistakes.

As you can see, I've always liked pushing the boundaries.

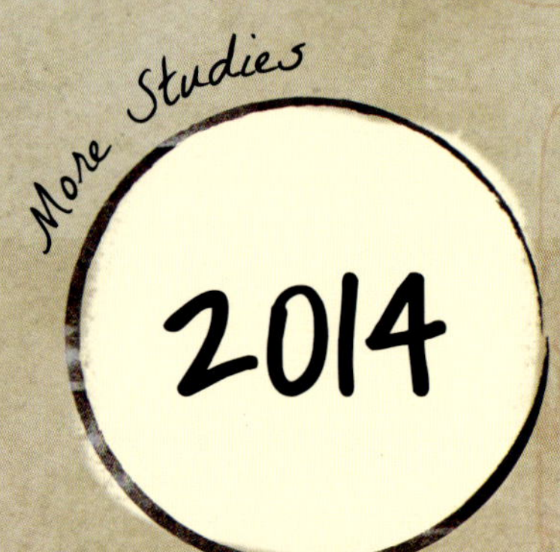

I tried out different styles, techniques ... a little bit of everything. You can see a red marker there to the left, and I still have it. Drawing the reality of things around me – from home, to trains, to parties – has been a great way for me to improve under pressure.

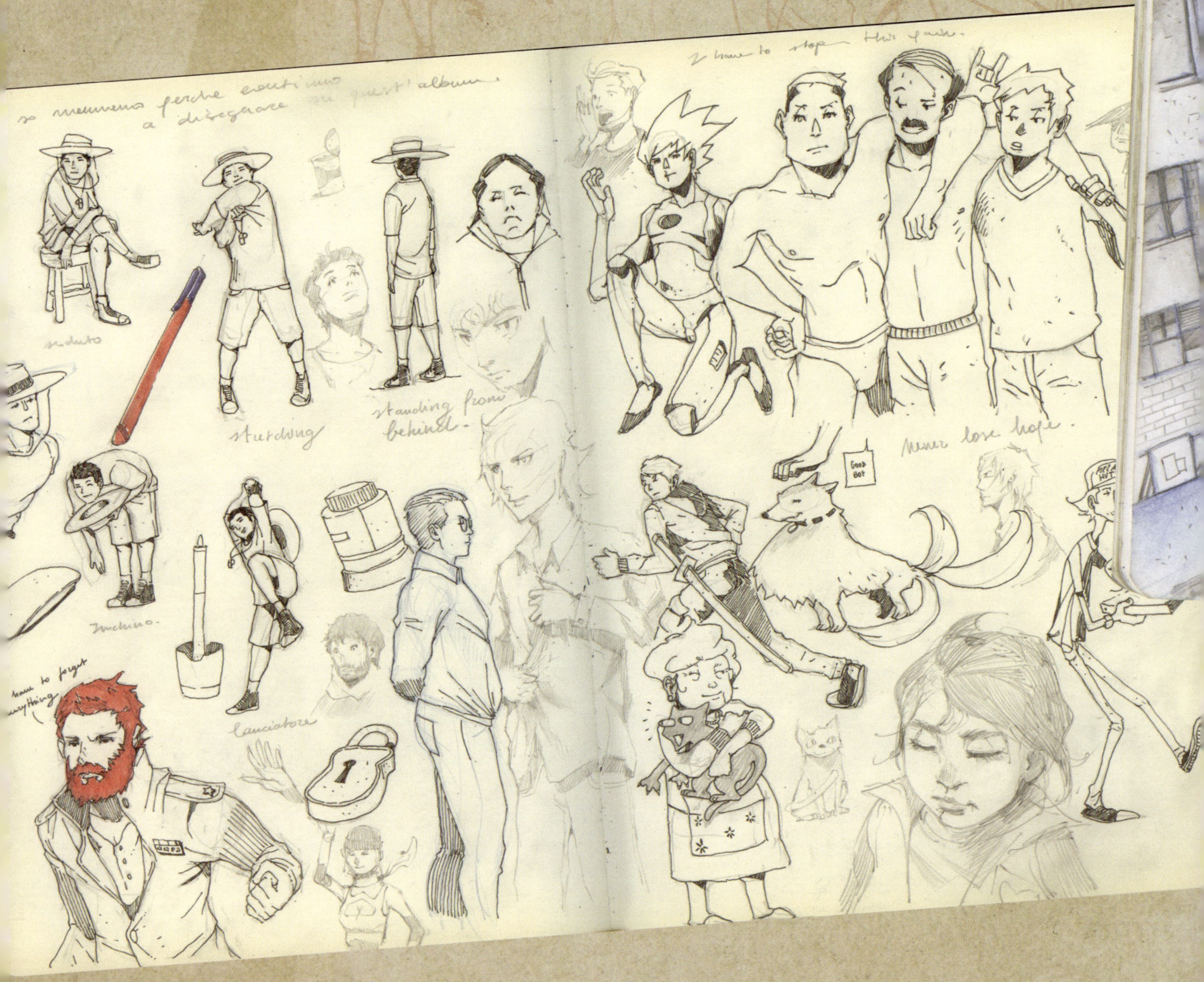

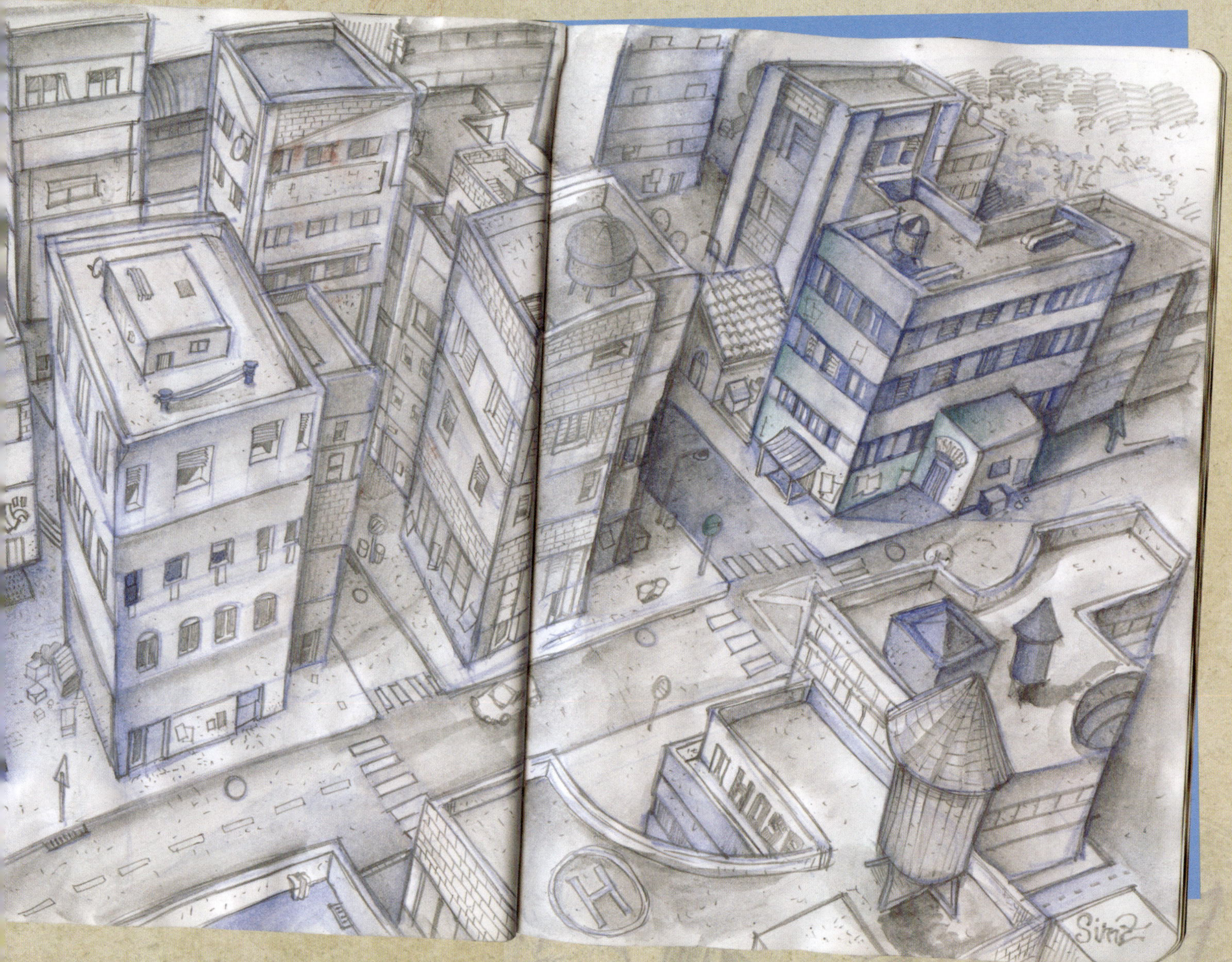

Perspective

2014

This is a perspective-focused doodle. It's not great, but it's a way to show improvement.

Experimenting

2014

There's a lot of back and forth in terms of quality, but at the end of the day, that's what experimenting is all about. I wasn't trying to finesse here – the aim was to figure out what worked for me and what didn't. Ideally, I want to express what I want, when I want to. The purpose isn't to produce a distilled product.

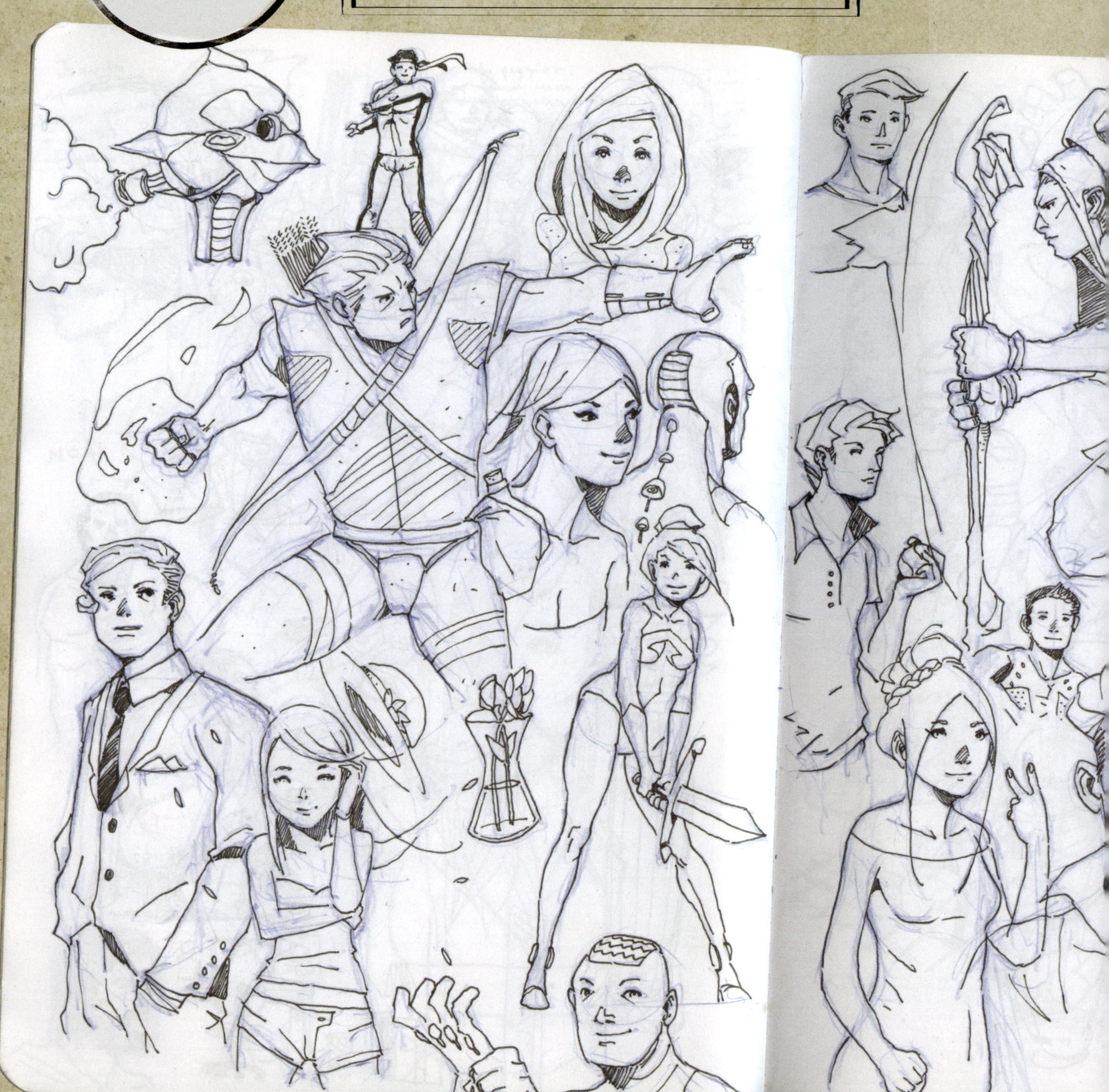

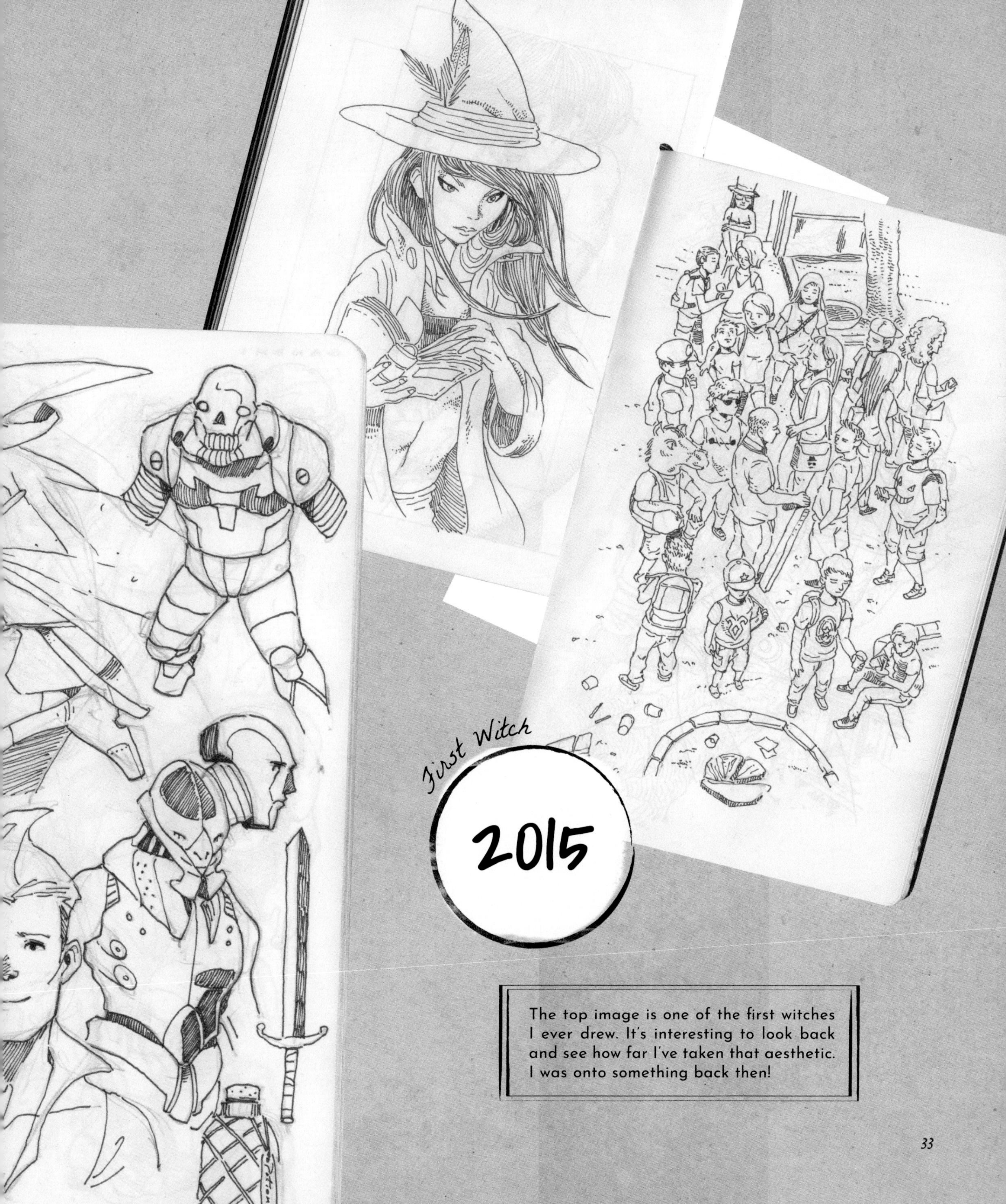

The top image is one of the first witches I ever drew. It's interesting to look back and see how far I've taken that aesthetic. I was onto something back then!

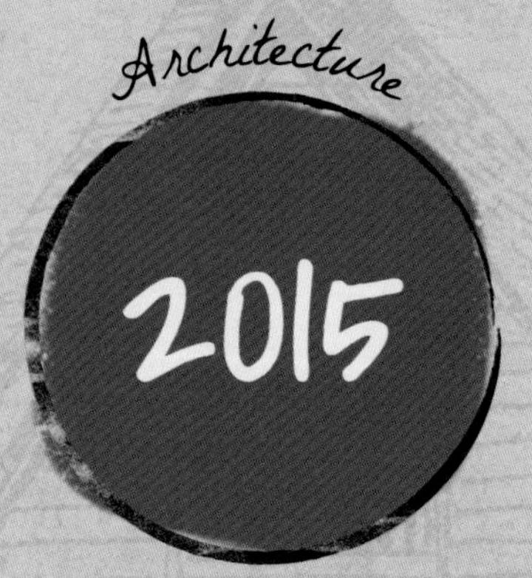

Here, you can see all the places I wanted to visit during my trip to London. To the right is the Globe Theatre. It's another example of how I always have my sketchbook with me, especially when there's a trip involved.

Drawing what you see helps to expand your visual library. When you illustrate a person, or a building in this case, you somehow remember the details a bit better – the unique elements.

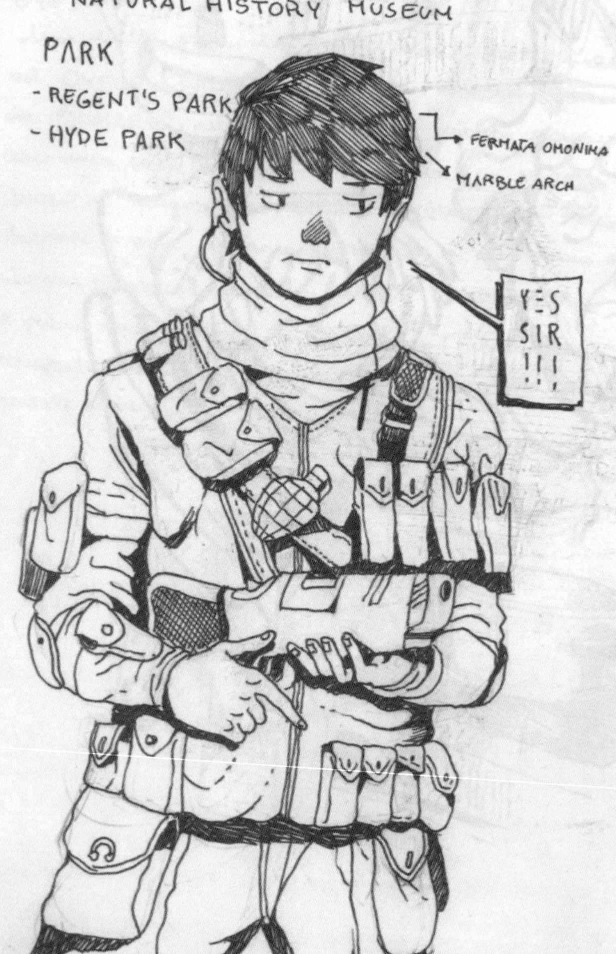

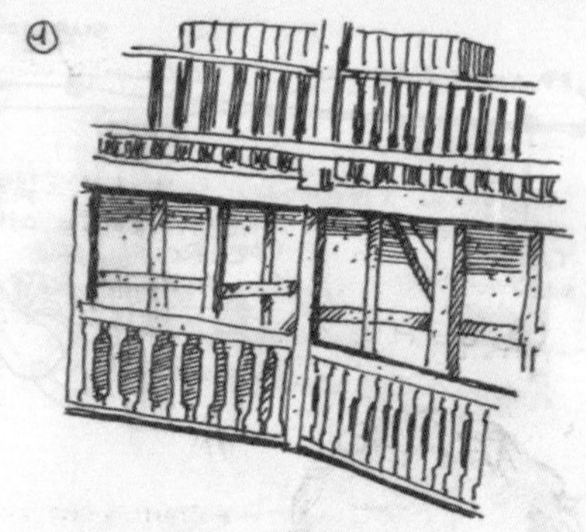

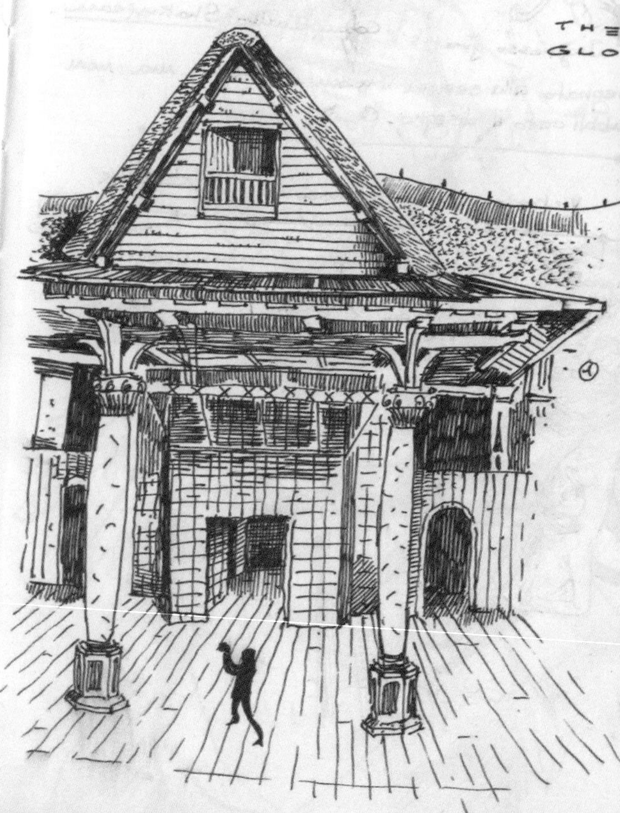

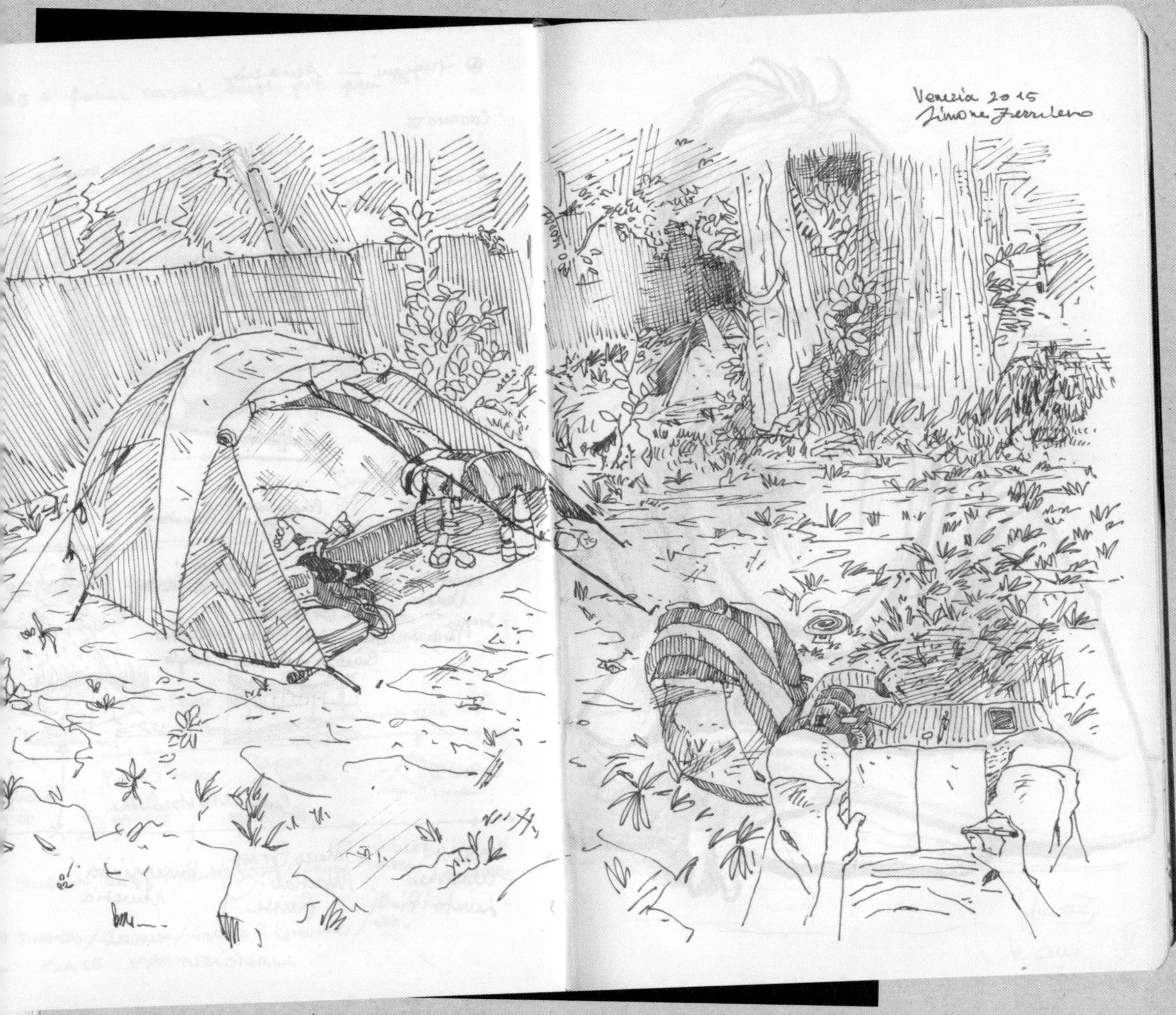

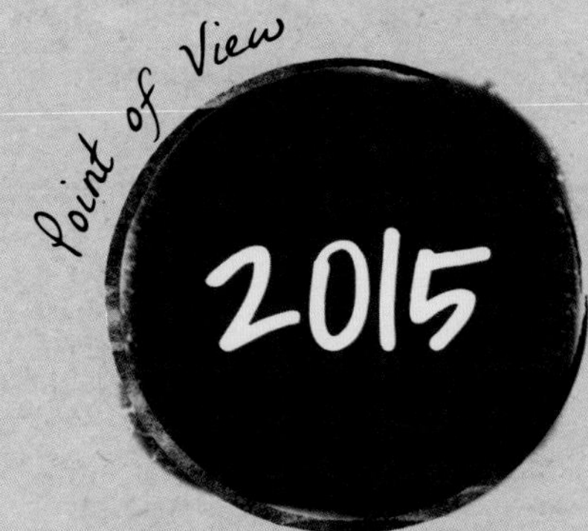

I really like sketching things from different points of view. It can feel complex, but it's good to understand how things look in real life instead of always using photographs or references. It's fun to play with perspective.

Vaults

2016

This is a sketch I made in the area underneath an old church I visited. I focused on depth and perspective by drawing the eye to the first column and the vaulted ceiling above.

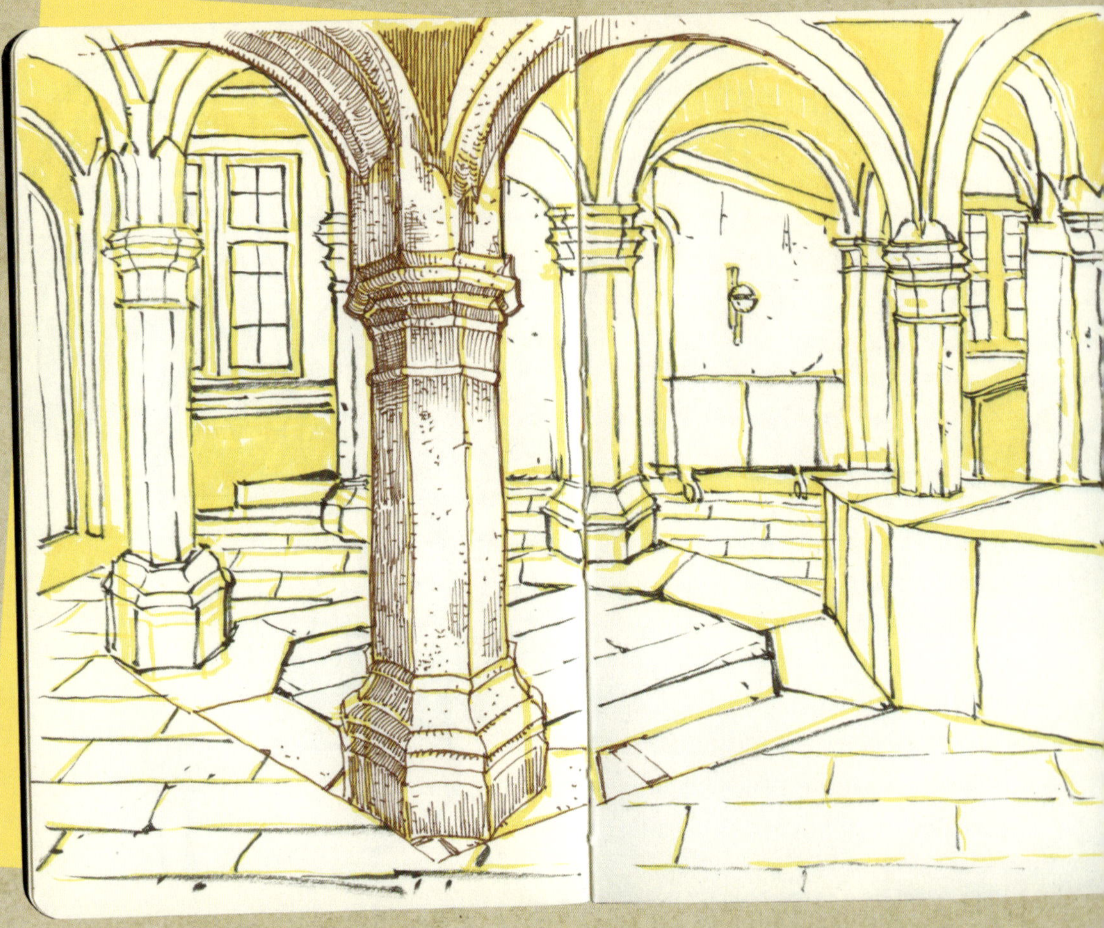

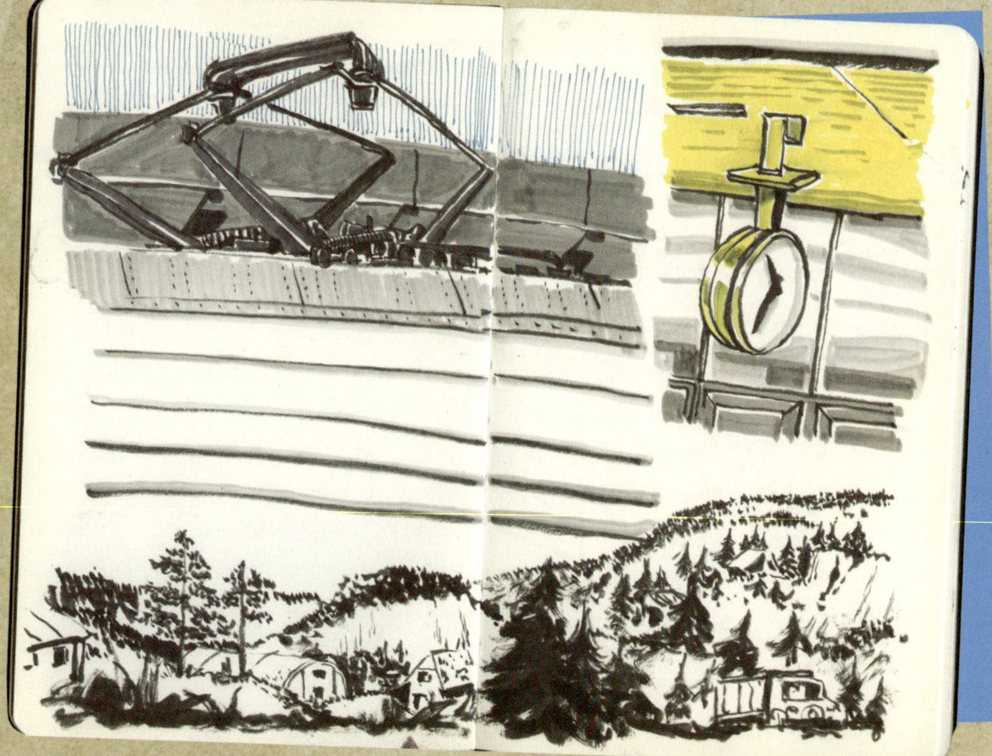

Creating Narratives

2016

I love the idea of creating a narrative through live sketching. You're not just drawing a random picture; you're telling a story. And in order to tell stories as you go, you have to be fast.

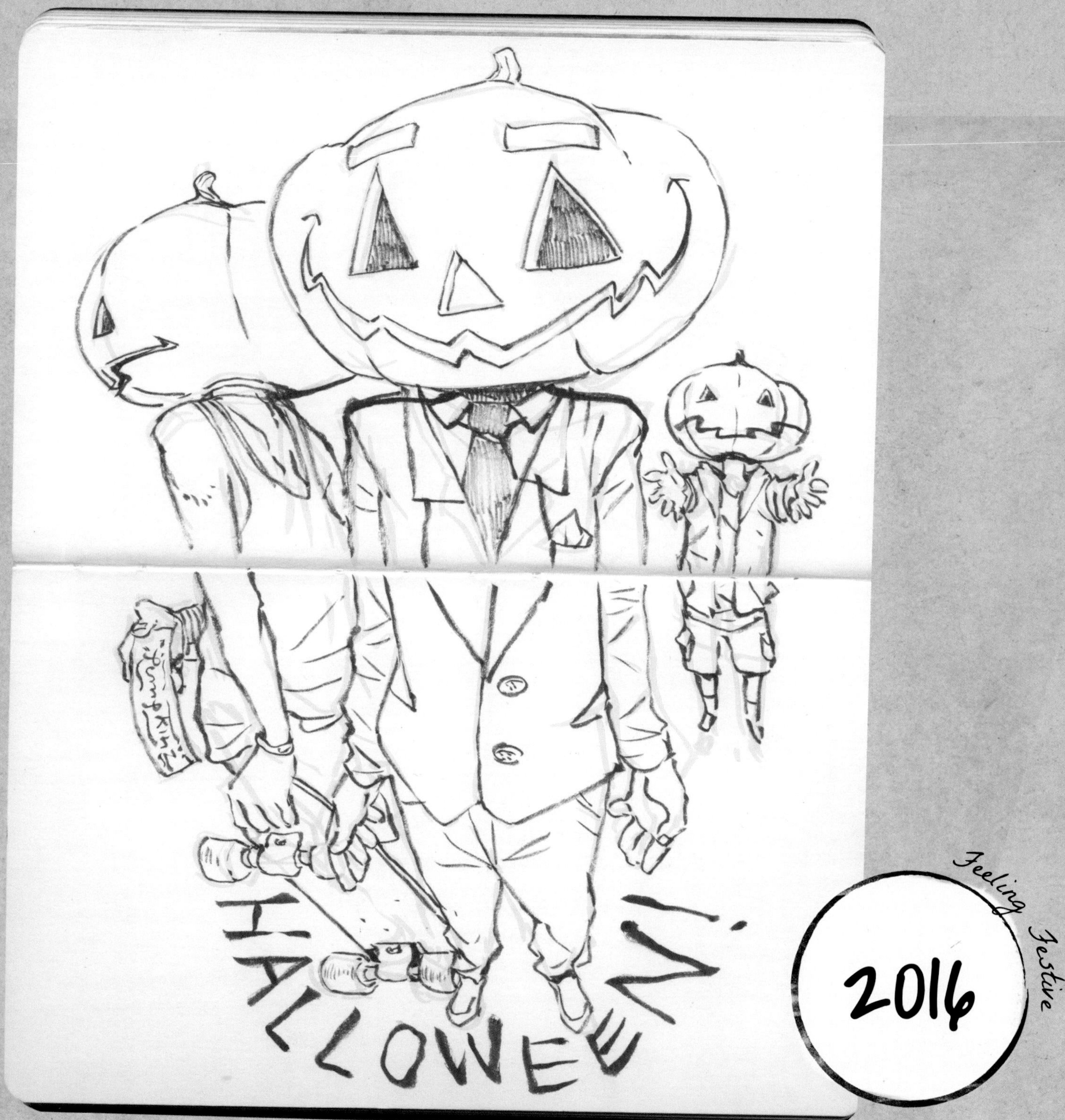

Can you guess what time of year I sketched this piece? I always have fun experimenting with perspective.

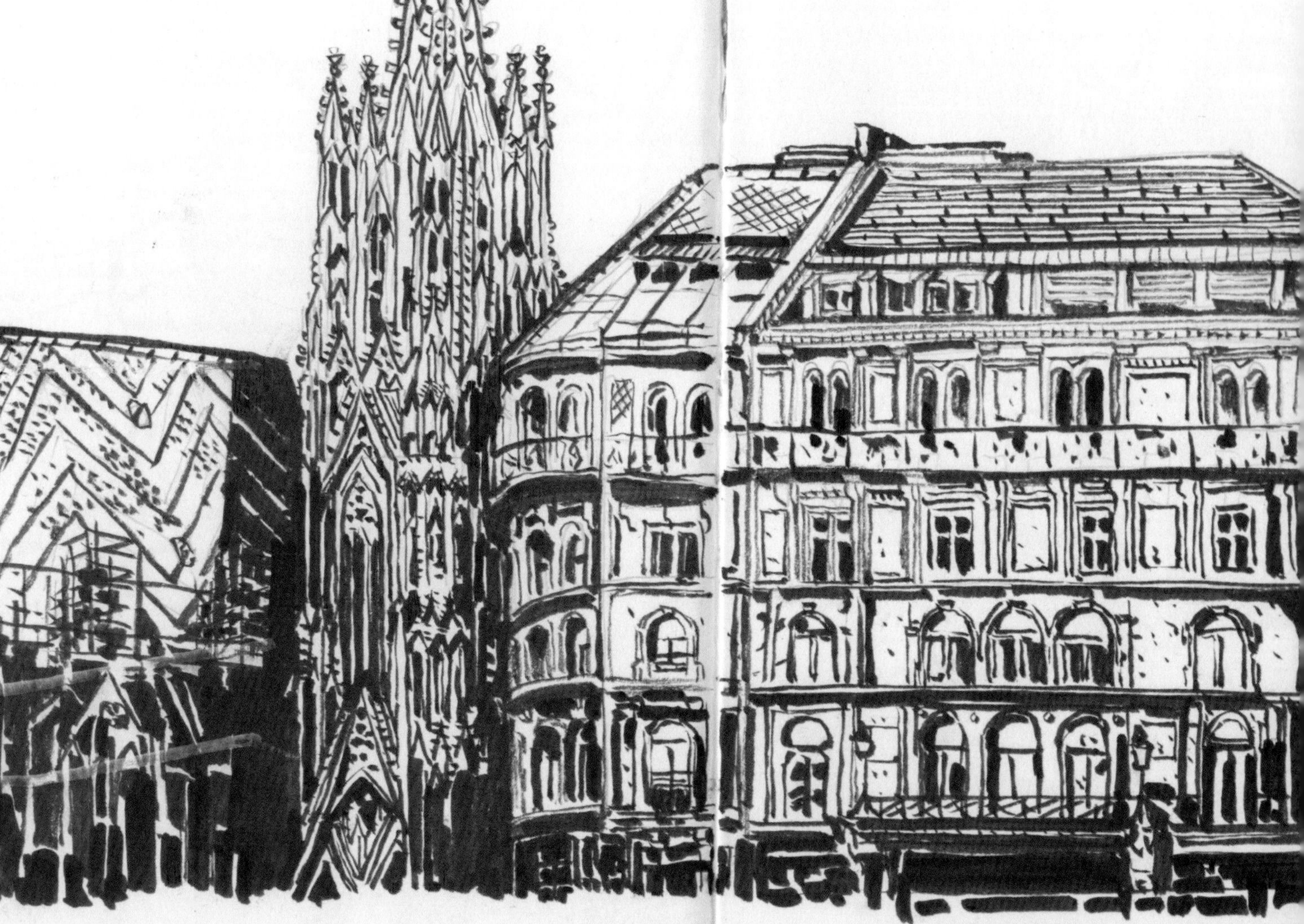
Stephansplatz
Wien.

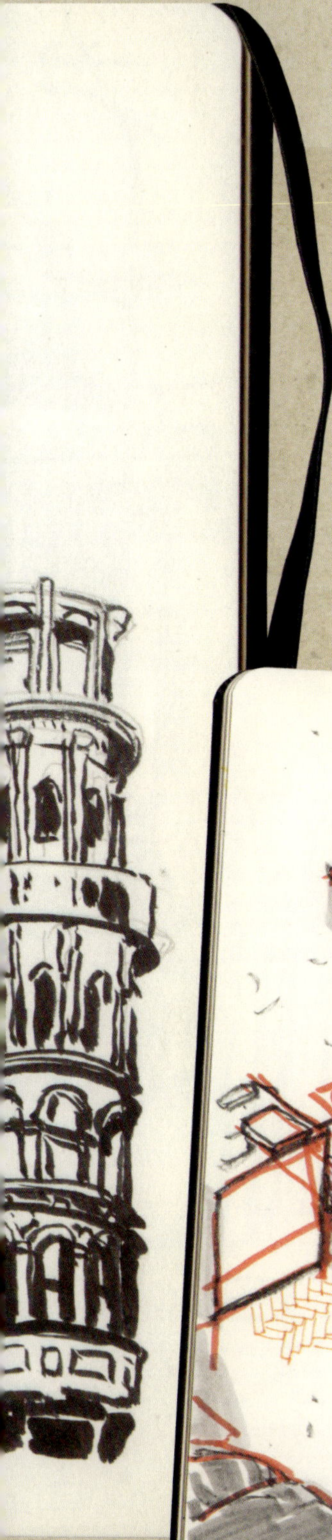

Public Sketching

This is Stephansplatz in Vienna, Austria. I remember drawing this on a bench outside, and passers-by stopped to watch me.

Interior Spaces

2016

The room I stayed in during my Vienna trip!

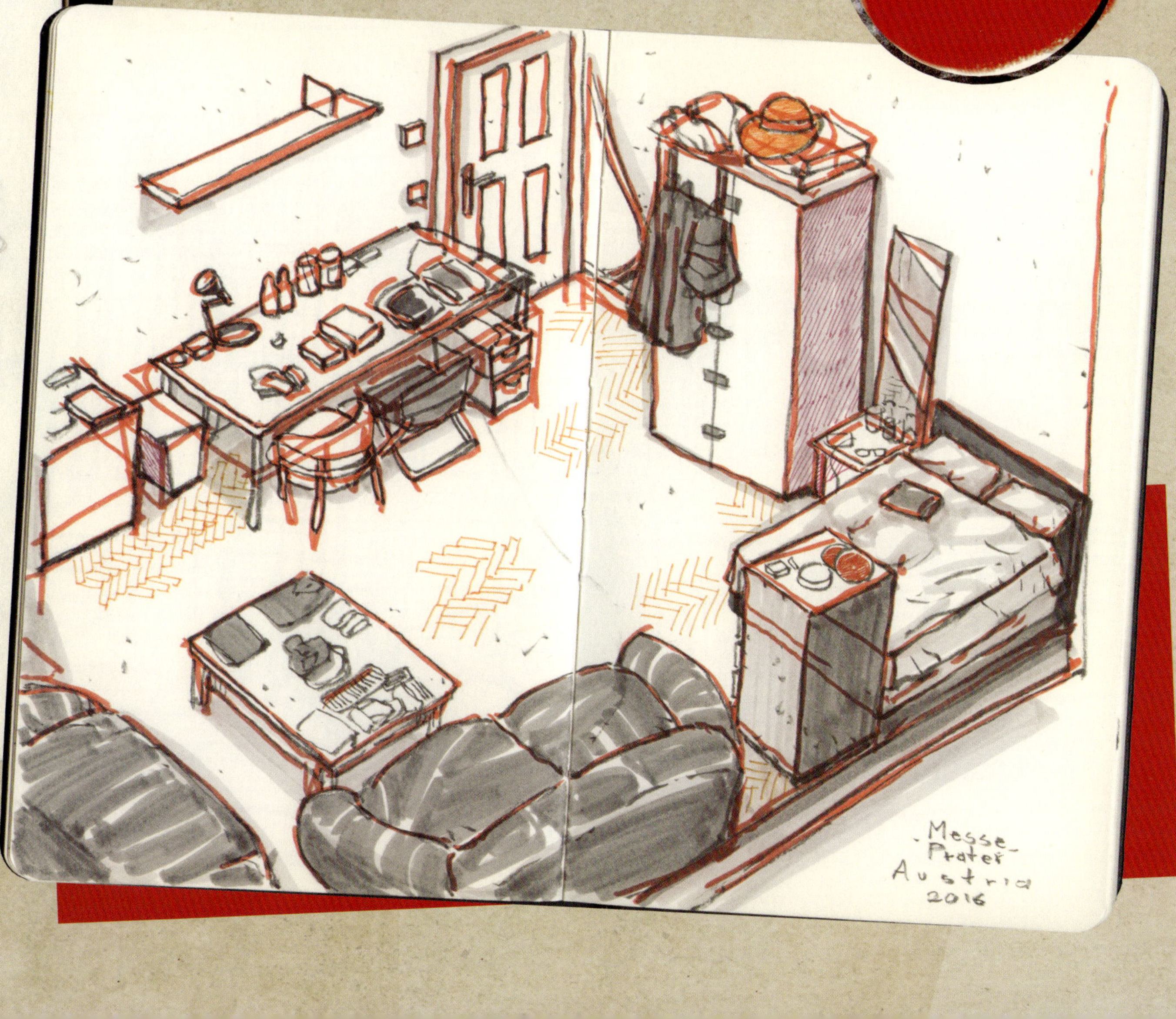

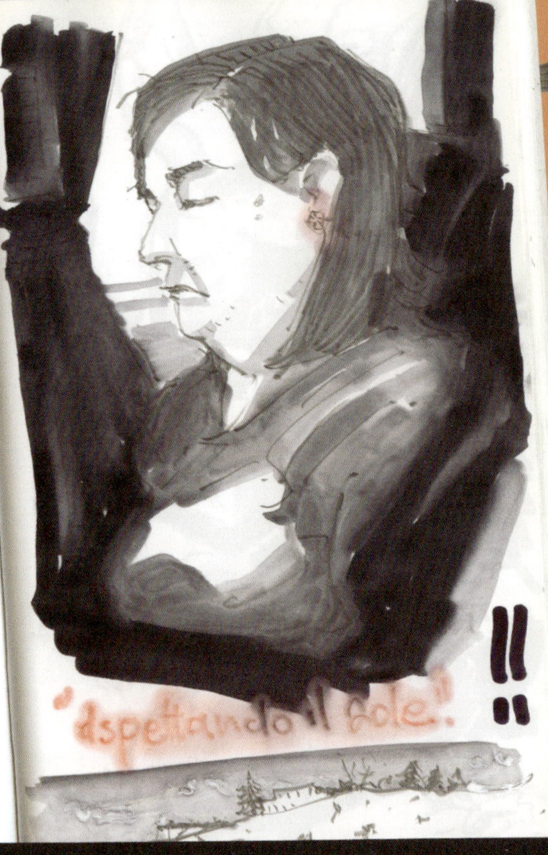

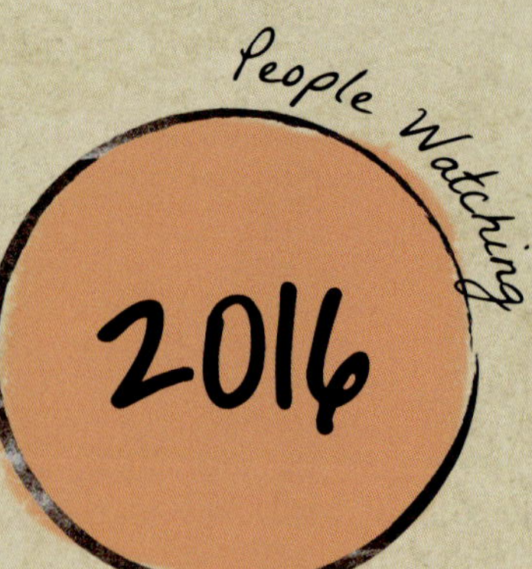

This particular sketch was made during a long bus ride. I was working away from home at the time, so every week I had to take a very tedious journey back. Of course, I used my time wisely, capturing people around me with my pencil.

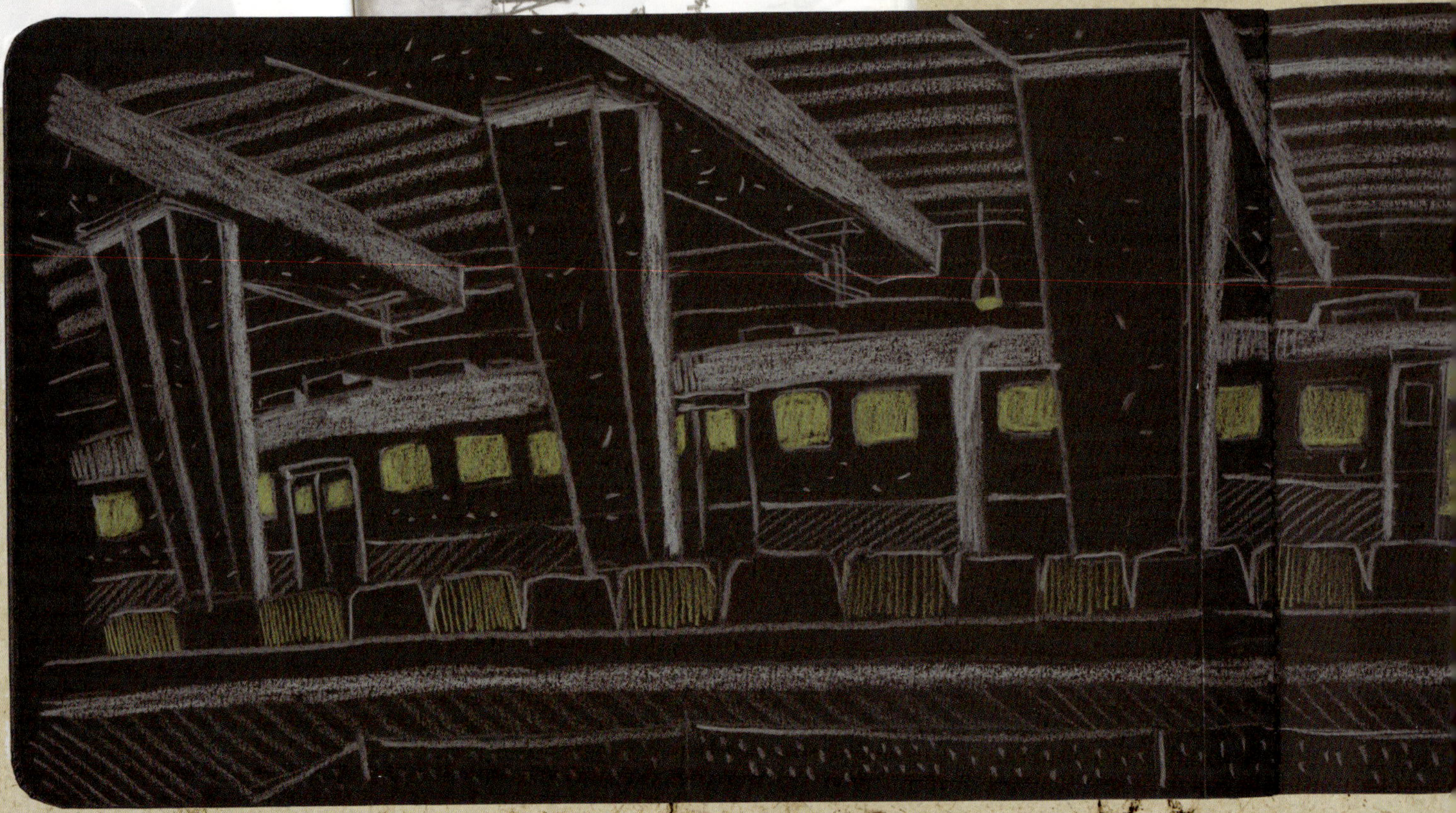

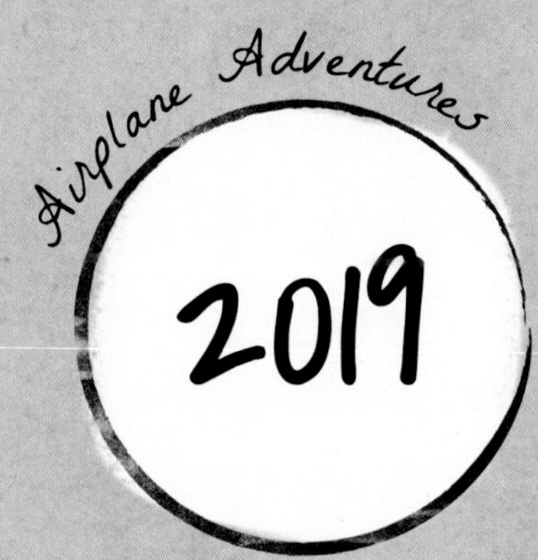

This is another example of how I took advantage of some quiet time. Playing around with perspective, I captured the interior of the plane from my aisle view.

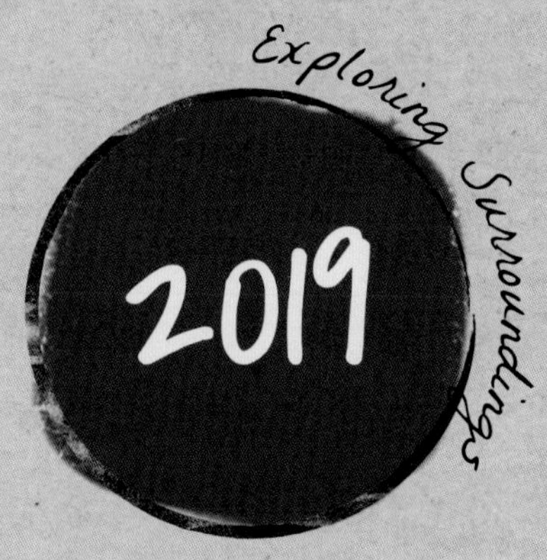

This is the station in Naples, Italy, the city where I live. It's another example of me trying something new. That's always been my goal in life – experimenting with new things, making cool things, collaborating with people, and networking with other artists. I live for it.

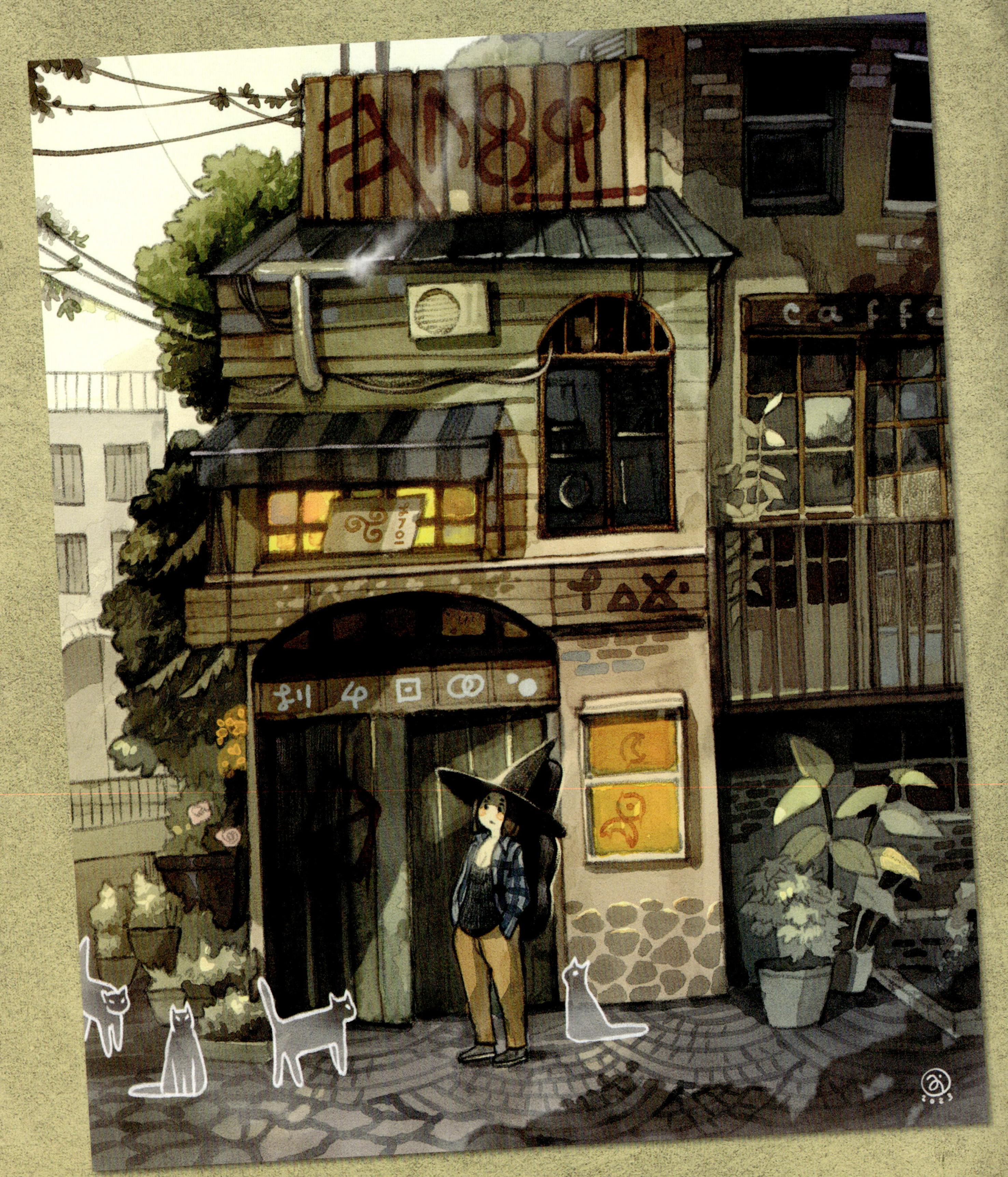
caffe

CREATIVE PROCESS

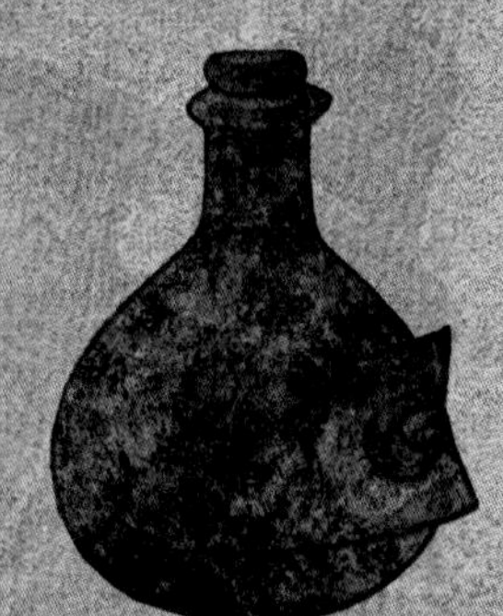

My perfect workspace ♡

From a digital point of view, I keep my interface as clean as possible. When using my illustrative software, I also try to keep an eye on the thumbnail – the small preview of your composition. Each time I stream, I always remind my viewers to look at the thumbnail. It's really important that the artwork looks good and readable at that tiny size because you can easily spot errors.

For my actual workspace, I have a mix of geeky devices like a tablet, buttons and boards for shortcuts, four screens, ring lights (for filming), a microphone, and other items used for streaming. It's a huge part of my career. For the past five years, I've been streaming on Twitch three days a week, every week, for three or four hours at a time. I have everything necessary for broadcasting. I'll use an external printing company if I need to print something physical, but I mostly use Redbubble as a third-party printer. I'm more about posting art in digital formats, so I tend to stick to that.

And there you have it – my not-so-secret secret work set-up and business technique.

Surrounded by inspiration

There's inspiration everywhere: my surroundings, the people and things I love, and other artists' illustrations. So many of the projects in my life are tied directly to these influences. Sometimes I'll find motivation to illustrate on a trip, or from a relationship, or even on video calls – it's that simple. If I feel like I need a boost, I'll get it from my artist friends, people in my community who update me on the latest trends, Pinterest, or other areas of pop culture.

My favourite tools

As far as digital software goes, I started off using Adobe Photoshop, but switched to Clip Studio Paint when I started working on the comic platform Webtoon. Although Photoshop has more colour-correction tools, filters, and is the best software for various editing effects, Clip Studio Paint has a powerful brush engine that I really enjoy. I've personalized it so much over the years that it's just become my go-to, and I use it almost all the time.

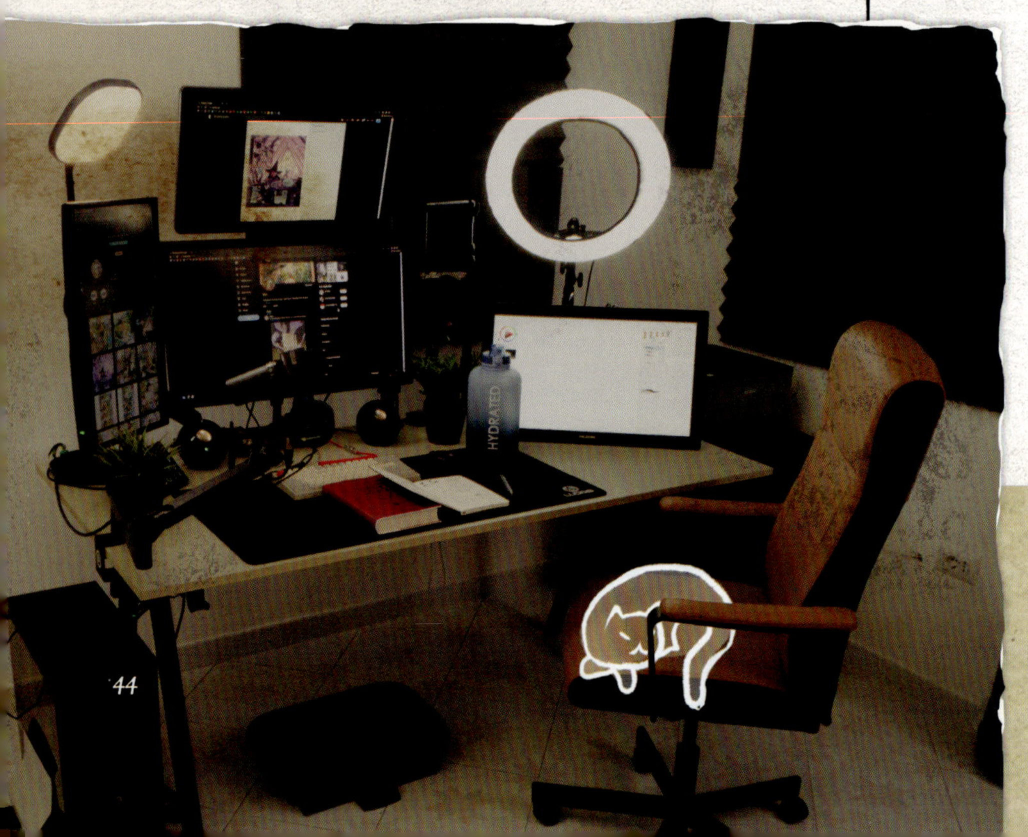

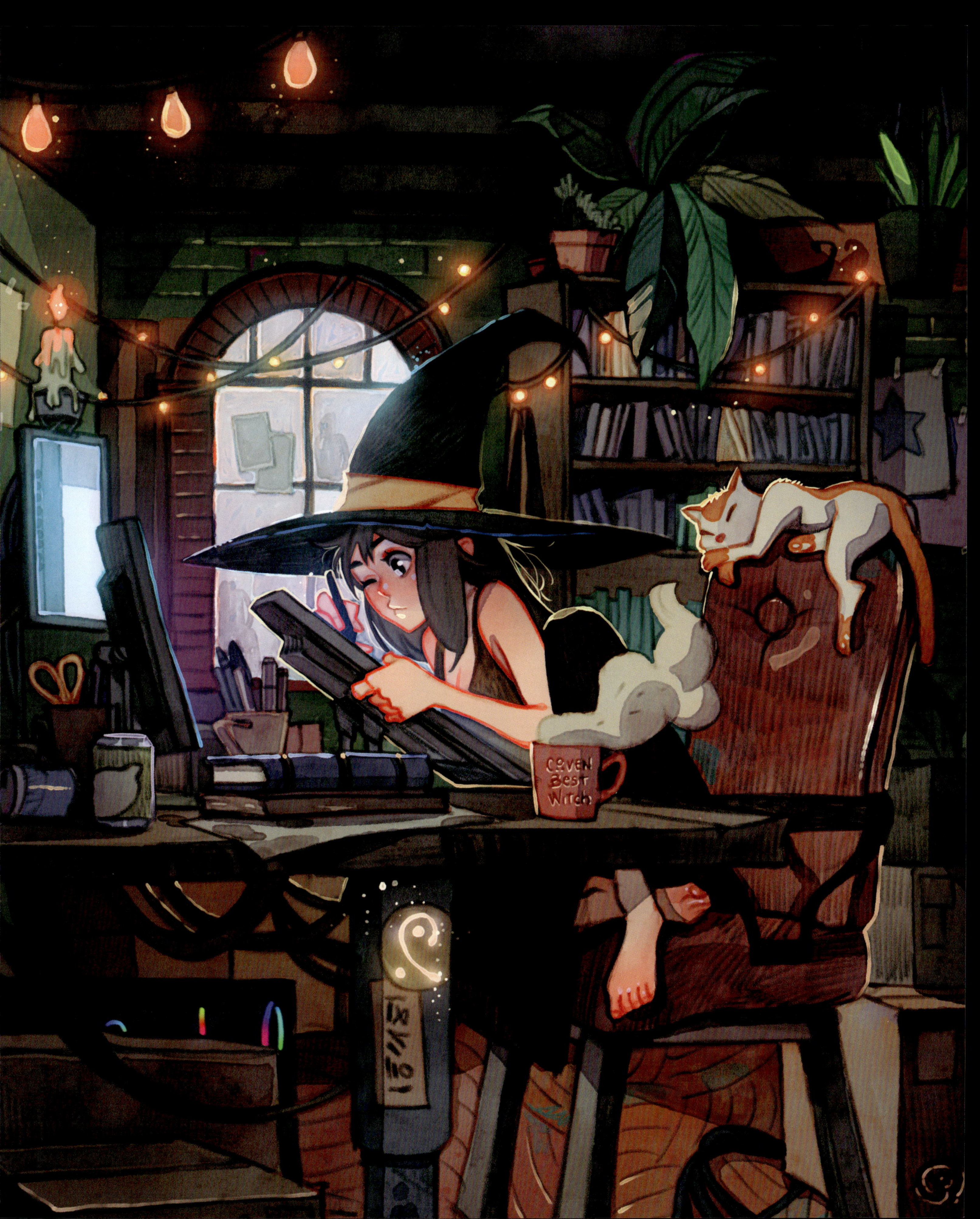
CoVEN Best Witch

Experimenting with different mediums

I started off traditionally, just like everyone else, and only moved to digital when I turned eighteen. A friend bought me my first digital tablet, so my medium transition was pretty late, considering where I am today. During art school, I did more graphic design than digital illustration, but I also kept drawing in my sketchbooks. I was twenty-six years old when I picked the digital tablet back up and made the jump to a freelance career.

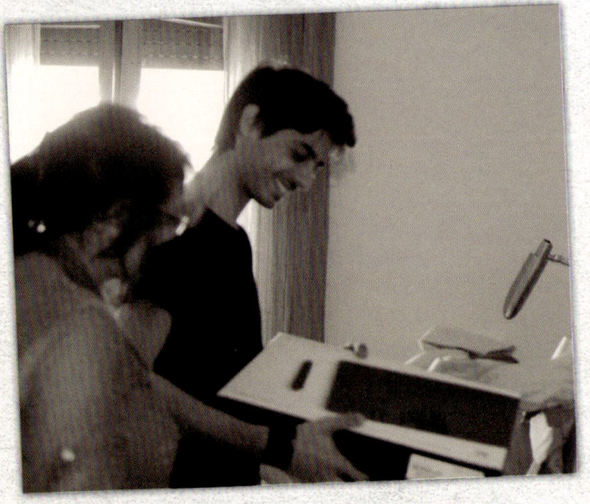

Working as a freelance illustrator really intensified my digital work, and I tried to incorporate many of my favourite aspects of traditional art. That's why many of my style choices gear towards watercolour and its technique. It was really important that my digital work looked as traditional as possible.

Choosing palettes & subjects

I've never really followed a specific colour palette, but seeing as I started my journey with yellow-tinged Moleskine pages, I like to apply the same vintage-like colour as a base and go from there. In the past, I chose a limited colour palette for comic projects such as *Falling in the Blue* on Webtoon, and for my current series, I use a lot of greens, sepia, and many other warm tones. The most comfortable way for me to approach colour is to follow the vibes I have in that specific moment – the 'colour under my eyes' that matches my mood.

The choice of subject really depends on what inspiring things I come across. Usually, I start with the pose or action; is my character sleeping, jumping, or running... waiting for the bus, catching the train? My illustration titles usually correlate to these actions as well. If I have a character eating a burrito, the name of the piece will most likely be *Burrito*. It's a running joke between me and my girlfriend, because she thinks I just pick out random names. But hey, identity is built through action!

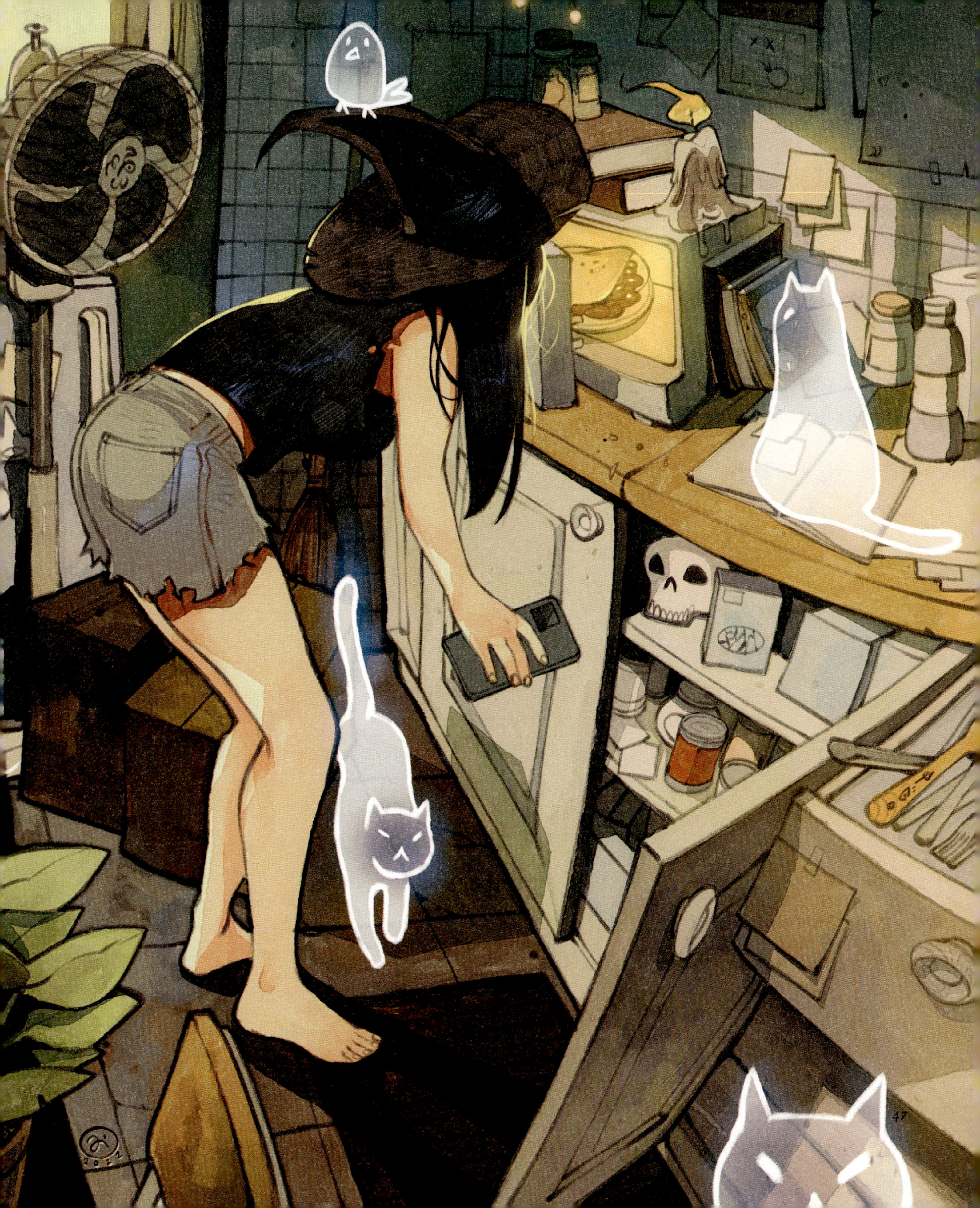

Mini tutorial

Whether you're working digitally or traditionally, painting processes can differ slightly from artist to artist. To get a better understanding of my method, I've broken down one of my favourite illustrations, *Out of Control*. I wanted to explore where the ghost cats came from, or at least the idea that the protagonists interact with them in different ways. I don't always draw characters with extreme expressions or poses because they may not leave enough room for the viewer's imagination. My main goal here was to expand this world's lore.

To better explain myself, I'll separate the illustration into layers. Let's break it down!

Sketch

To start, I roughly sketch the idea down. Normally, I add the ghost cats during the final stages of the illustration, but here they're part of the main concept. As they are exploding out of the cauldron, it's important to sketch their bodies to resemble an ethereal, liquid-like substance.

I quickly sketch the character's alarmed expression, and add in small details I can fine-tune later, such as the potion bottles, witch hat, and room layout.

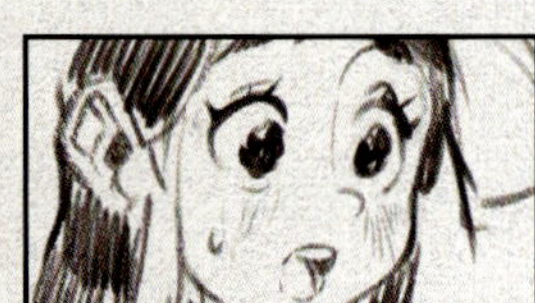

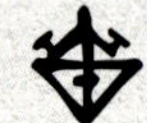

Line work

I'm a big fan of images that showcase interior spaces. They provide opportunities to include elements that emphasize the concept of modern witches living like normal people. I make sure to keep the lines soft and organic; it's important that they don't appear too stiff. I leave out the erupting ghost cats for now (they're translucent, so I won't be jeopardizing any detail).

During this phase, I also focus on perspective and depth. The composition is split into three planes: the foreground with the table and cauldron, the middle ground showcasing the witch, and the interior background. These volumes will make my illustration appear much more dynamic.

I'm not worrying about it looking perfect. Instead, I focus on perspective and storytelling.

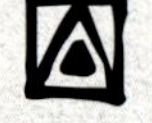

Colour

To begin the colouring process, the first thing I do is flatten the character and set the liner to a blending mode called Color Burn. As the word suggests, flattening refers to filling all the areas with flat colours. These areas have no shading. I start from the foreground, making sure my palette has muted, earthy tones. Once all of the colours are applied for the background, middle ground, and foreground, I can add shadows to create a better sense of depth.

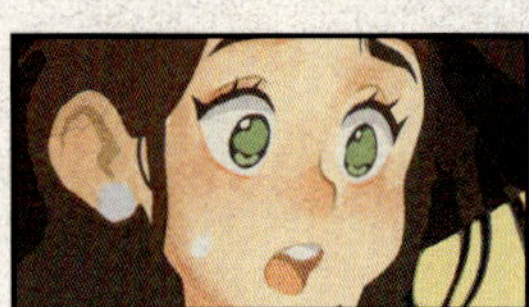

To finish, I add some rim light and highlights around the character's head and hair. These small details will ensure that the face captures attention.

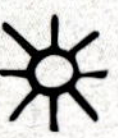

Translucent cauldron cats

I give the cauldron cats their own layer to better focus on the details. The fun thing about working with layers is that you can add or amend elements without compromising the rest of the illustration. Having the cats on a separate layer also makes the colouring process easier. I fill the line work in using a blue hue, and amend the layer opacity so the cats appear translucent.

Although my artwork has a 'traditional' feel, I still make use of the convenience and power of digital software.

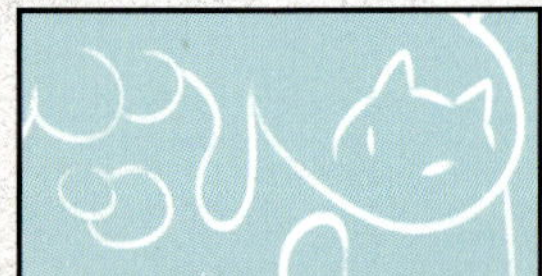

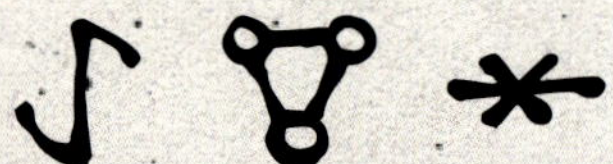

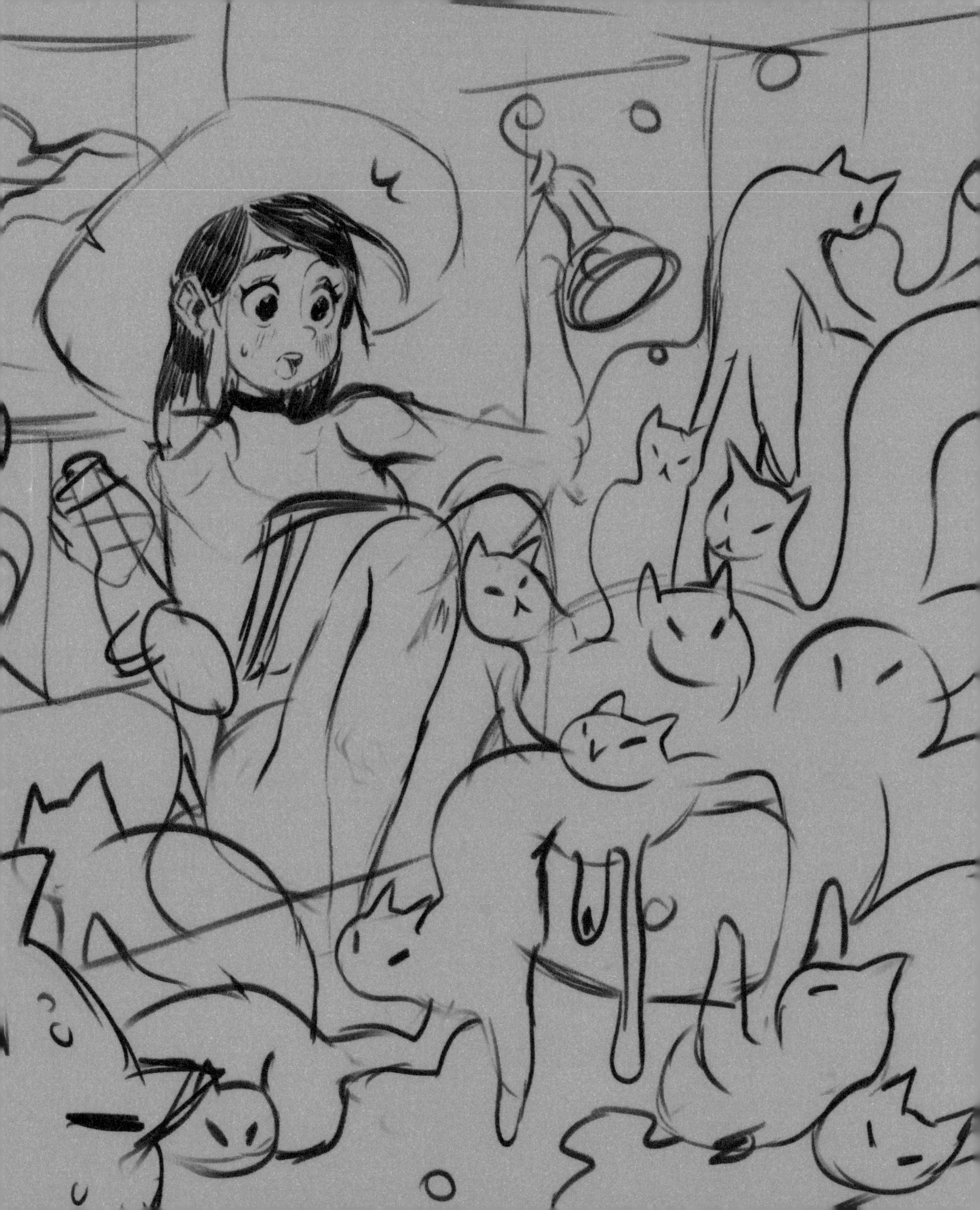

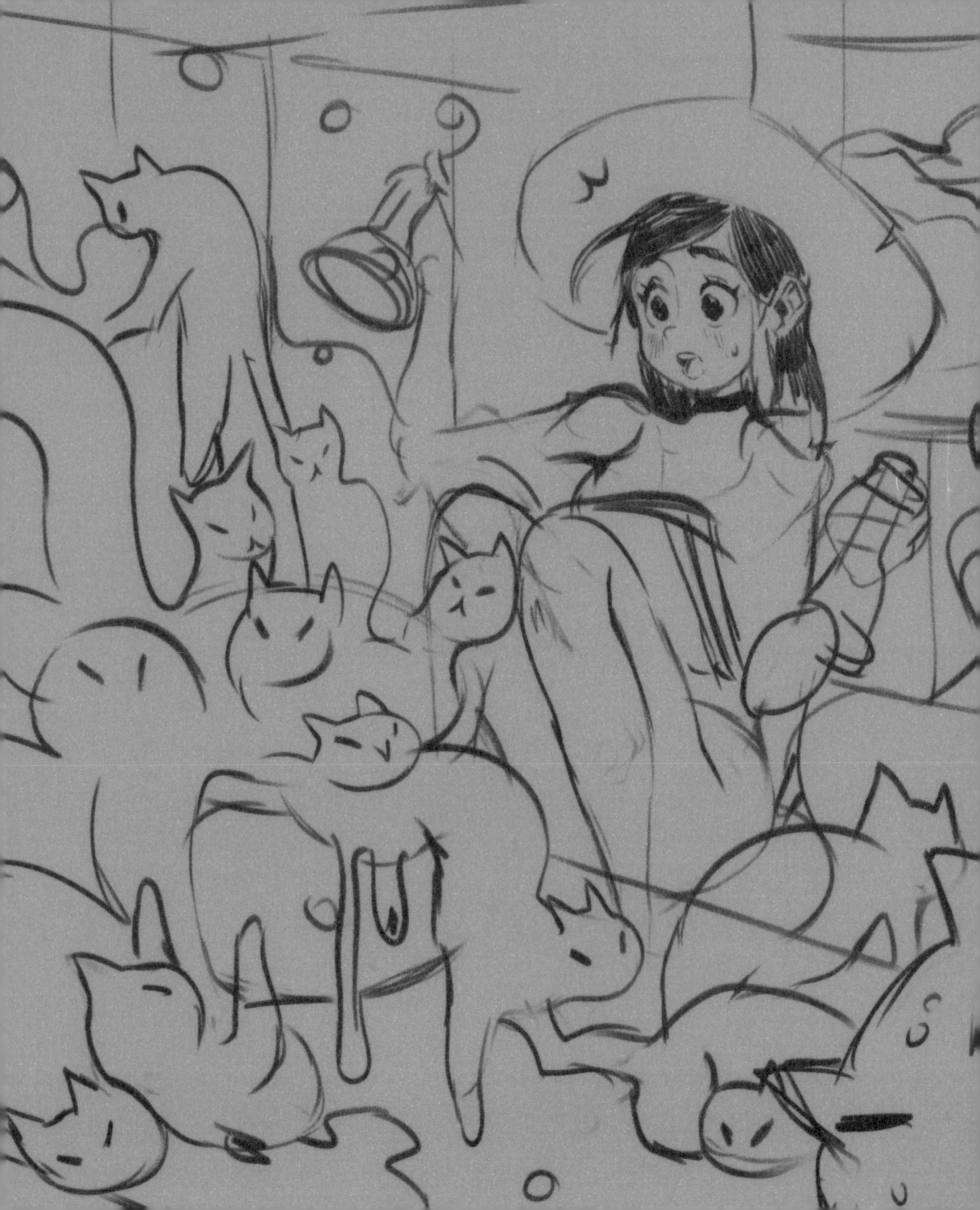

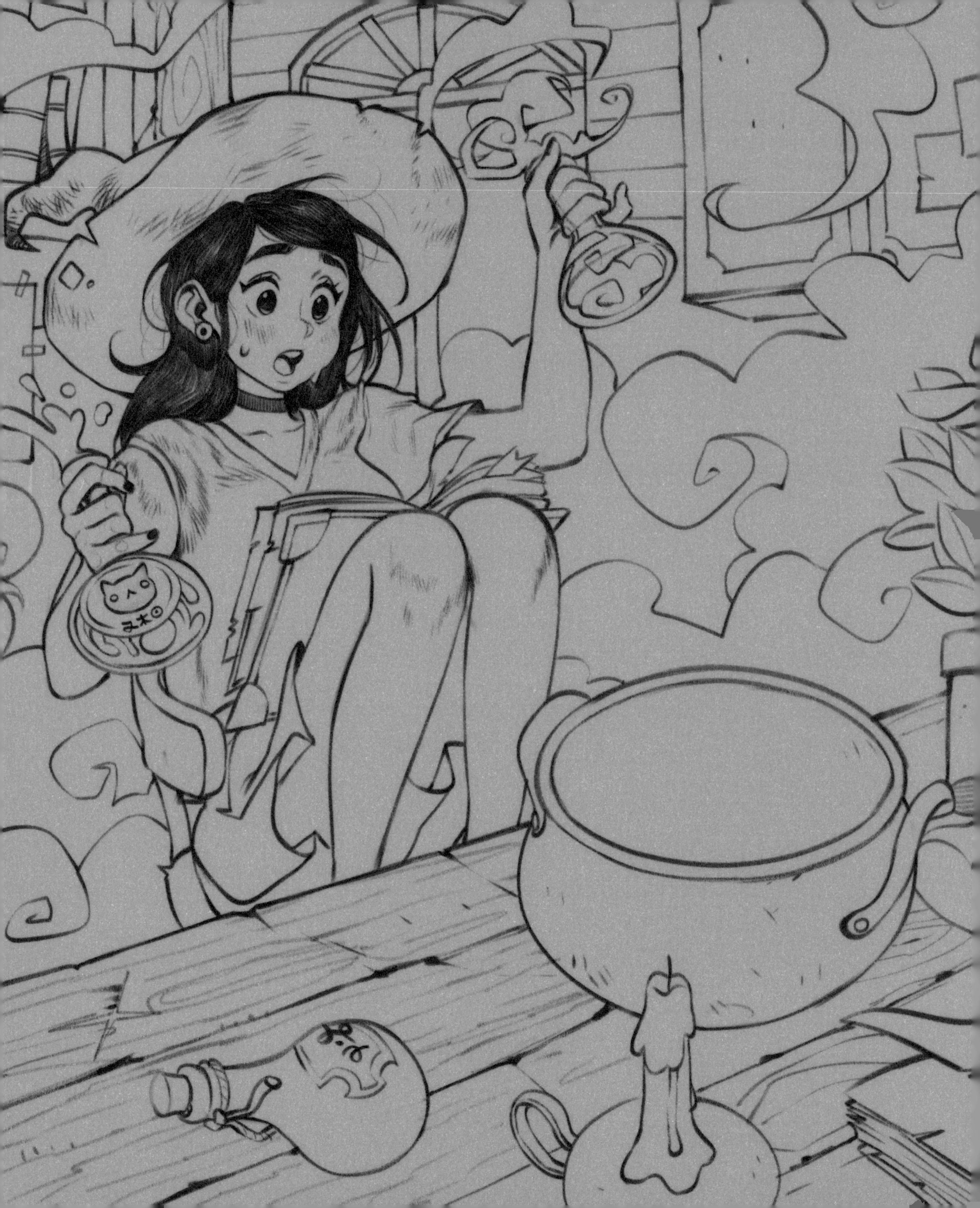

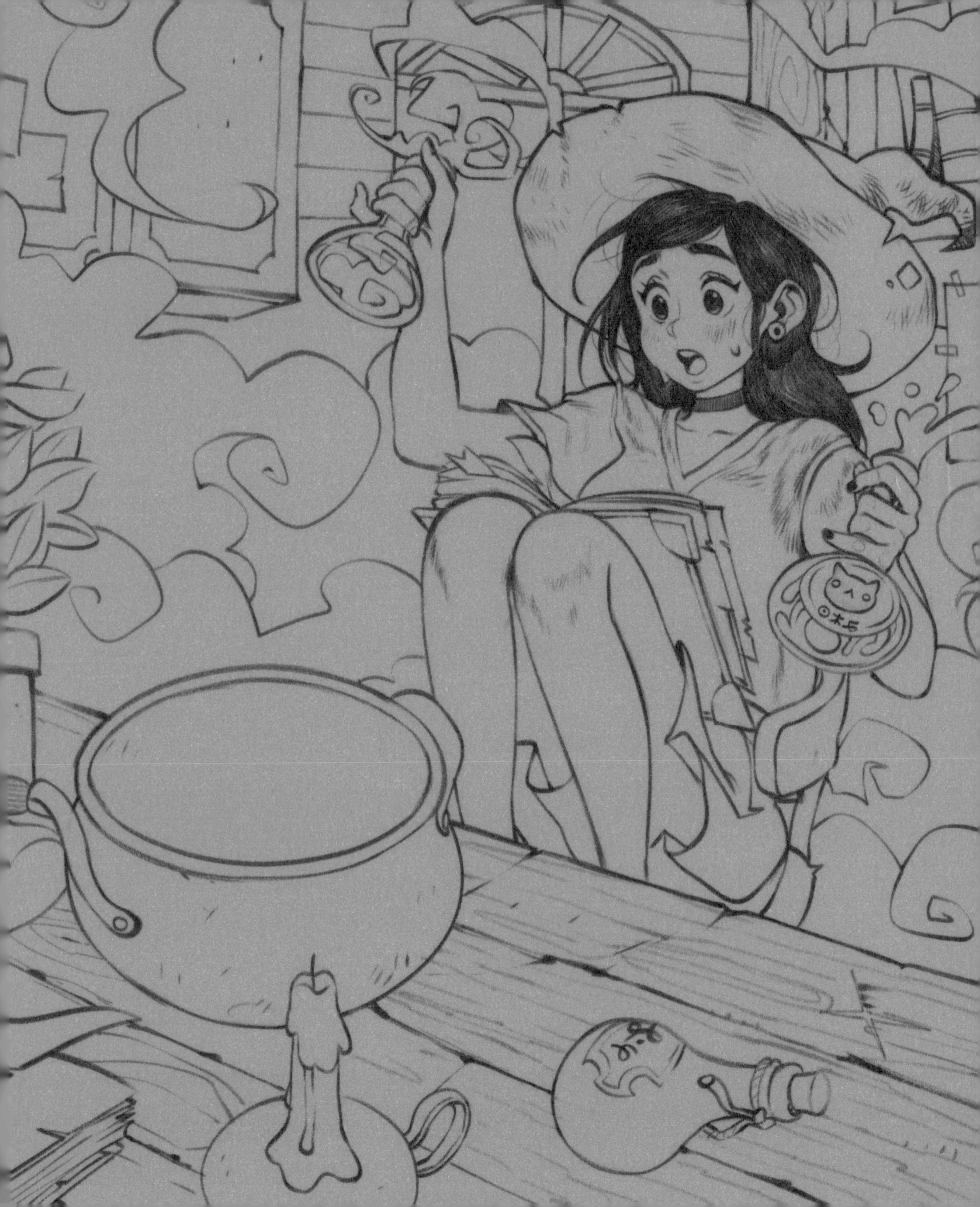

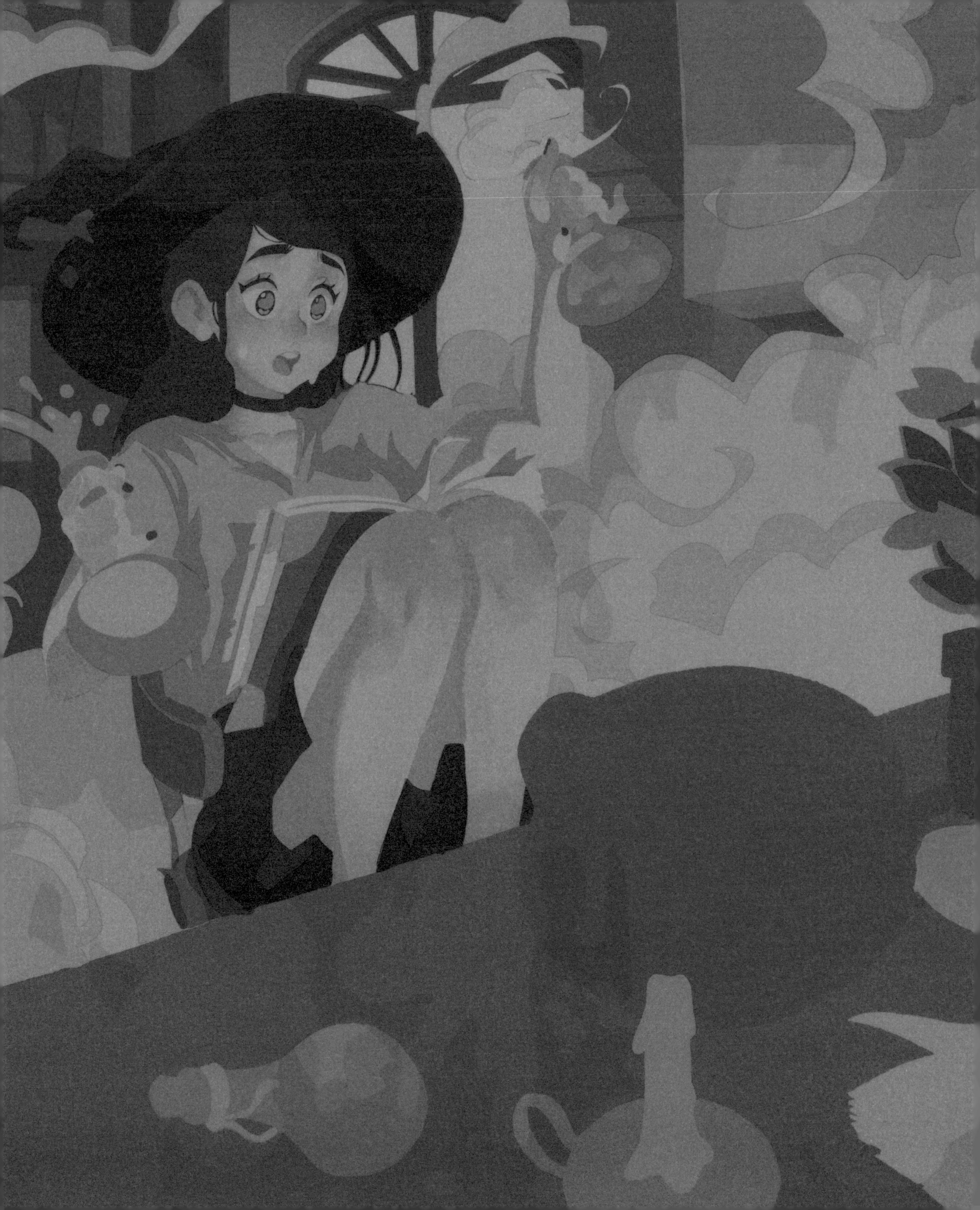

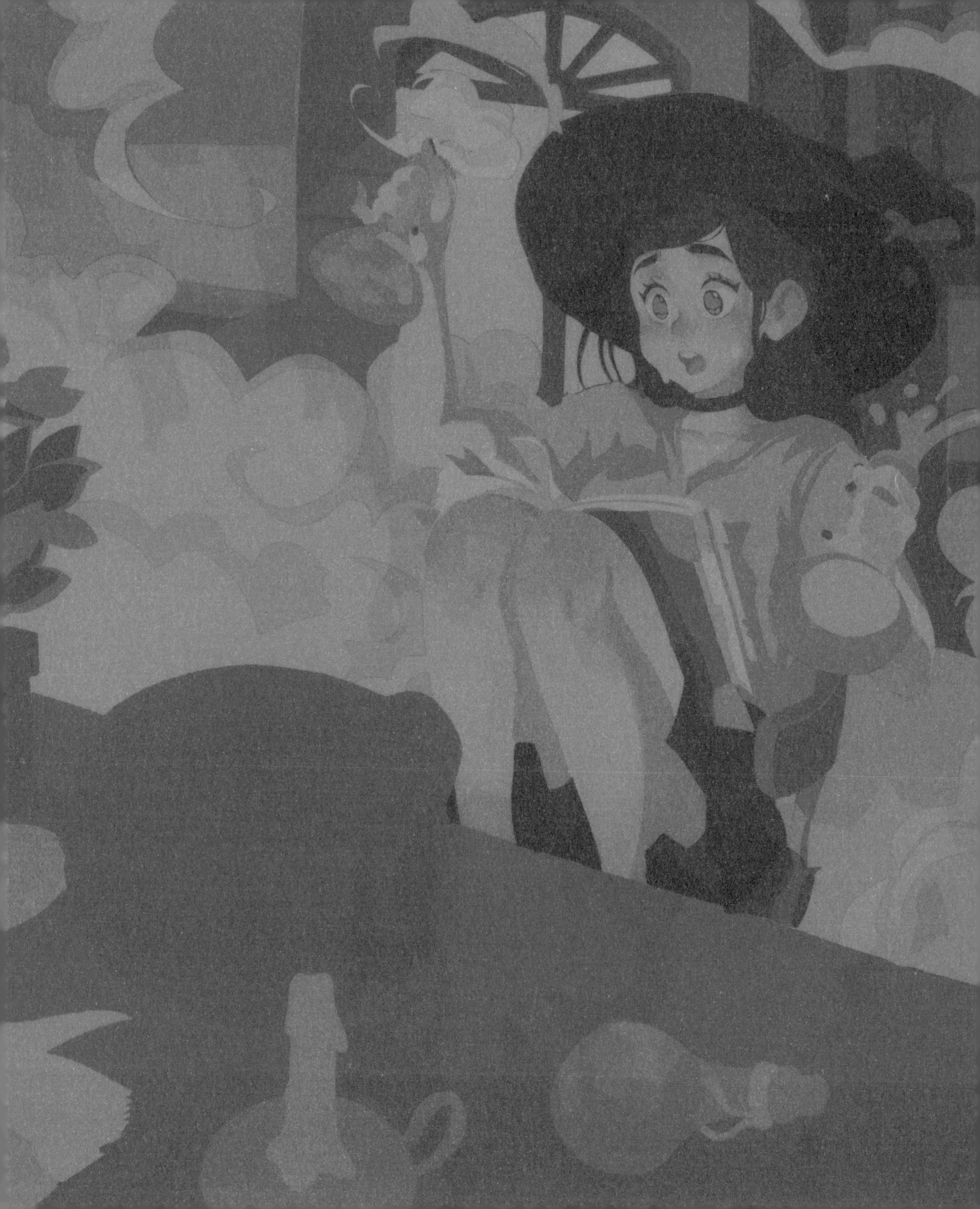

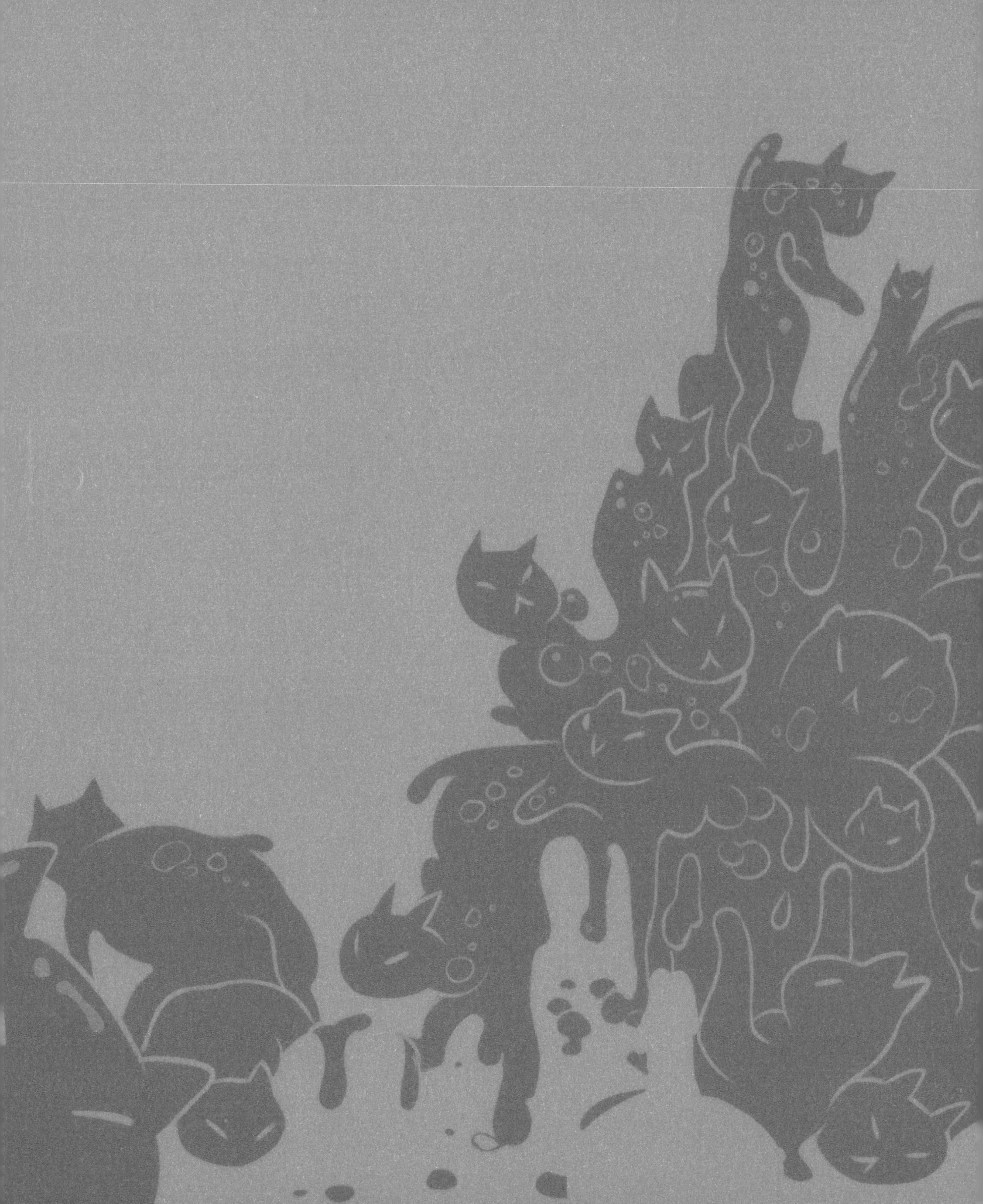

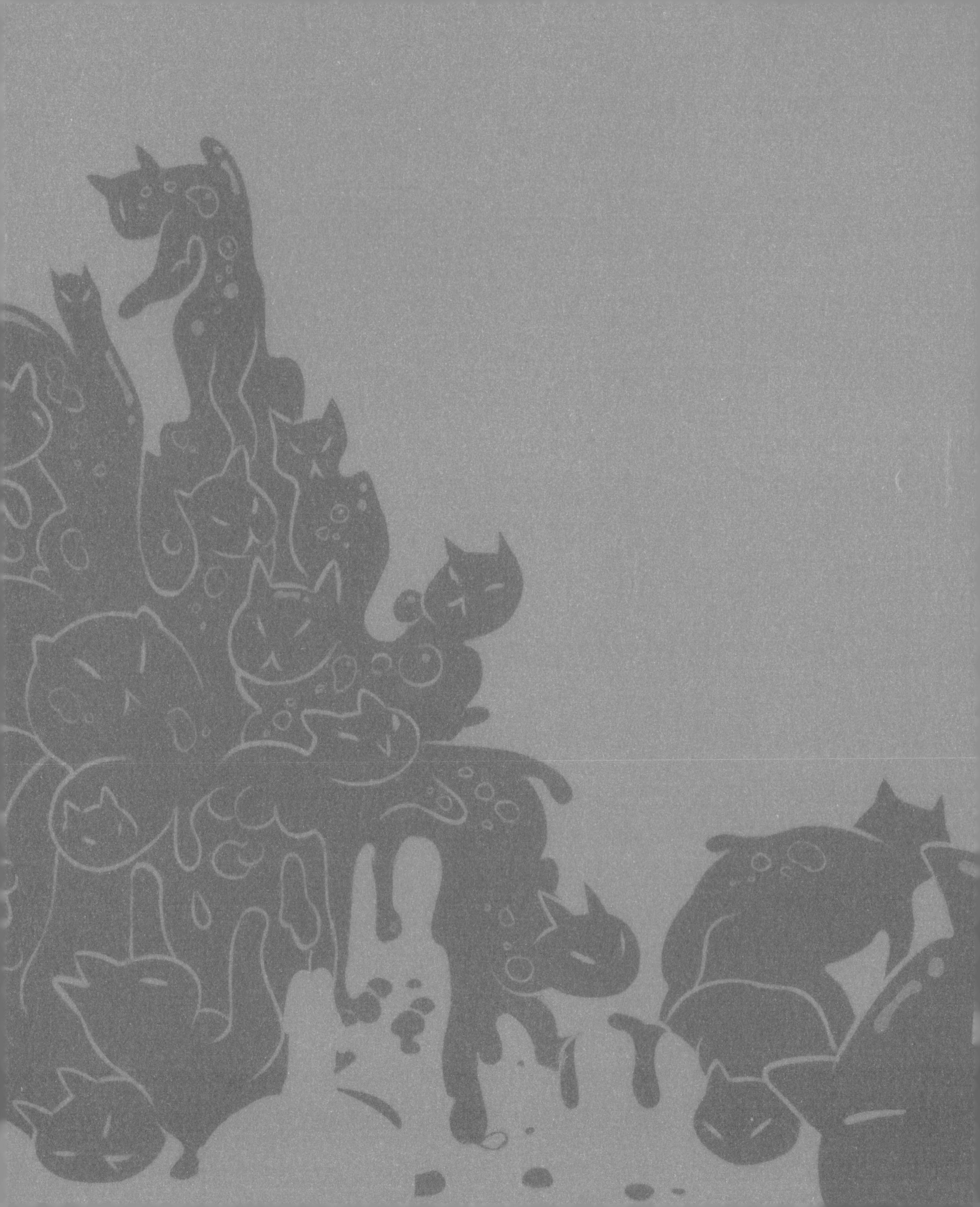

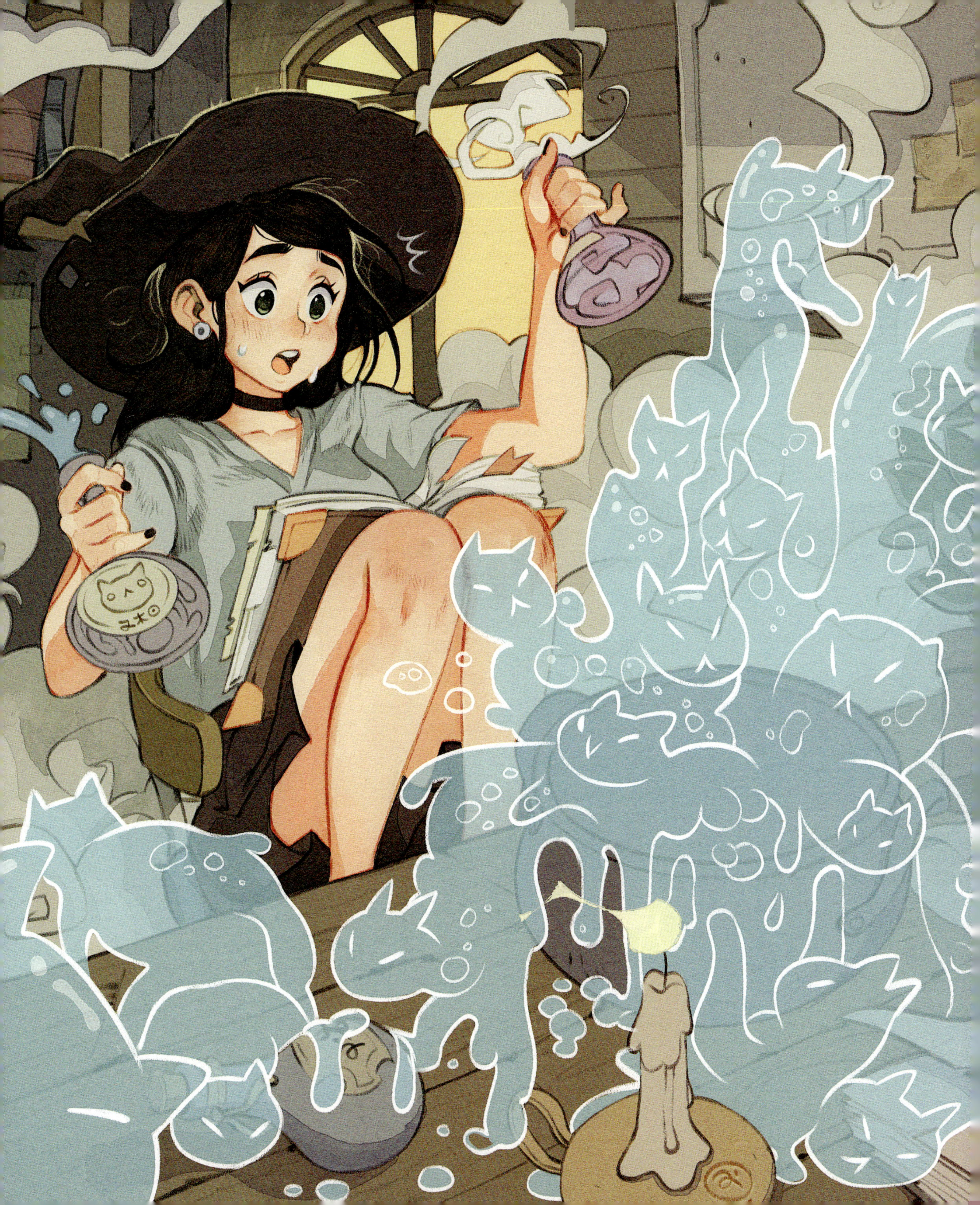

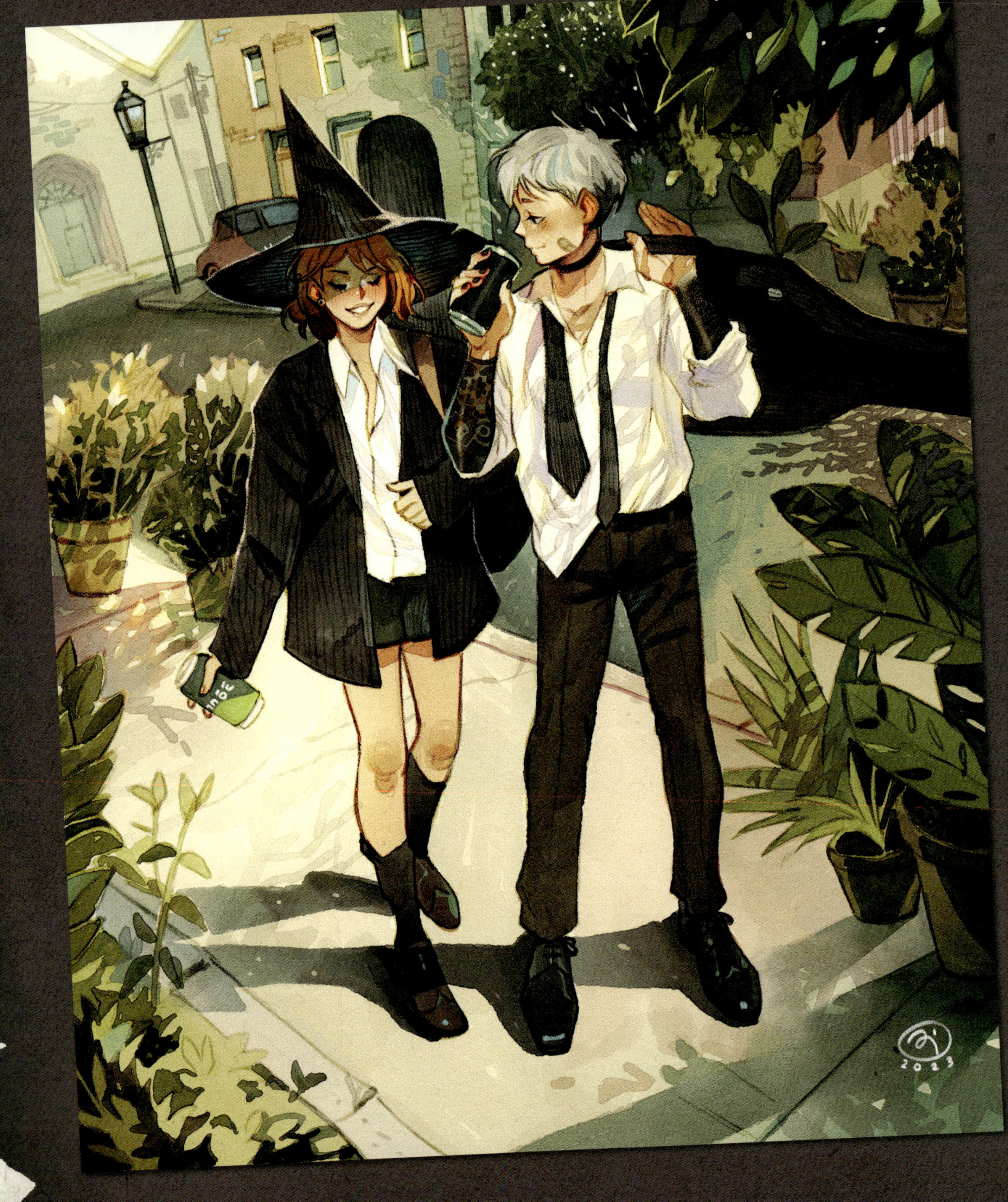
2023

COMICS

Before I began working on my witch project, I had another one that involved two characters and a kiwi bird. If you look at my older work from around 2020, you will come across the orange and teal palette I used for the illustrations.

My initial idea was to make a comic and then find a publisher for printing purposes, but I was approached by a writer before I got to that stage, and we ended up publishing together on Webtoon. It didn't take long for one of their editors to approach us, and soon after, Webtoon bought the rights for the project. They published it as a Webtoon Original called *Falling in the Blue*, which you can still find on the site.

My whole experience with Webtoon has been a bit of a rollercoaster ride, as well as a learning curve. The project has a really unique aesthetic, which was especially reflective of my style at the time, and I think it still holds up today. Maybe I'll continue working on it in the future, who knows!

Since my work for *Falling in the Blue* was copyrighted, I couldn't share those comics on my social-media channels, so that's when I started working on my witches. What began as a side project soon turned into *Ghost Cats and Tea* – a continuing story about a witch who is the only person with the ability to see these phantom felines.

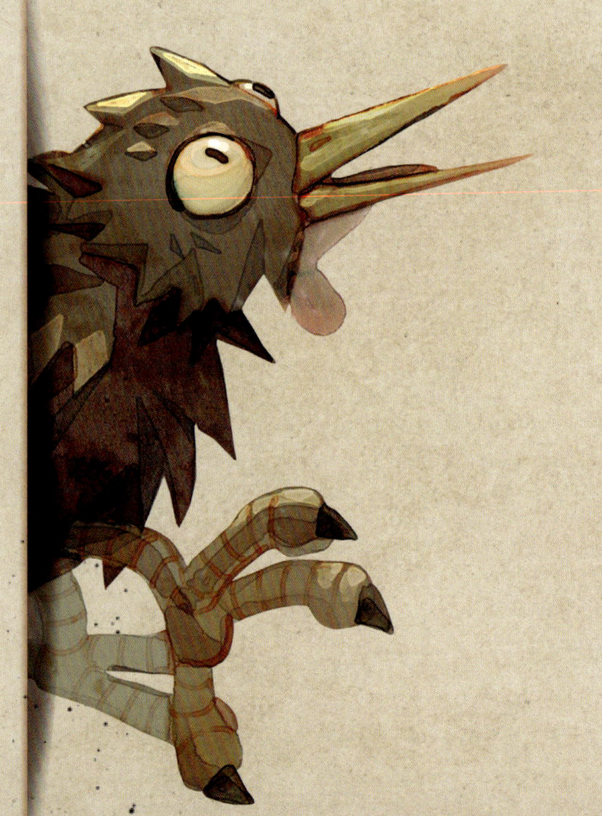

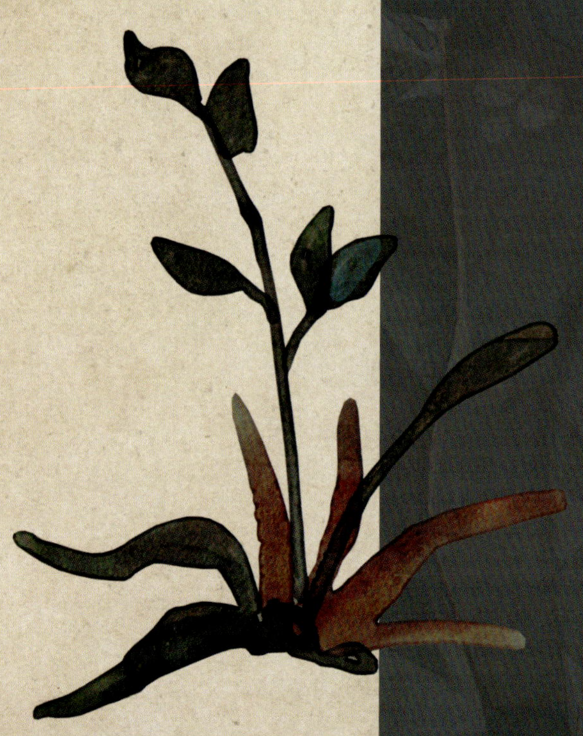

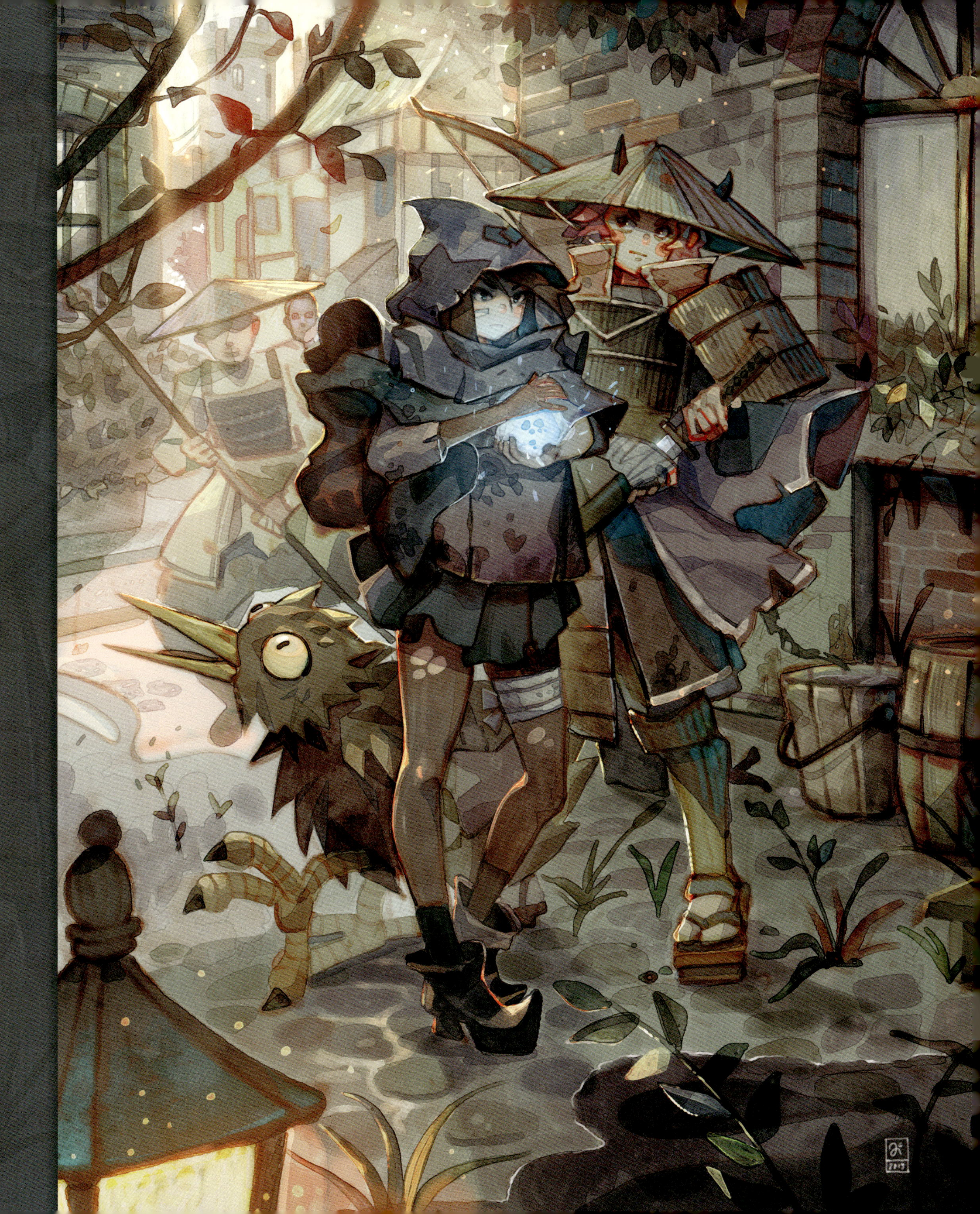

Webtoon comics

1 **A Day Like Any Other**
This is the first episode from a comic series based around a rough idea. I decided to test the water and see how people would react. I posted it in April 2022, and the second episode a few days later, then I took a hiatus until 2023. The idea was to showcase a possible scenario of how the overarching story would start, and when I revisited the project, I decided to continue the story from here.

In this episode I created my main character, Ony, and established a very clear aesthetic mood and concept.

2 **Arcane Innovations**
This episode came a year later. I tried to use the same aesthetic as shown in the first episodes, but this one has a script and ideas that I wanted to develop further. In this case, my main character Ony and another called Christina meet each other in a flashback. I didn't announce that it was a flashback, and didn't give away too many hints; I let people make their own minds up by reading and enjoying the story.

Creating comics is a totally different process to creating illustrations. The resolution for Webtoon is smaller and the tools are slightly different, so I calibrate the images for web comics to be read on a phone. The aesthetic has to work on a small screen.

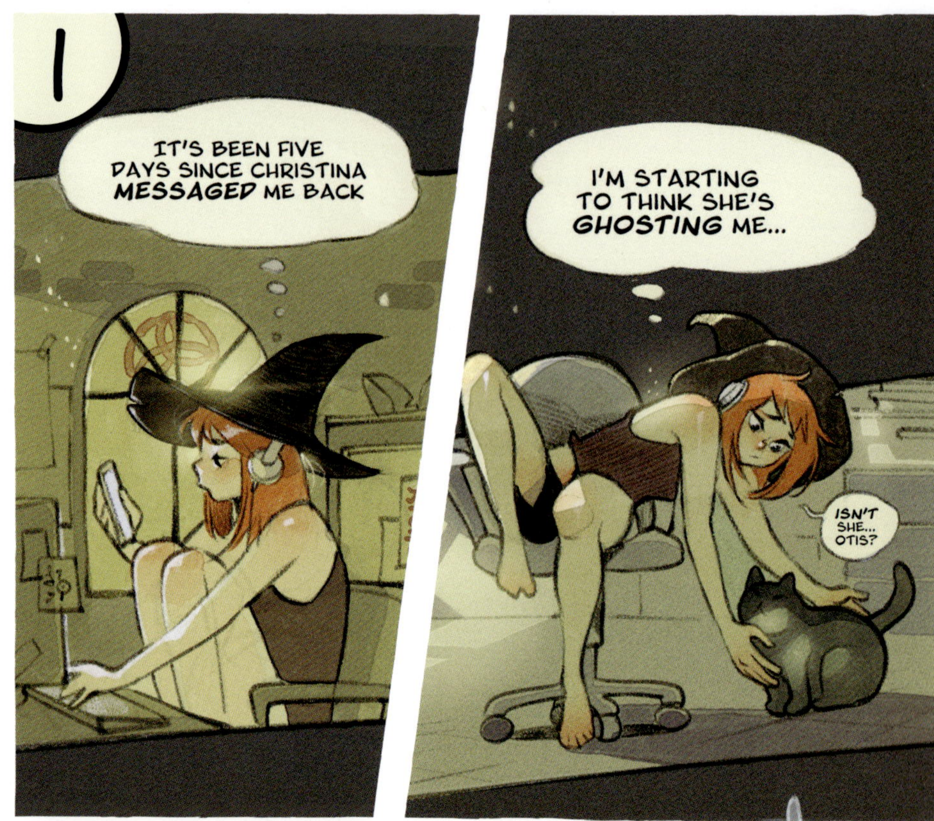

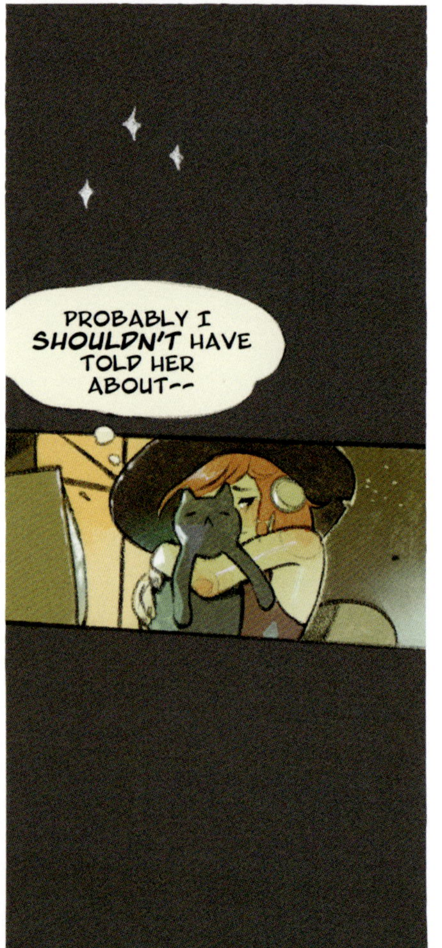

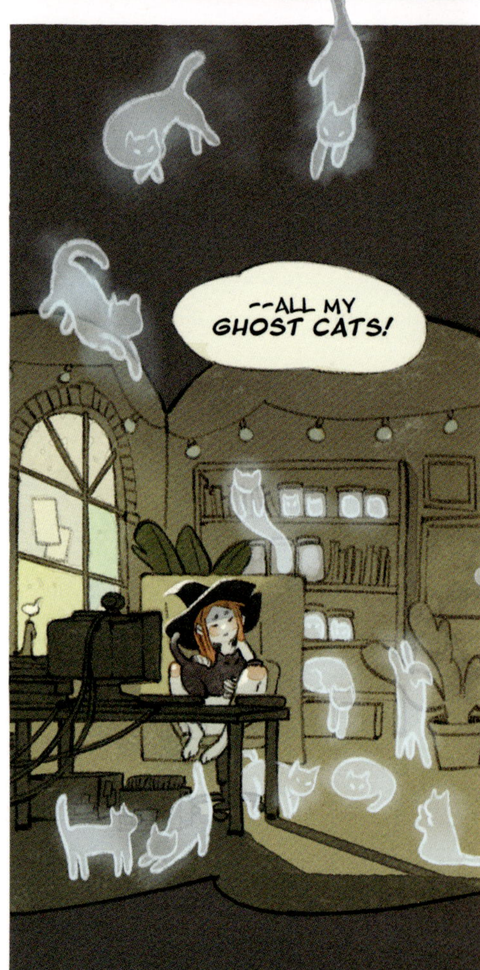

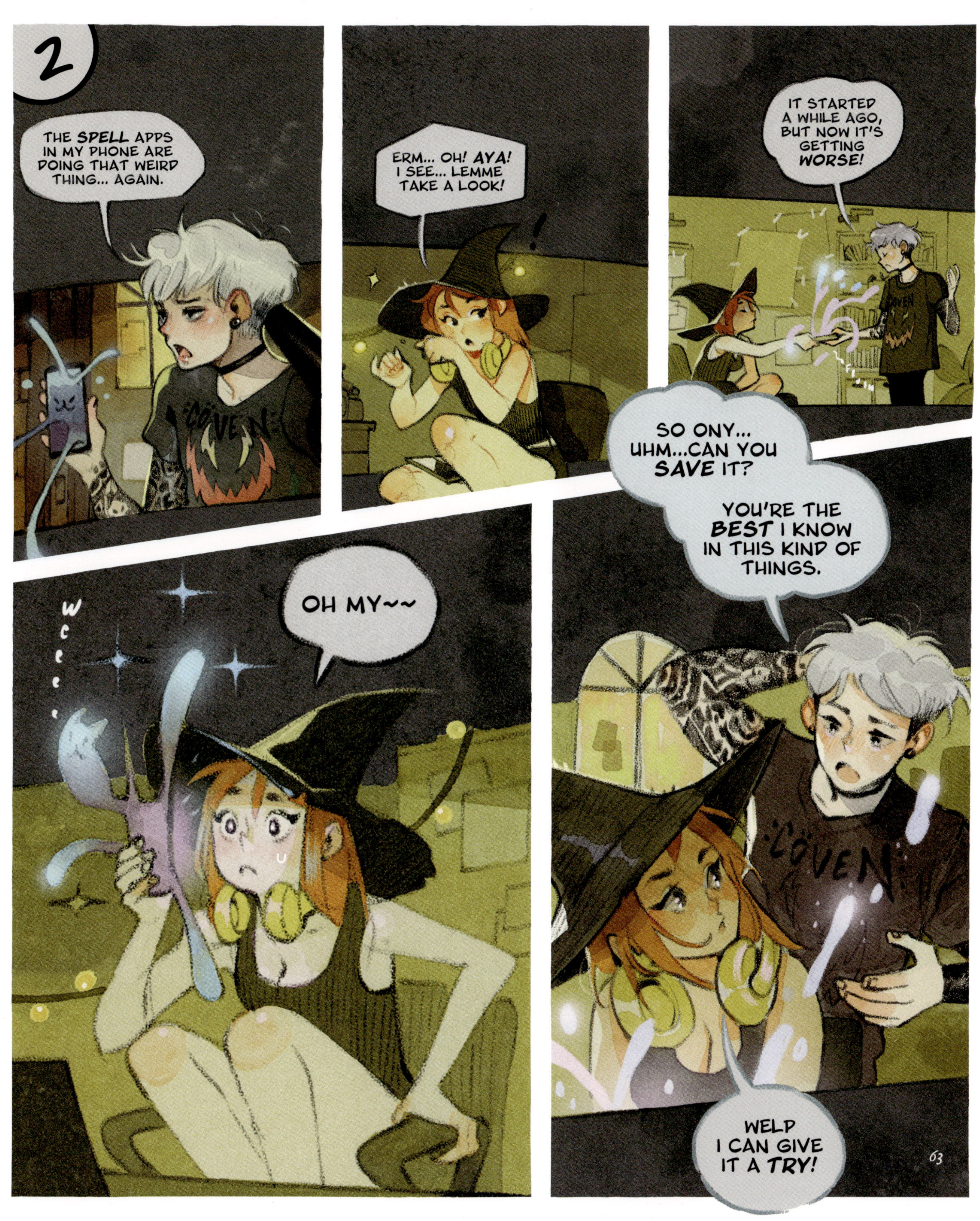
2
THE SPELL APPS IN MY PHONE ARE DOING THAT WEIRD THING... AGAIN.
ERM... OH! AYA! I SEE... LEMME TAKE A LOOK!
!
IT STARTED A WHILE AGO, BUT NOW IT'S GETTING WORSE!
COVEN
OH MY~~
SO ONY... UHM...CAN YOU SAVE IT?
YOU'RE THE BEST I KNOW IN THIS KIND OF THINGS.
COVEN
WELP I CAN GIVE IT A TRY!

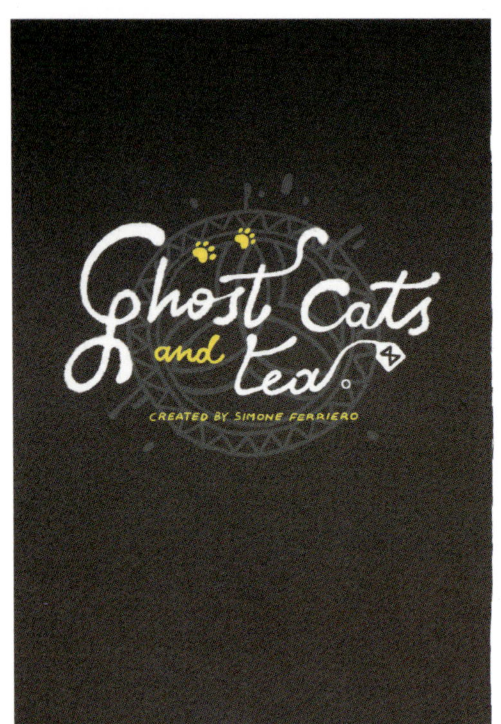
Ghost Cats and Tea
CREATED BY SIMONE FERRIERO

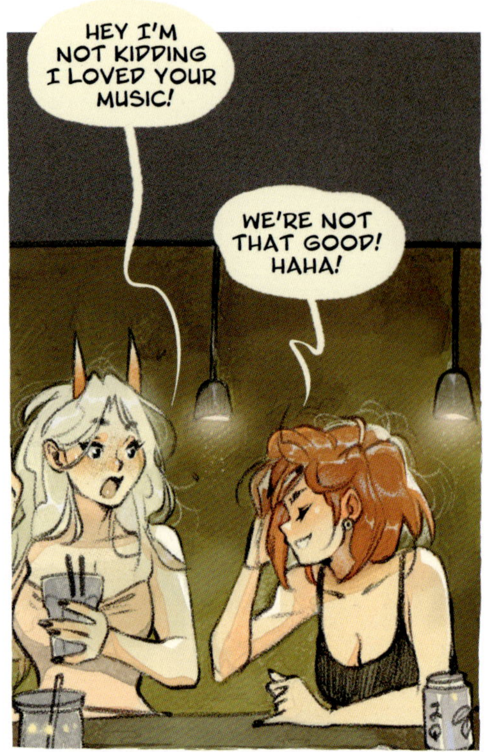
HEY I'M NOT KIDDING I LOVED YOUR MUSIC!
WE'RE NOT THAT GOOD! HAHA!

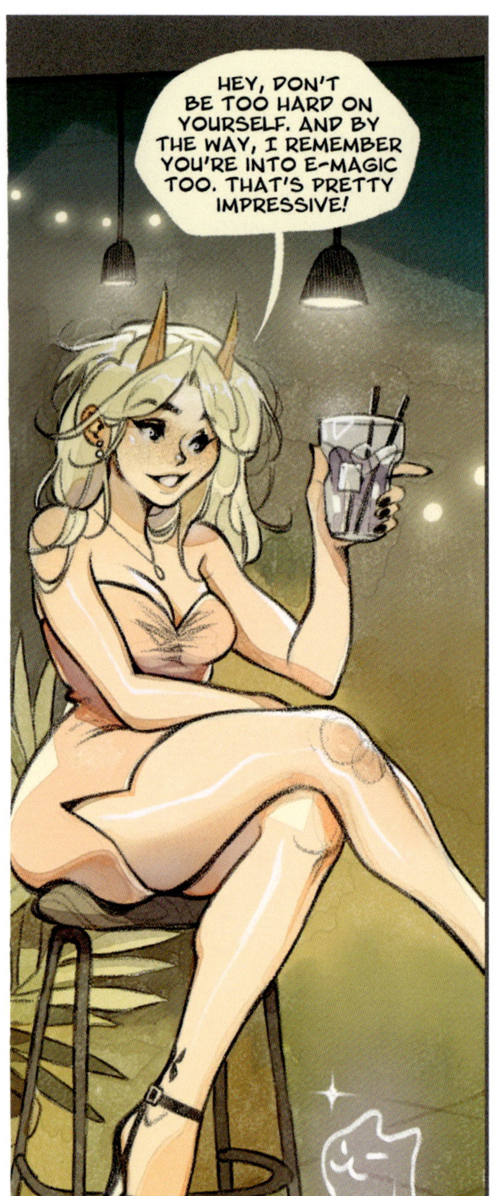
HEY, DON'T BE TOO HARD ON YOURSELF. AND BY THE WAY, I REMEMBER YOU'RE INTO E-MAGIC TOO. THAT'S PRETTY IMPRESSIVE!

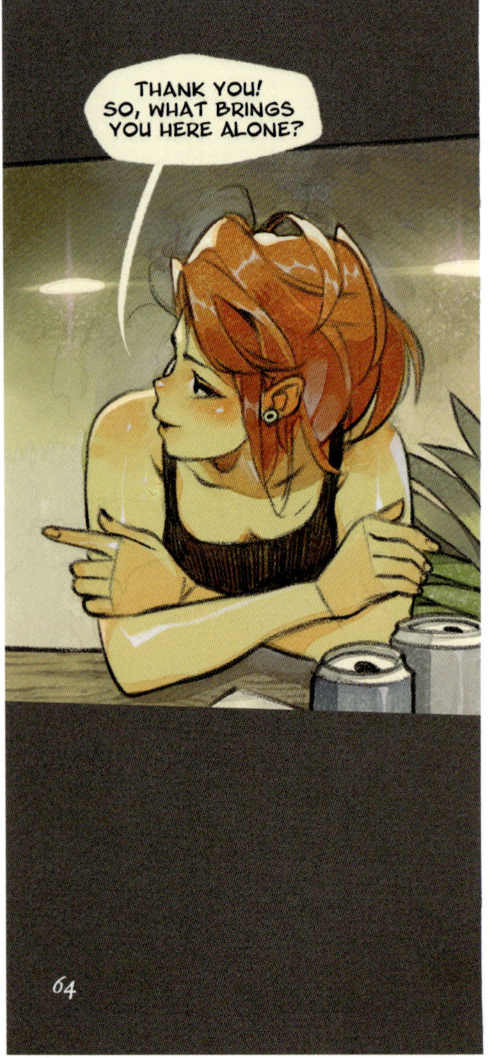
THANK YOU! SO, WHAT BRINGS YOU HERE ALONE?

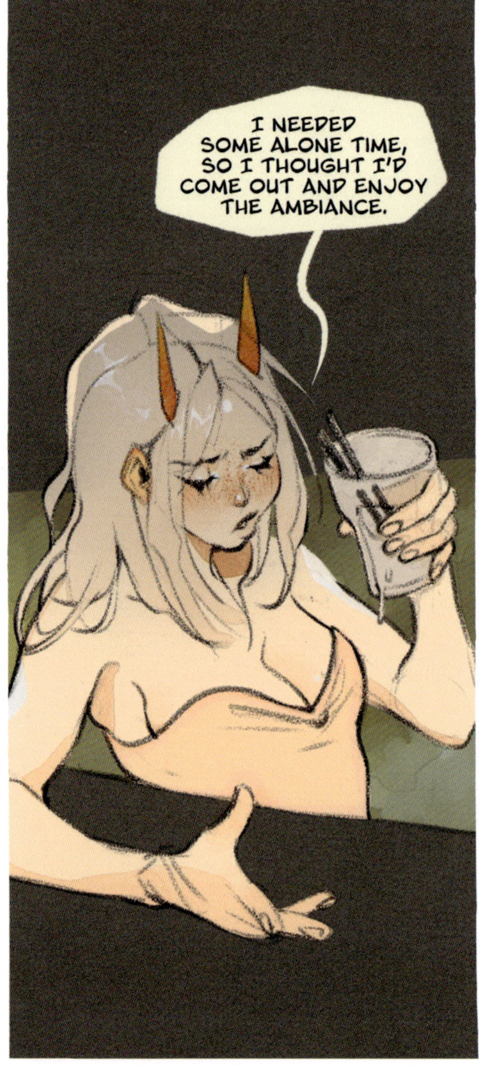
I NEEDED SOME ALONE TIME, SO I THOUGHT I'D COME OUT AND ENJOY THE AMBIANCE.

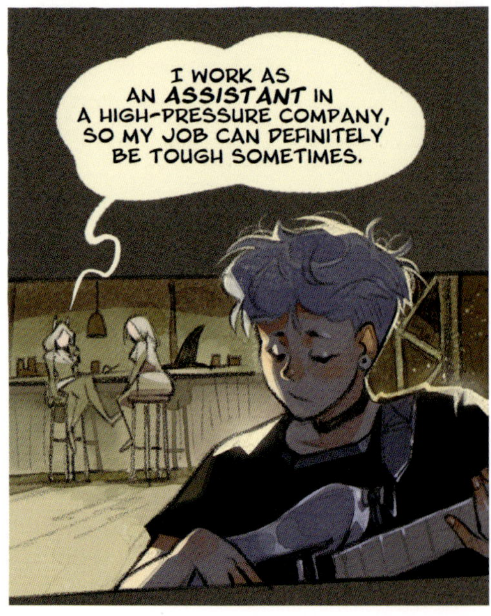
I WORK AS AN **ASSISTANT** IN A HIGH-PRESSURE COMPANY, SO MY JOB CAN DEFINITELY BE TOUGH SOMETIMES.

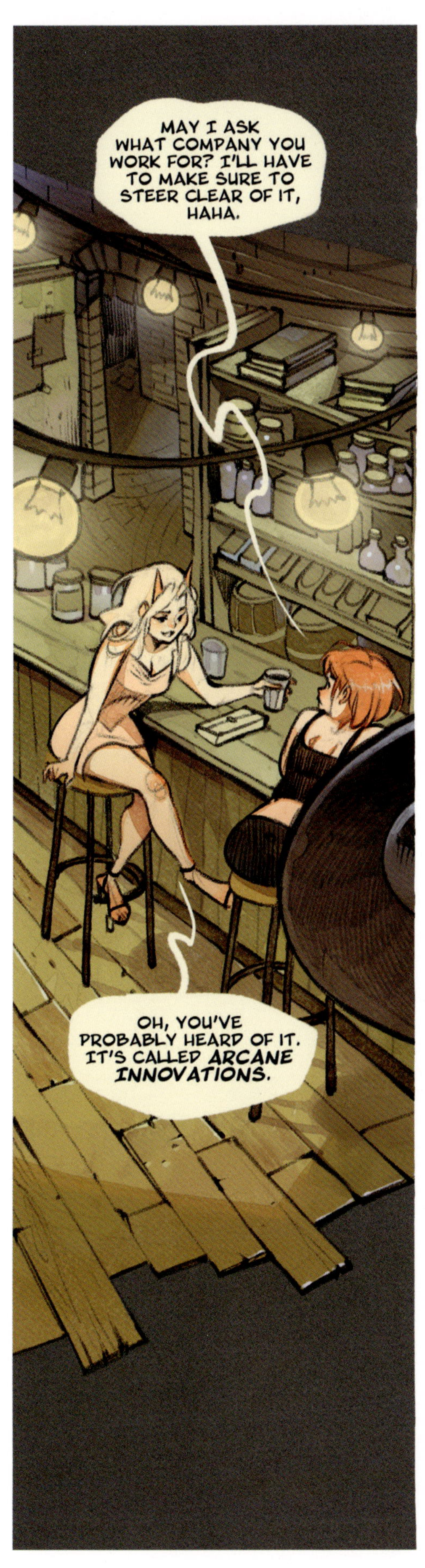

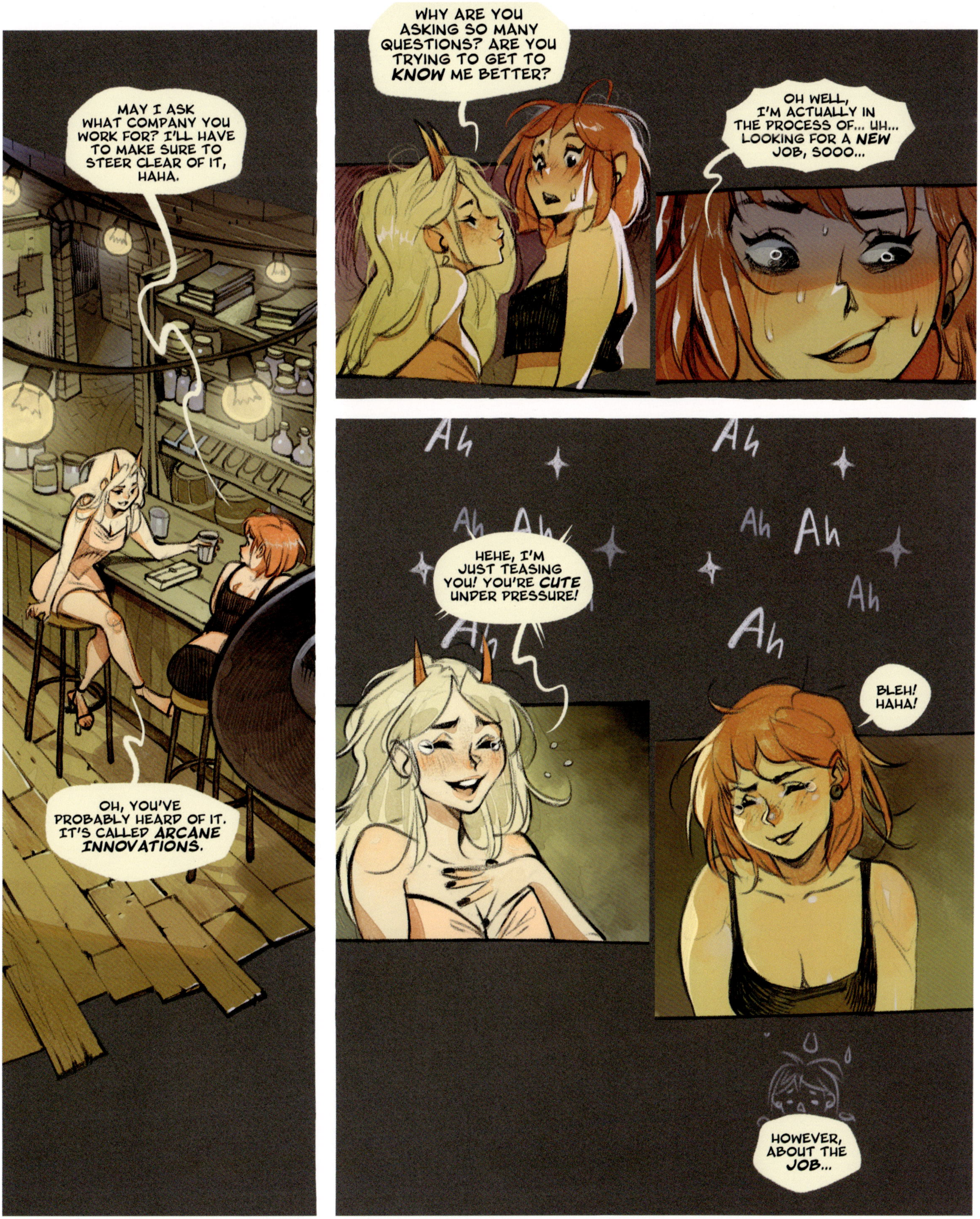

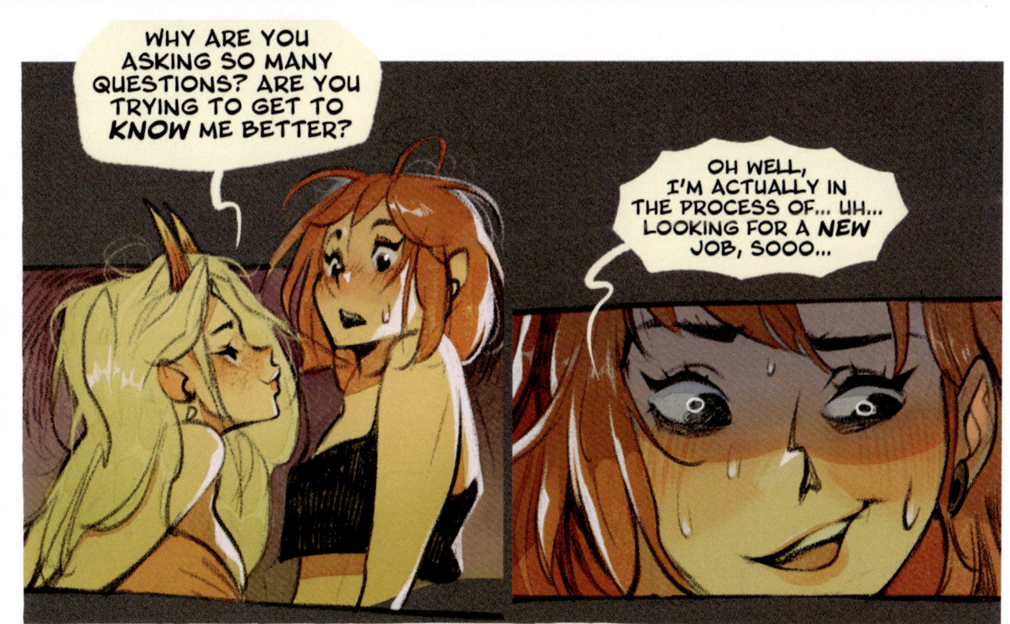

Ah
Ah
Ah Ah
Ah Ah
HEHE, I'M JUST TEASING YOU! YOU'RE ***CUTE*** UNDER PRESSURE!
Ah
Ah
Ah
BLEH! HAHA!
HOWEVER, ABOUT THE ***JOB...***

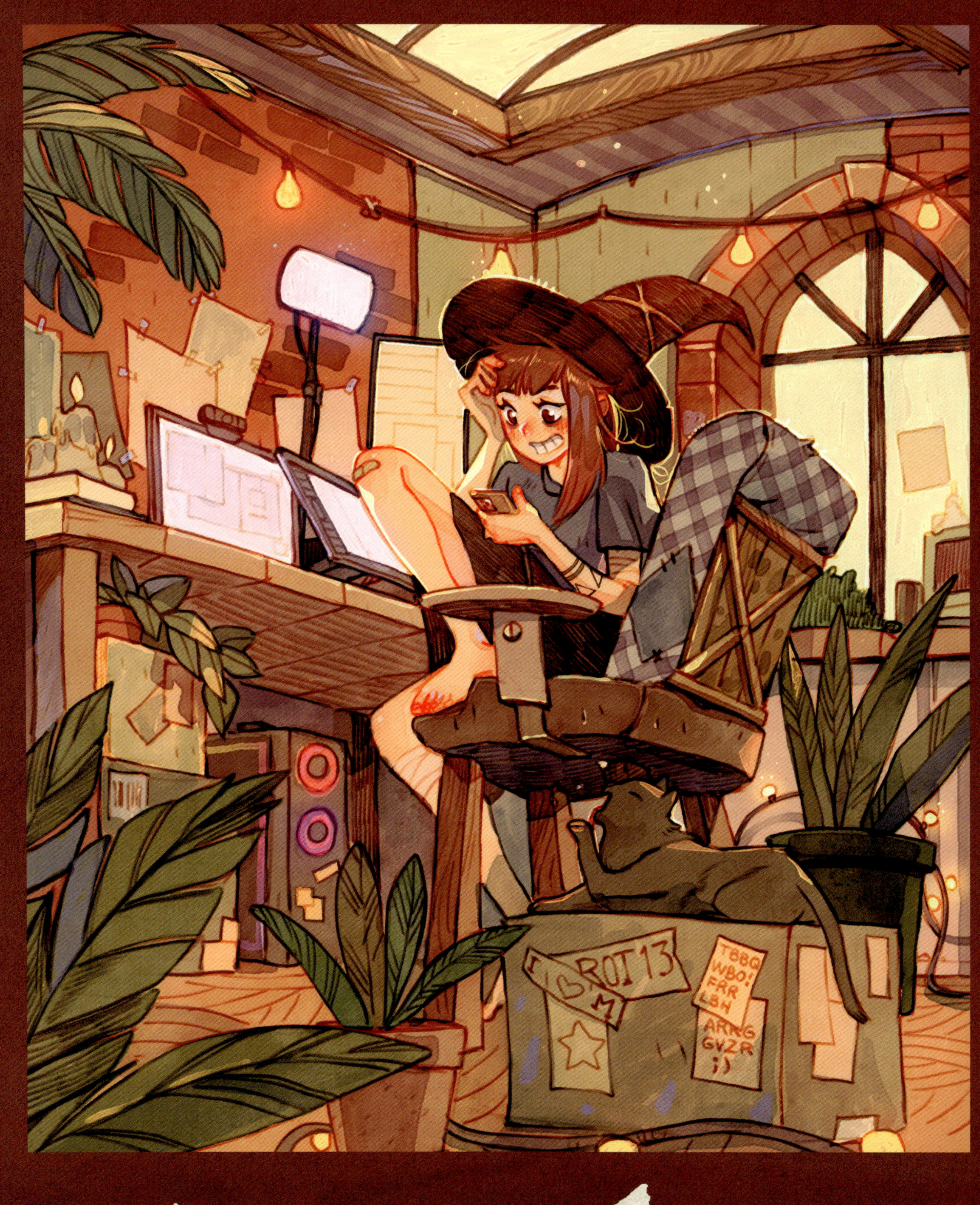
ROT13
I ♡ M
TBBQ WBO! FRR LBH
ARKG GVZR ;)

FINDING YOUR FEET

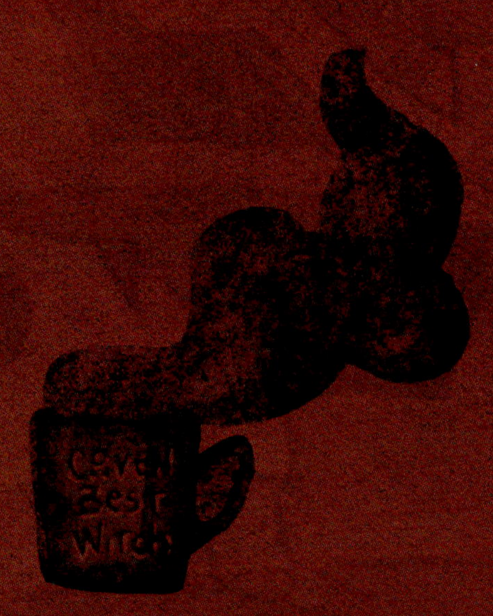

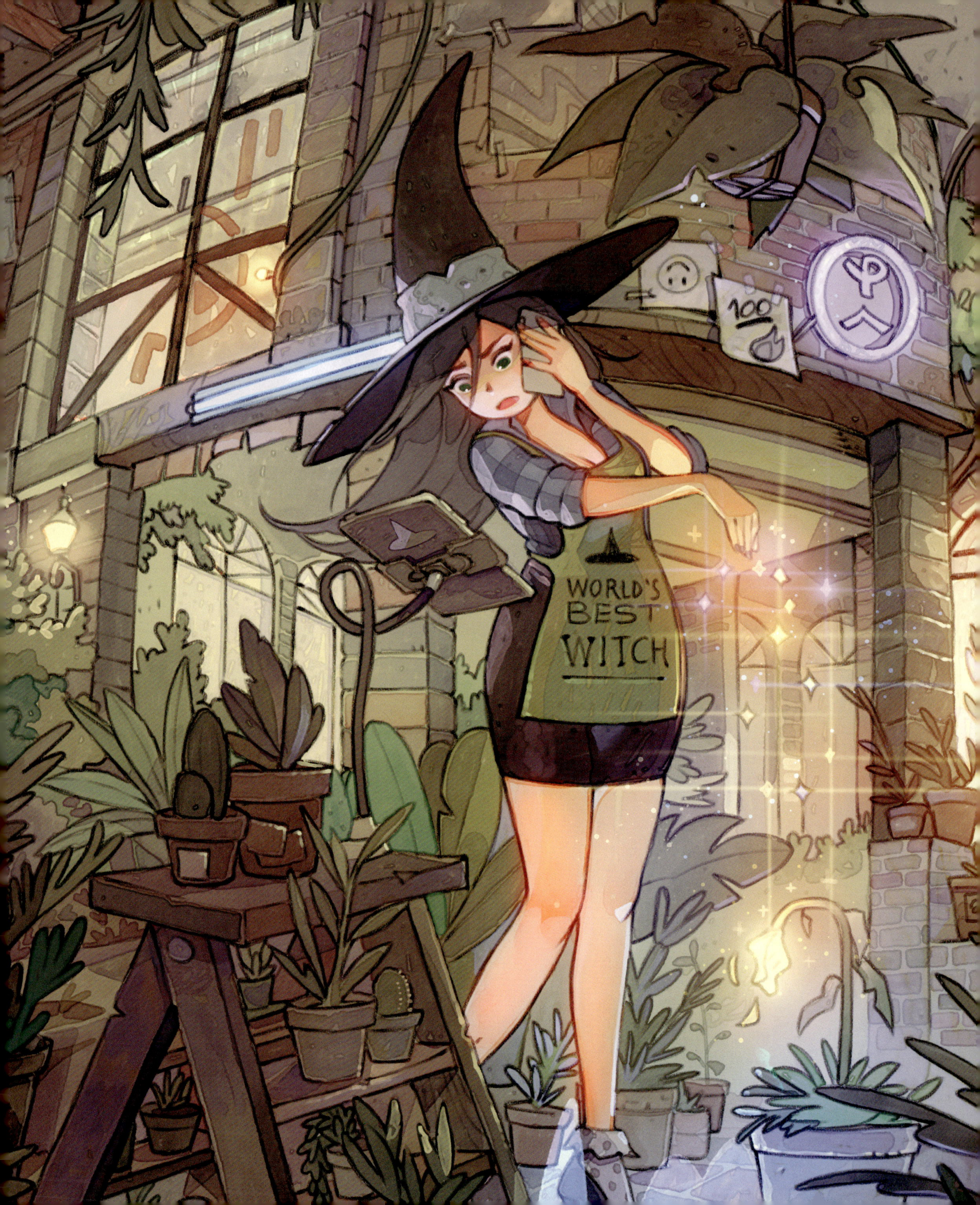
100
WORLD'S
BEST
WITCH

Making mistakes

I make mistakes as much as the next person – *constantly*. In order to preserve my mental wellbeing, I just go back to the basics: focus on what I want to say with my art, and where I want to go with it. If the picture has a mistake, I'll do better next time and I'll not lose sleep over it. That's not to say I don't obsess over details – I'm still learning to go easier on myself. But when it comes to an illustration, there will come a point where I think, 'I did my best, I can't realistically add anything significant to make this better, so it's time to move on.' Know that you will always make mistakes. You can't make a perfect picture because perfection doesn't exist. Instead of focusing on the 'issues', focus on the good you'd like to convey in the illustration.

'Know that you will always make mistakes. You can't make a perfect picture because perfection doesn't exist'

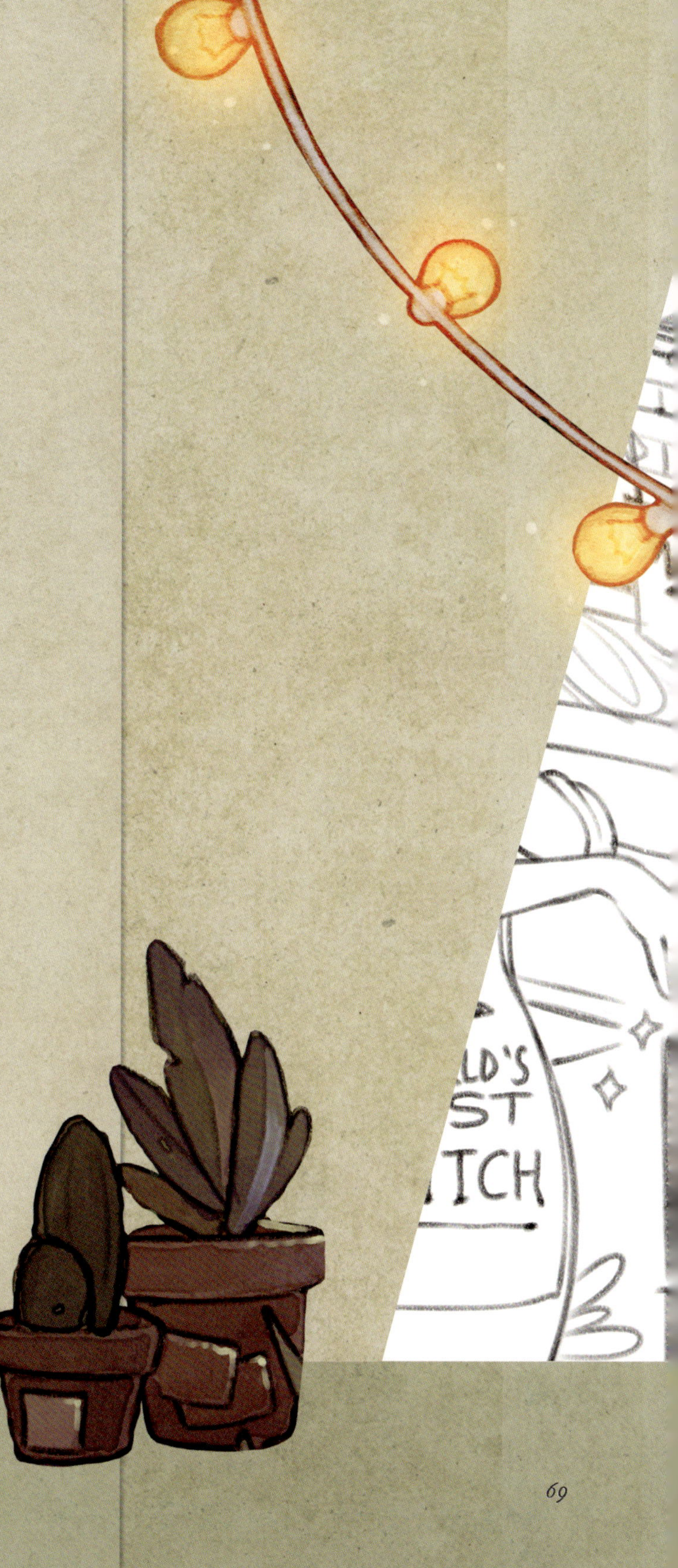

Tips on staying motivated

1. If you're just starting out and want to stay motivated when nobody (except your mother) cares yet, the best remedy is to find a way to enjoy the process. That should be the crux of why you're illustrating in the first place. You don't draw for money, or to find popularity, or because someone forced you. You do it because you like to draw, and that's the best way to approach this career. Remember that you're doing it for yourself.

2. It's important to have a little nest egg that will allow you to focus on finding your artistic personality instead of worrying about art-related income. It can be difficult to navigate, and everyone's financial situations differ, but if you are in the position to do so, I would recommend saving up to allow yourself the freedom to explore and find your artistic voice.

3. Once you get the ball rolling, support from the community is invaluable. Make sure to foster those important relationships. I am so grateful for everyone who has supported me throughout the years, whether that be through subscribing to my Patreon or Twitch, donating on Kofi, creating fan art from my work, or just sending friendly messages on my social platforms. Someone even tattooed one of my pieces on themselves! It all motivates me to keep going.

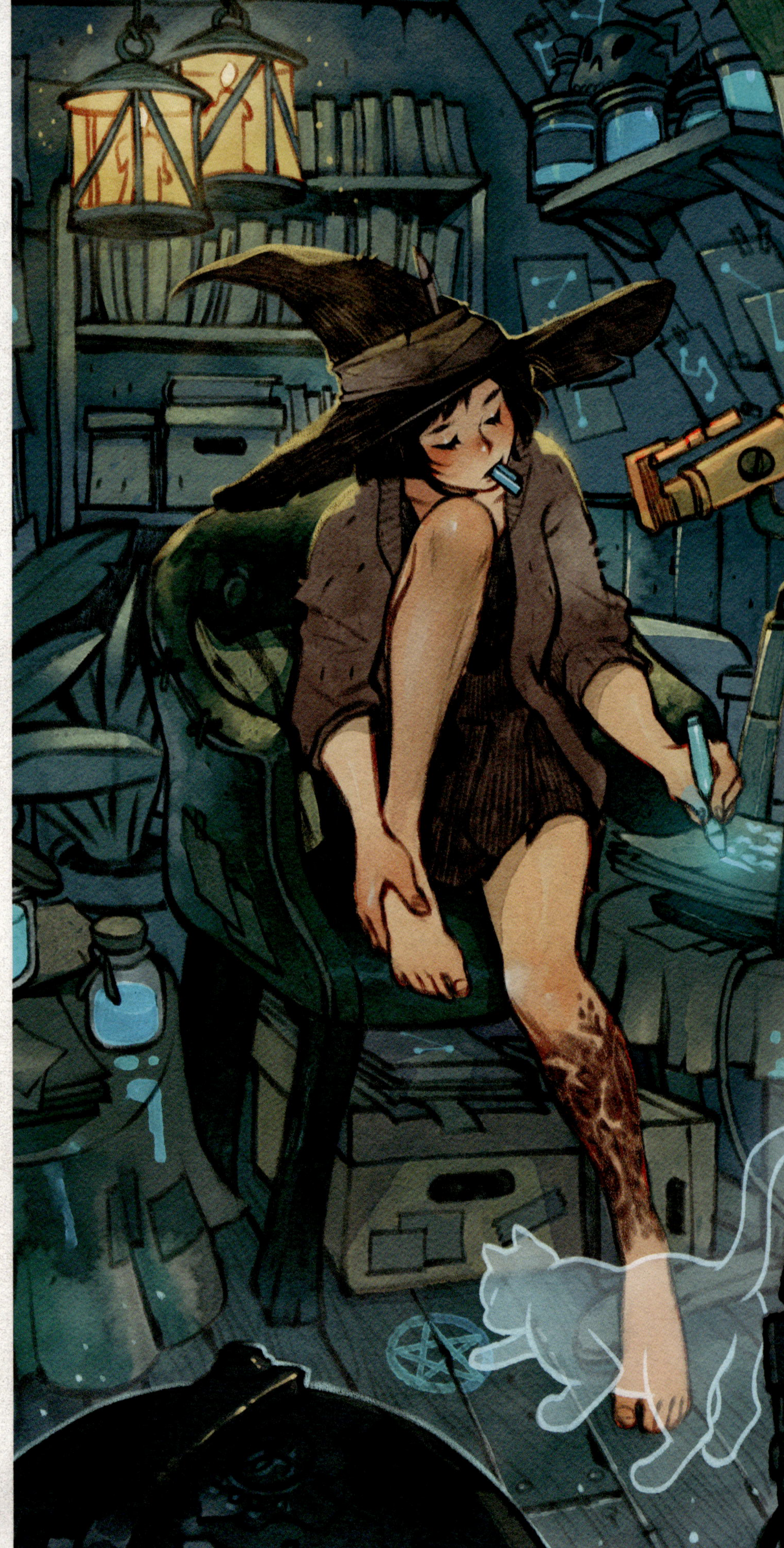

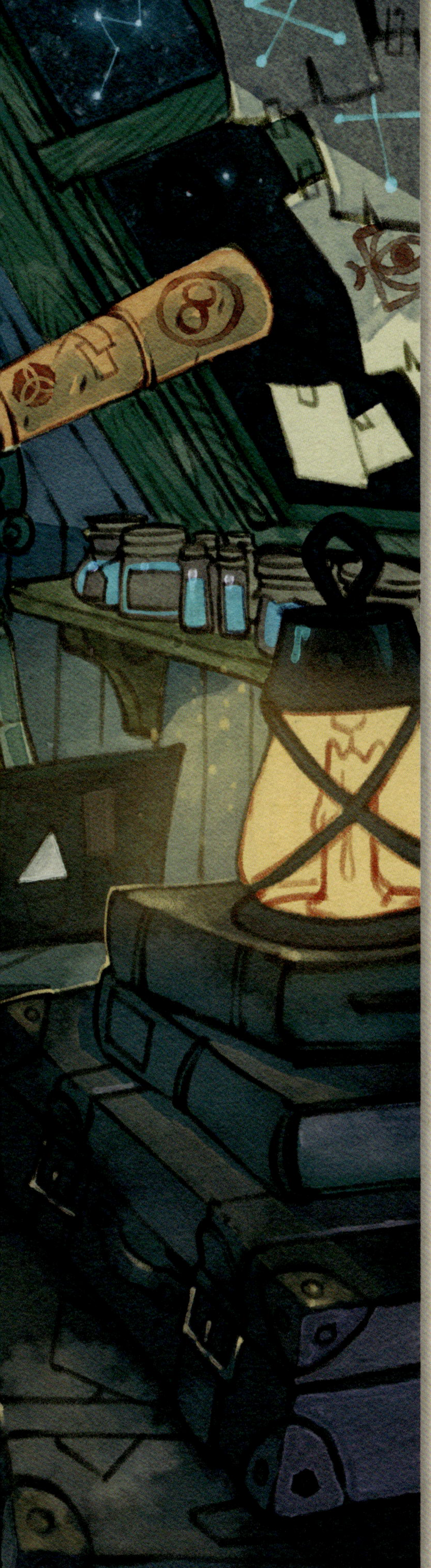

Discovering your own signature style

So many people think art style is how you draw things; how far you stretch the anatomy, or how much you exaggerate the perspective. In my opinion, that's just a technical aspect of style. Realistically, I think the only identifier of art style is your personality. If you have a strong personality, it will manifest itself in your stylistic choices. You will naturally take your art in a certain direction. There is no style if there's no personality.

Often when people start drawing, they don't have a clear idea of who they are (artistically), or where they're going. They just want to draw, which is completely understandable, but unfortunately, they won't find their style until they find their personality. The deeper you dive, the better the style. At some point, you'll start questioning yourself – why am I using this specific ink, or this particular brush, for this desired effect? I know it probably sounds like art mumbo jumbo, but that's how to do it. Discover why you do what you do, and where you'd like to go with it. Once you set off in the right direction for you, your art style will follow.

Since my whole love of illustrating began with pencils, ink, watercolour, and Moleskine sketchbooks, it was my mission to emulate them digitally. The sudden thought of 'What if I can get this exact look on a tablet?' sent me down a rabbit hole that I'm still in six years later. I constantly ask myself, 'How can I achieve that organic randomness that naturally happens in traditional mediums?' And it's that research that helped me develop my signature style.

The modern witches theme came to me just as spontaneously. After drawing a few here and there, I decided to explore the concept further. What if I made it mine? How far could I delve into this aesthetic? How could I introduce and incorporate things that inspire me, like dark academia, cottagecore, or even trends like tech-wear? I loved facing these challenges, and still do as I continue to research and grow.

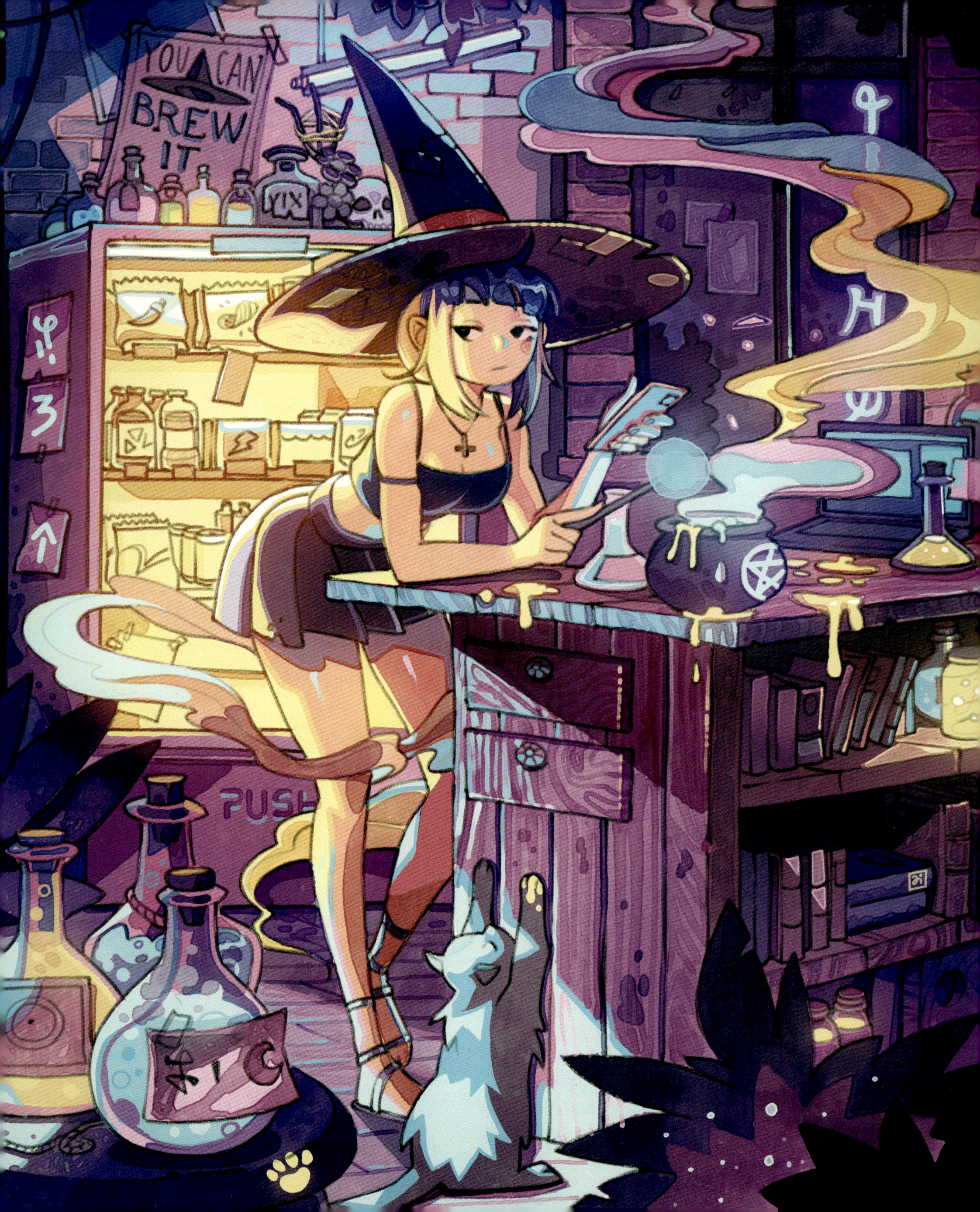
YOU CAN BREW IT
PUSH

Art influences

Having someone to look up to in the art community is really important, too. Role models are inspiring and offer direction for where you might want to go. Kim Jung Gi has been one of those integral influencers for me, as well as Hector Sevilla, Elsevilla, Rebecca Sugar, *Steven Universe*, and Dan Harmon from *Adventure Time*. As I mentioned before, my dad is an architect, and he's definitely shaped my style, especially when it comes to settings. Together, we visited many churches and abbeys across Europe, as well as museums and notable buildings. The architecture of these places stuck with me and positively altered the mood and aesthetic of my art. You can see it in the way I draw windows, or a room, or a vine-covered wall.

However, it's important to filter influences as much as possible, as many beginners tend to want to emulate these creators. Sure, you can appreciate a person, movie, or TV show. But you then must ask yourself how you can take the bits you like and use them in your own illustrations. A good way to do this is through research – fill up those sketchbooks and study who you admire and what it is about their work that makes you tick. That's what I did!

That being said, I've never felt pressured to create art for the mainstream. I dabbled in fan art for a short while, but stopped because I felt people weren't liking my work so much as the show or characters it was based on.

I've always illustrated what I enjoyed; I might find it cool, or interesting, or stimulating for the viewer. It's always my intention to take something and make it mine, transforming it in my own style. At some point in my career, I settled on a bunch of techniques and that turned into my style, but it changes constantly. I feel like I'm still growing, changing. I experiment by looking at other people's art and techniques.

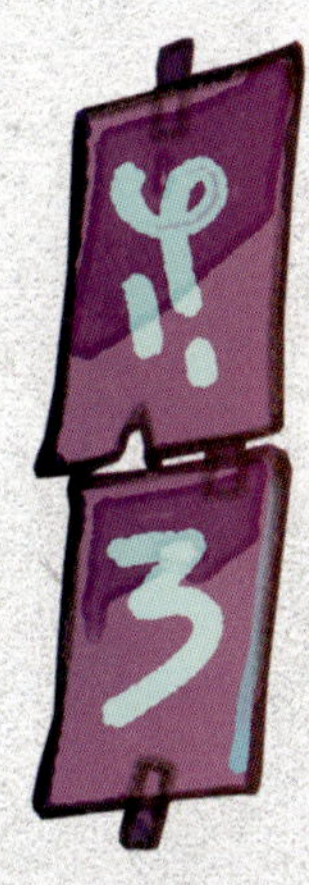

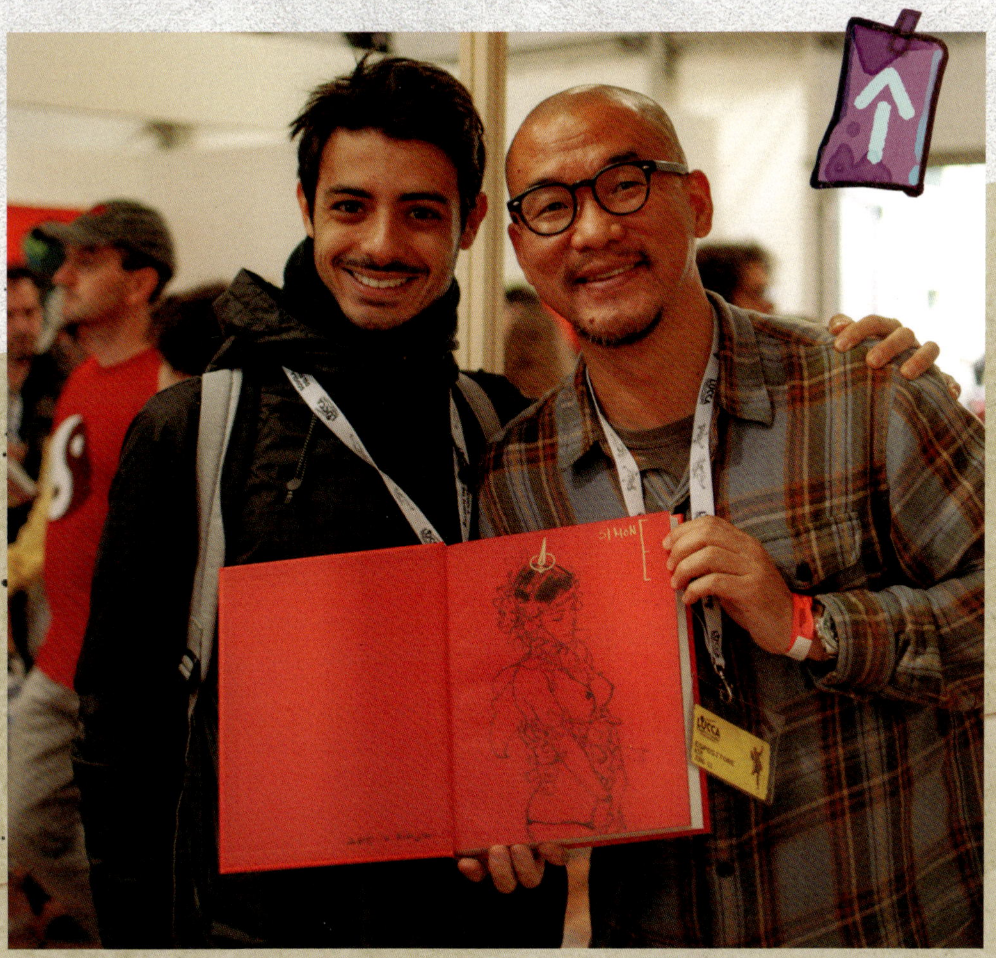

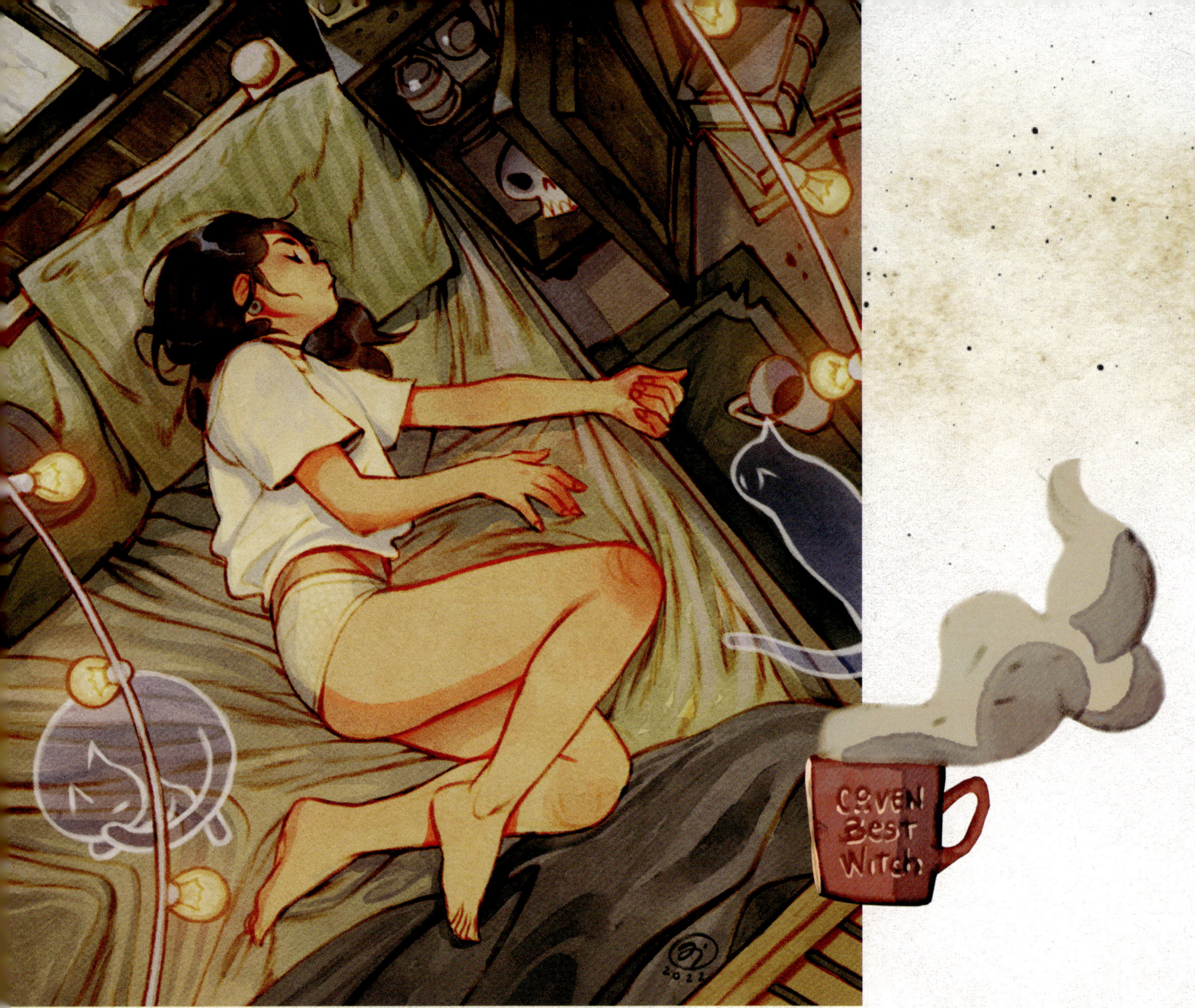

Client work vs. personal work

I don't accept anything that's not my perfect aesthetic. If a client contacts me, 99.9 per cent of the time, they want something in my style. They'll usually send me examples of my own work, and request that I create something in their desired scenarios. I'm very lucky because it's what I wanted from the beginning: to have a personality, a signature style, and to make sure I draw what I want each time, even if it's something for someone else. I had to fight hard to get to this point.

When you start out as a freelancer in this industry, the best way to make money quickly is to accept everything and anything that comes your way, but that would have seriously slowed my progress. I wouldn't have enjoyed working on something I didn't feel was mine. So, I worked hard and refused many commissions. I still haven't reopened them to the public, because I'm afraid they might ask me to deviate from my style and what I love to illustrate.

As I grew on social media, big brands contacted me for collaborations, and that's when I realized my style was recognizable.

Finding your niche

For this specific niche that I'm following right now, I took plenty of influence from the classic witch tropes, but I also found inspiration from Gandalf in *The Lord of the Rings*, and other fantasy books and films. I've also pulled ideas from horror movies, and I really like the United States college aesthetic that you often see in American movies. There is something I love about normal, everyday environments that have sci-fi or fantasy elements. When I was a teenager, *Buffy the Vampire Slayer* was a huge source of inspiration for me – especially the witch character Willow – and the witches I draw tend to be around the same age as those characters. My ghost cats evolved in a slightly different way; I was working on an illustration that I felt needed a splash of magic, so I gave my witch character a wand, and from that wand came a strip of light, which turned into a shape, and... you can guess what that shape was. A simple white line became one of my most used elements.

Social media seemed to really like the addition of ghost cats, so I began experimenting, drawing a lot of inspiration from the techy things around me. My niche seemed to spring from there – what if witches were among us? And what if they used a phone like everyone else? What if they took selfies, slept in an IKEA bed, and shopped for things on Etsy? Breaking the dark stereotypes and normalizing these misconstrued characters was a very fun concept for me to explore, and turned out to be a gold mine for content.

'It's always my intention to take something and make it mine, transforming it in my own style'

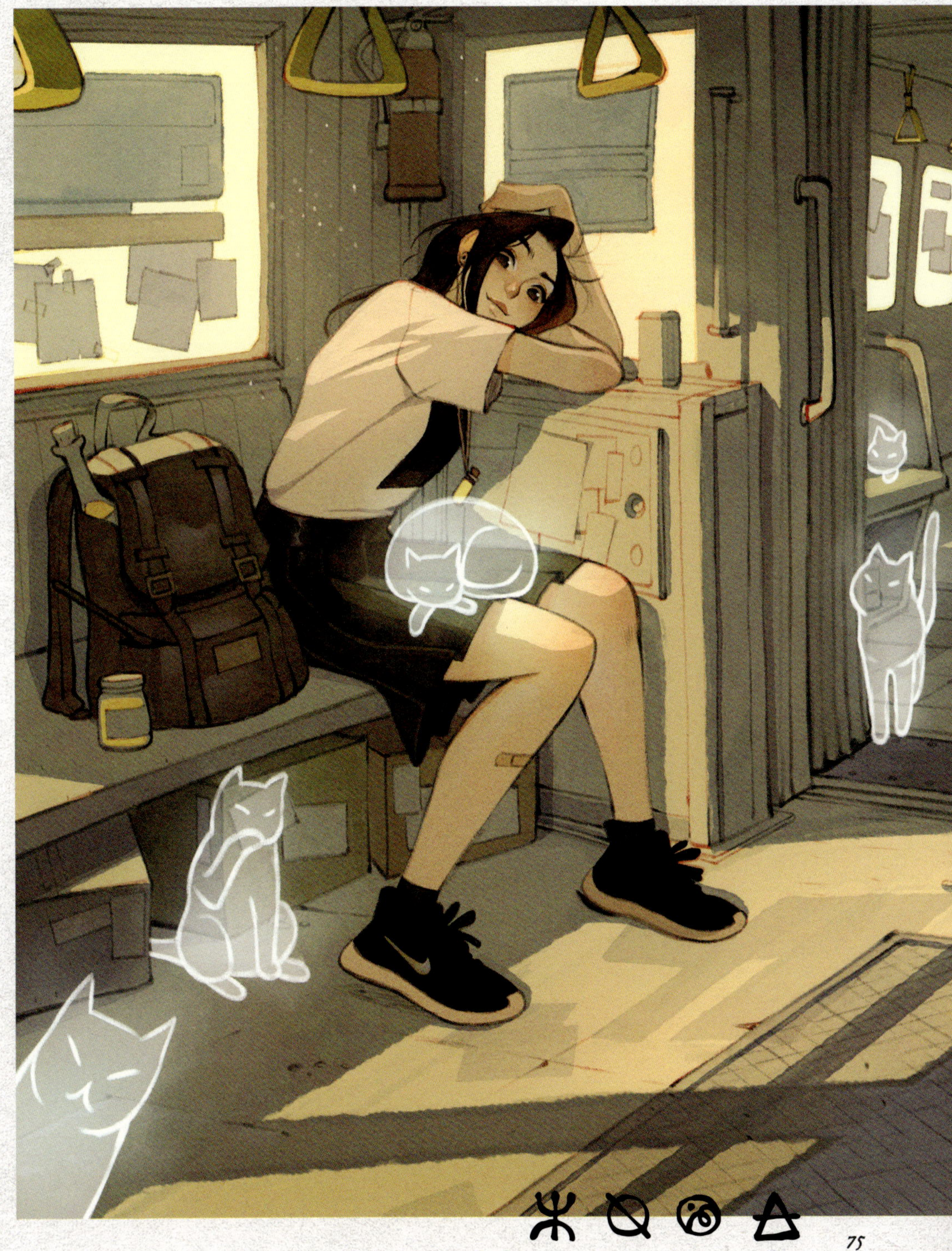

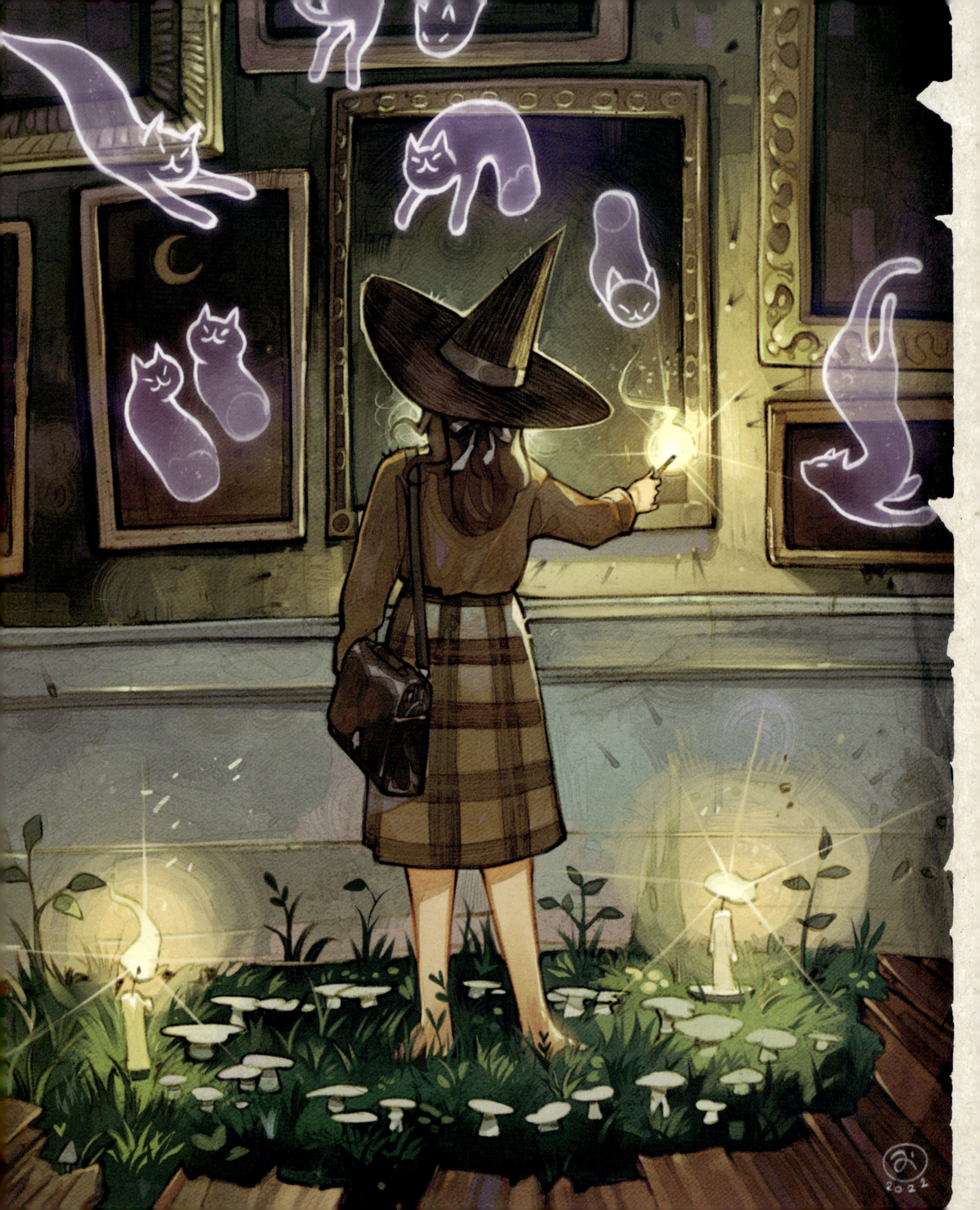

WITCHES GALLERY

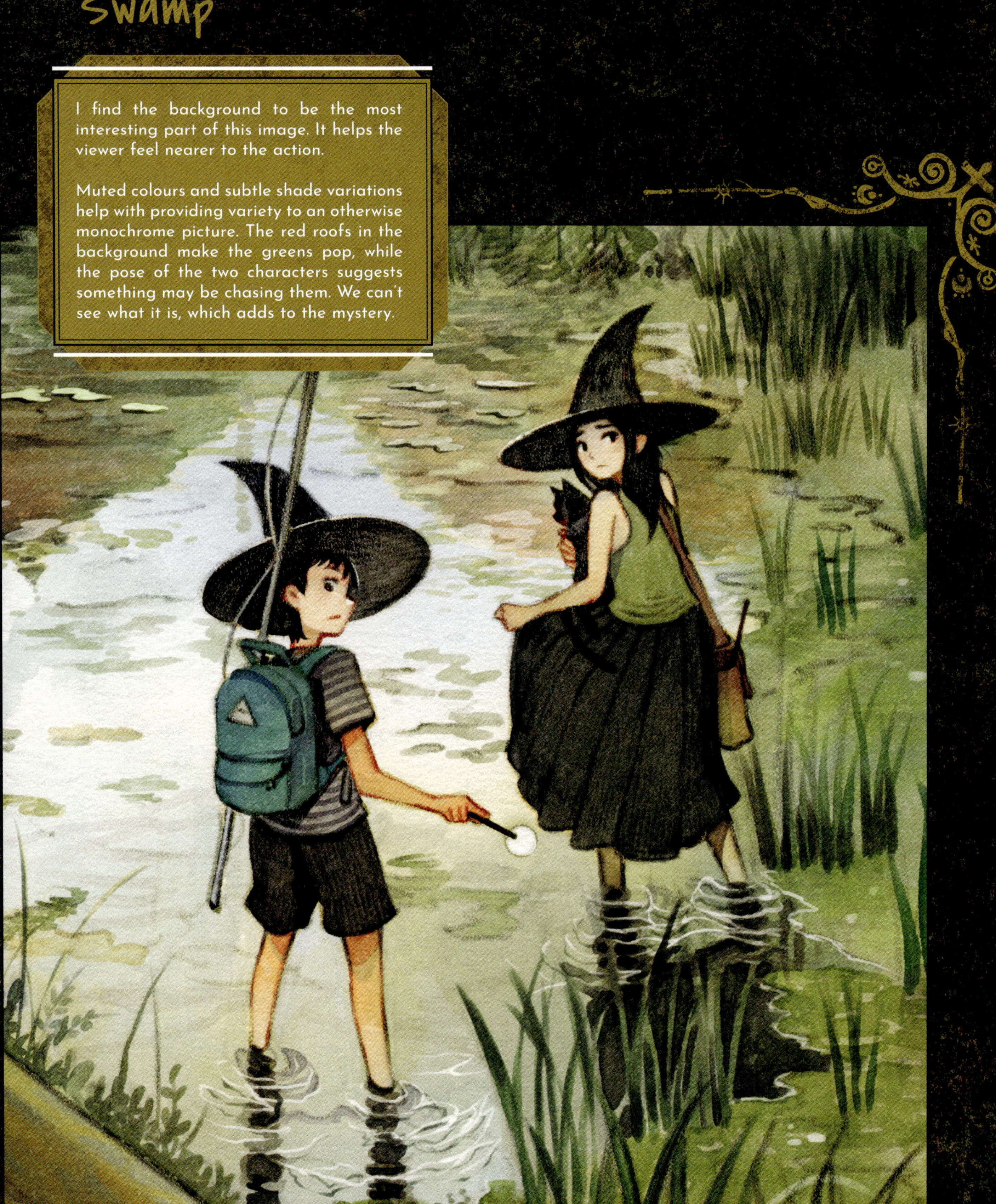

Swamp

I find the background to be the most interesting part of this image. It helps the viewer feel nearer to the action.

Muted colours and subtle shade variations help with providing variety to an otherwise monochrome picture. The red roofs in the background make the greens pop, while the pose of the two characters suggests something may be chasing them. We can't see what it is, which adds to the mystery.

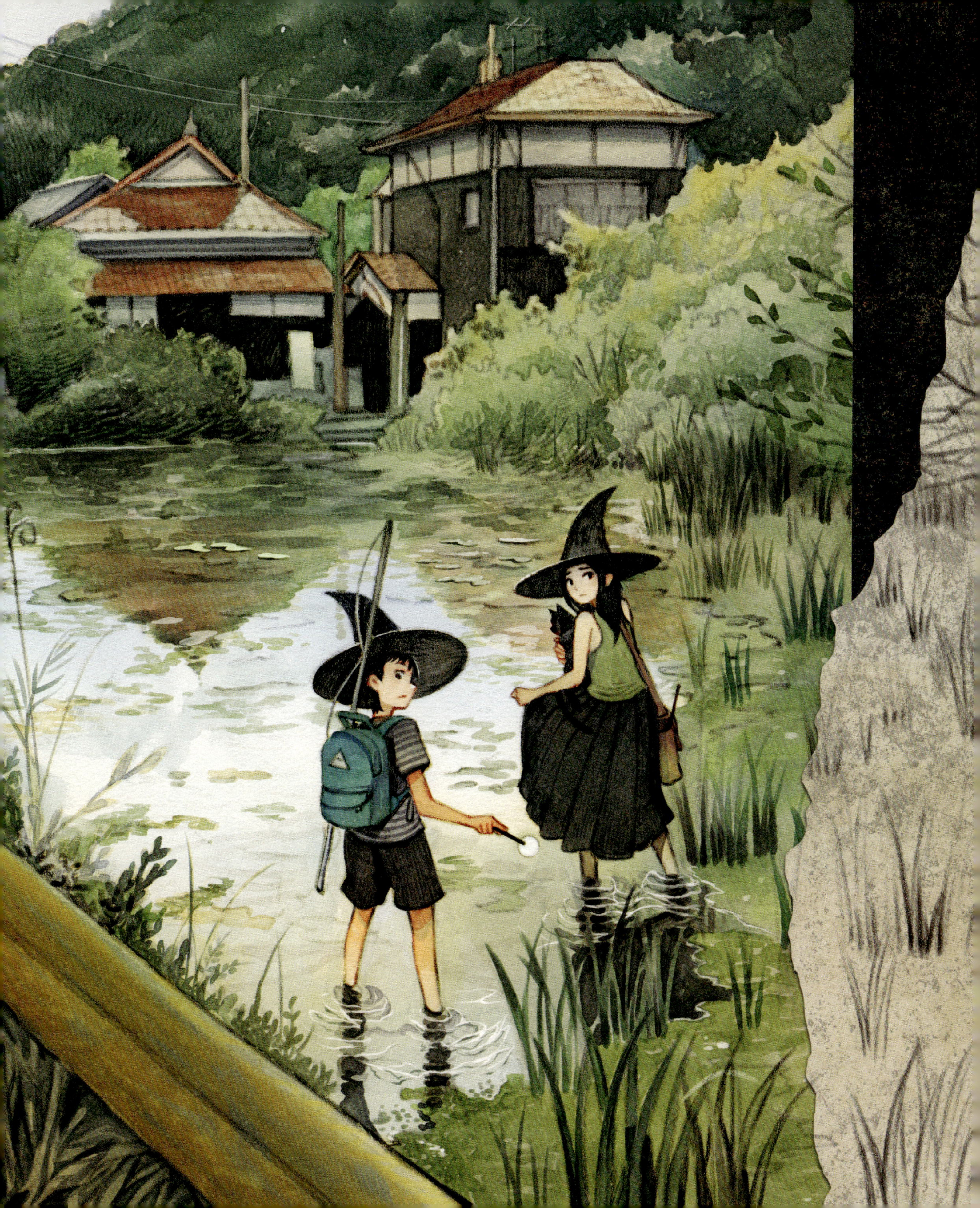

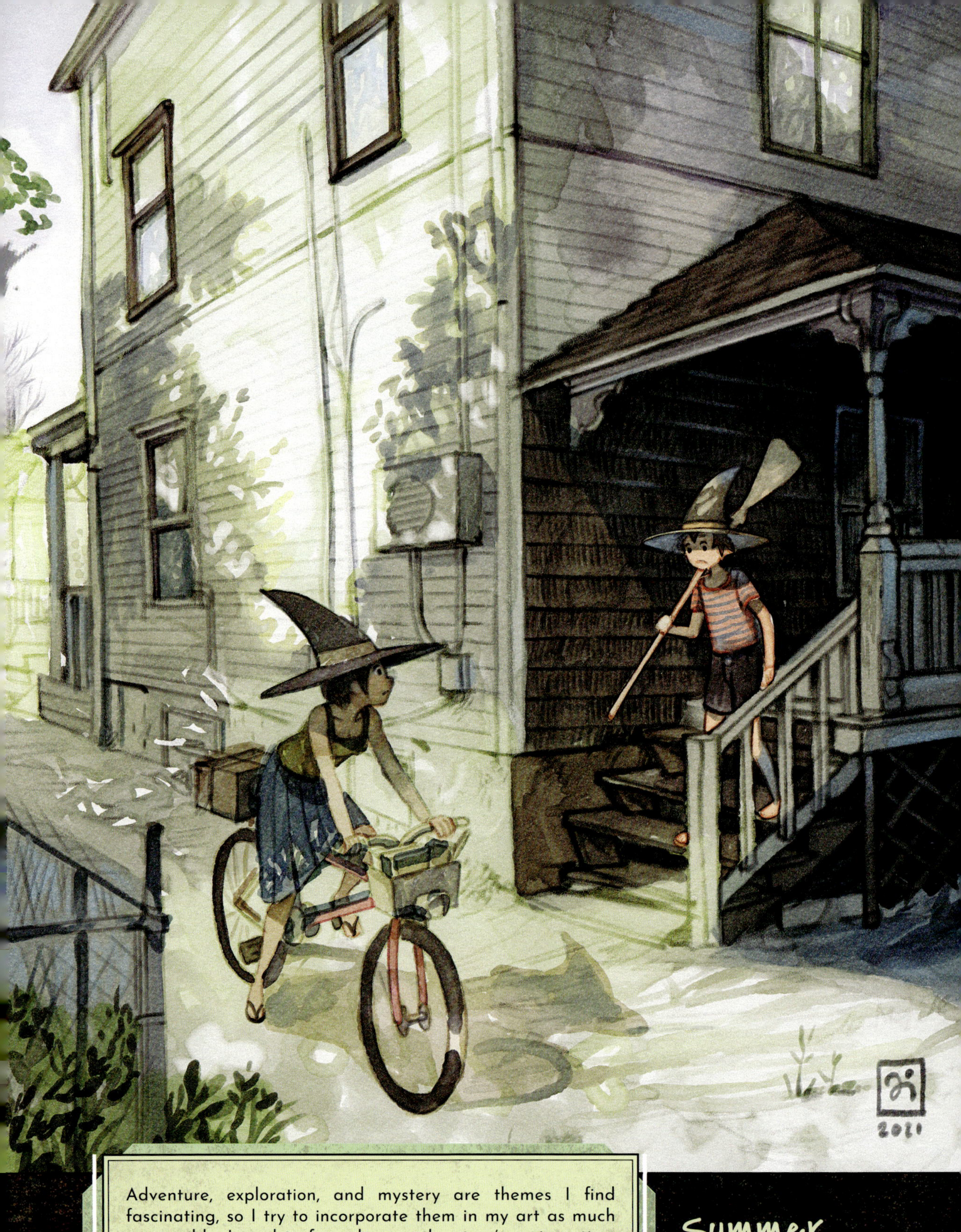

Adventure, exploration, and mystery are themes I find fascinating, so I try to incorporate them in my art as much as possible. I tend to focus less on the story's main action, and more on the discovery that inspires the action. In this image, I also focused on light, using high contrast and lots of whites to reflect what you'd see on a typical summer's day.

Summer Adventures

Potion Machine

Drawing in high-key is always something I find really challenging. It's scary using a higher contrast, as elements can sometimes be completely whited out. However, when it works, I'm really happy because it gives a light, whimsical look to the images. Using pastels is also particularly hard because there are very small tonal changes between each colour. If you choose the wrong colour, it can appear too saturated and break the light aesthetic. I try to pay close attention to this!

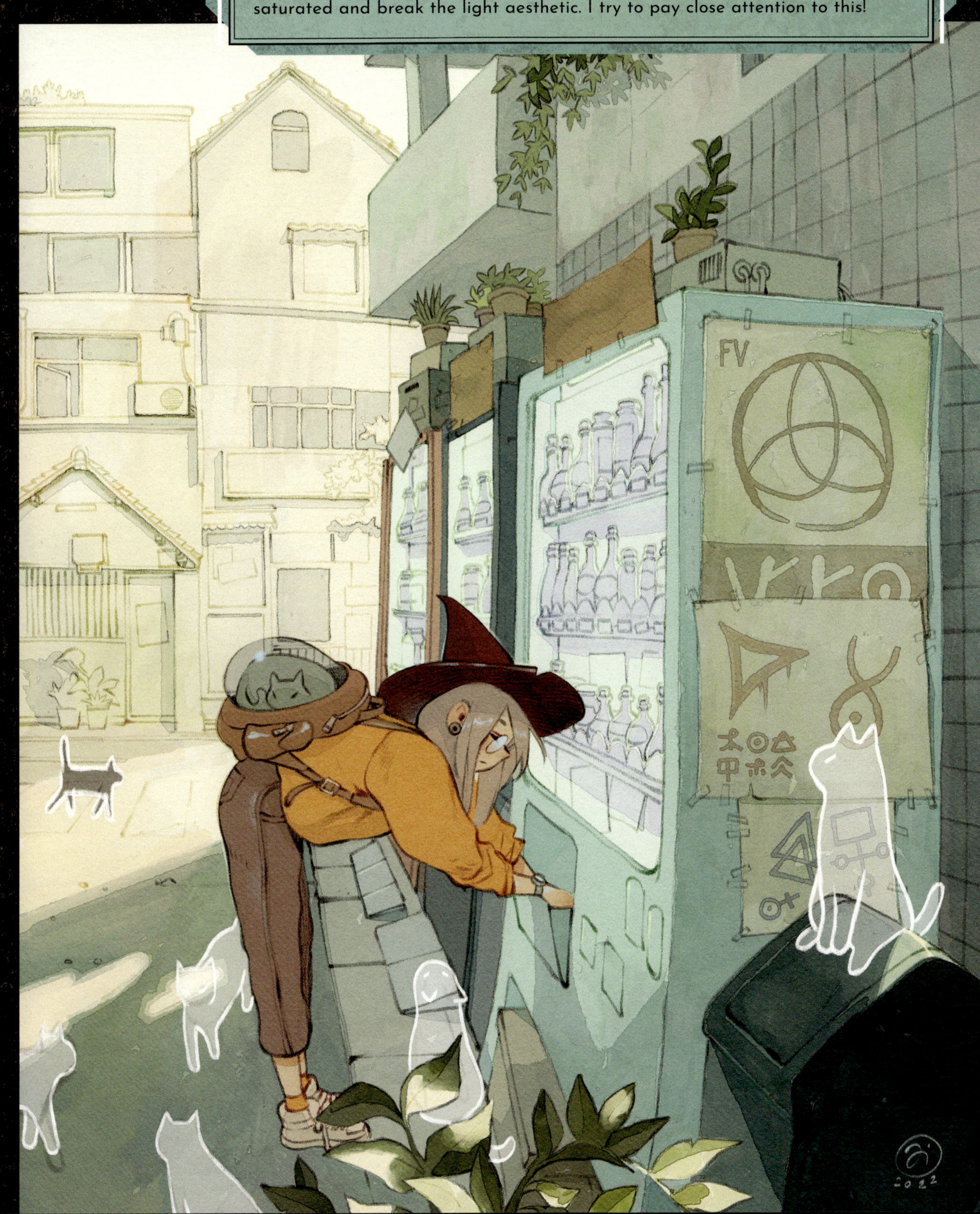

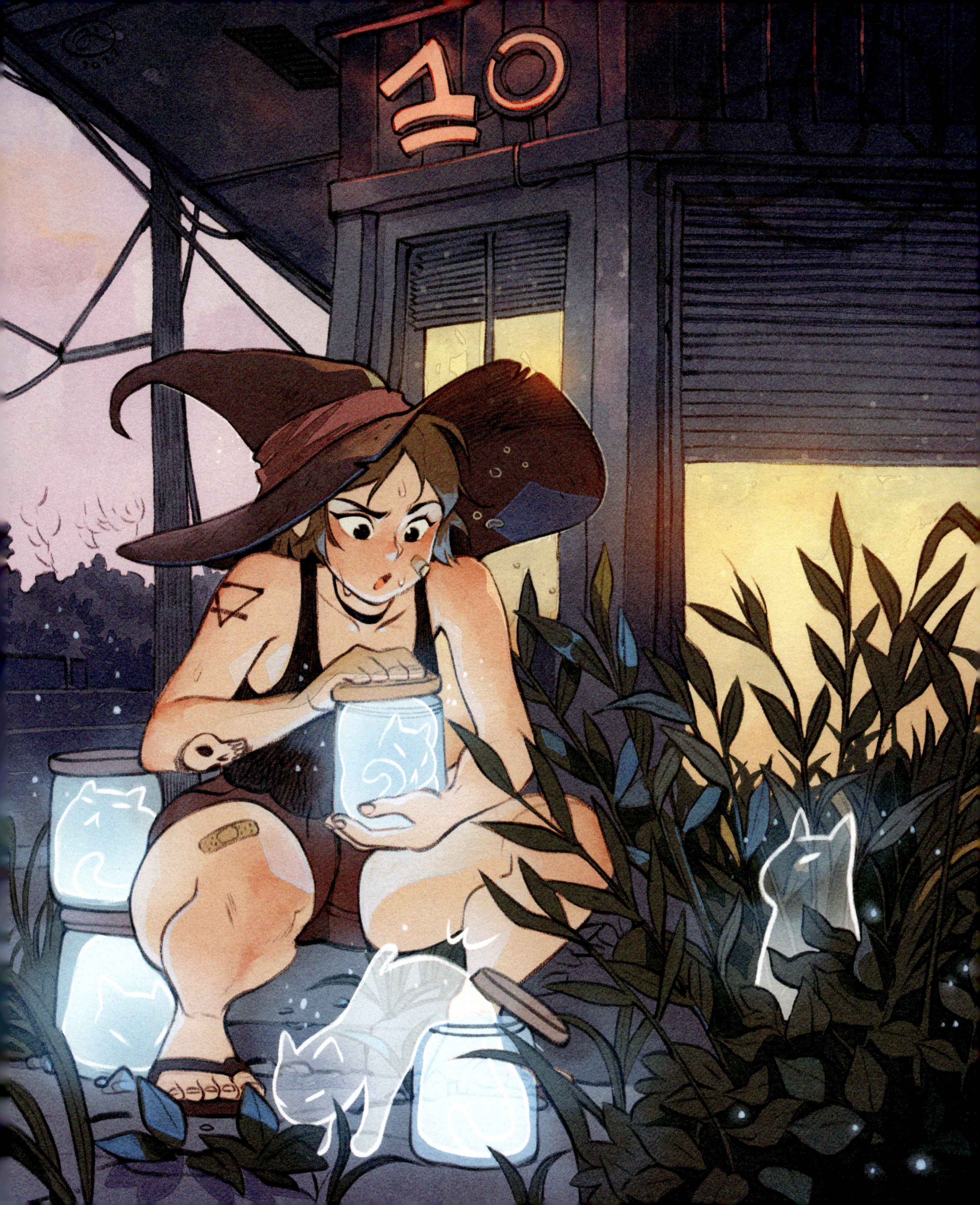
10

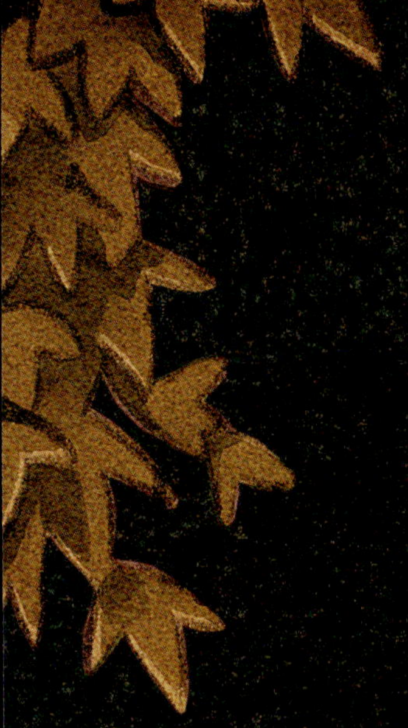

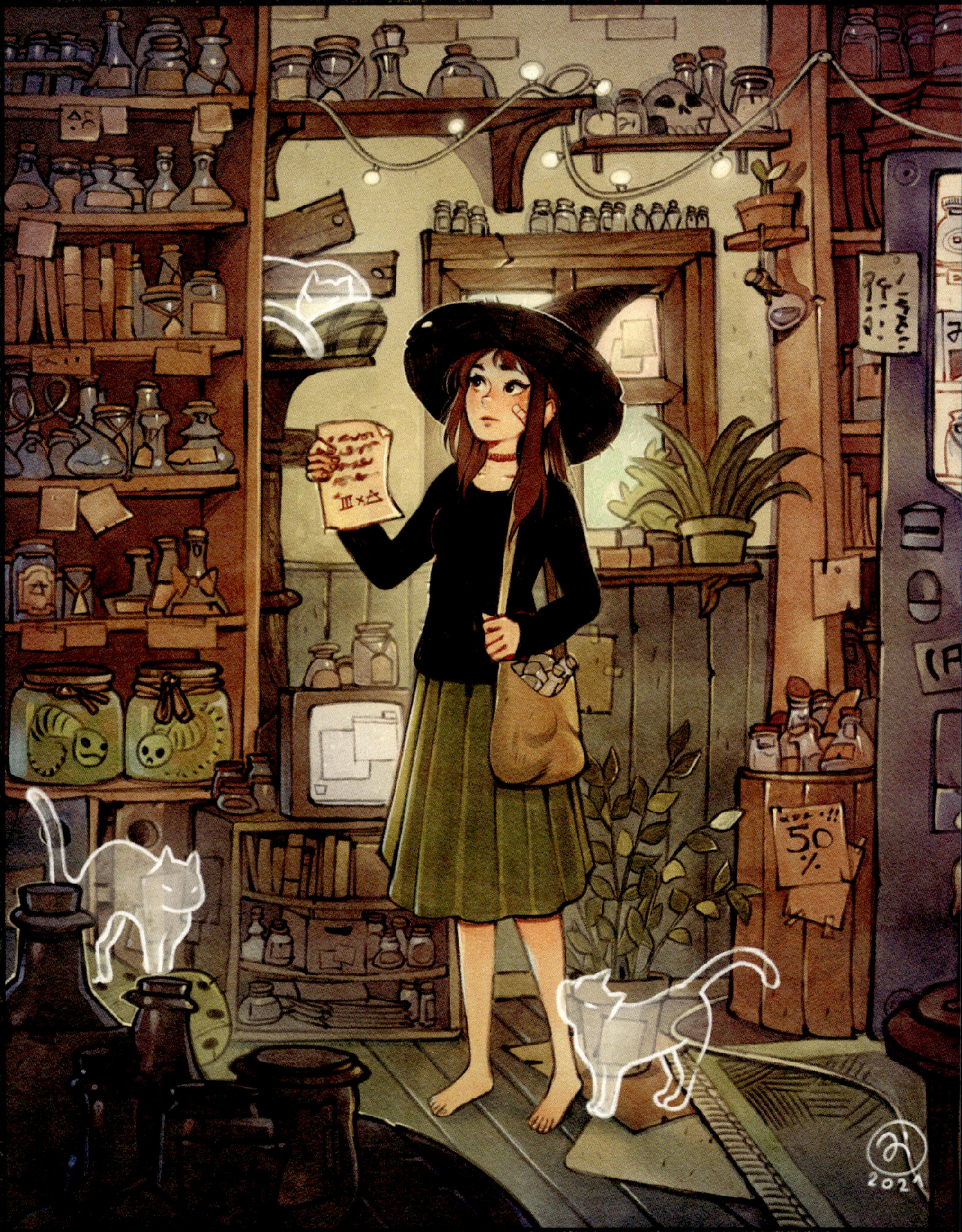

Capturing Kitties

Once I established that ghost cats existed in my world, I toyed with the idea of them having relationships with the outside world. From this point, they no longer have a passive role in the series, and instead interact with the characters in different ways. I also try to drop possible hints as to why they exist, but always leave it open to the interpretation of the viewer.

Potion Shop

Here, I went for a traditional shop with modern elements, which I feel worked well. There are shelves filled with potion bottles that look like they are straight out of a medieval apothecary, but there's also a PC monitor and a vending machine. This type of contrast can make illustrations more interesting.

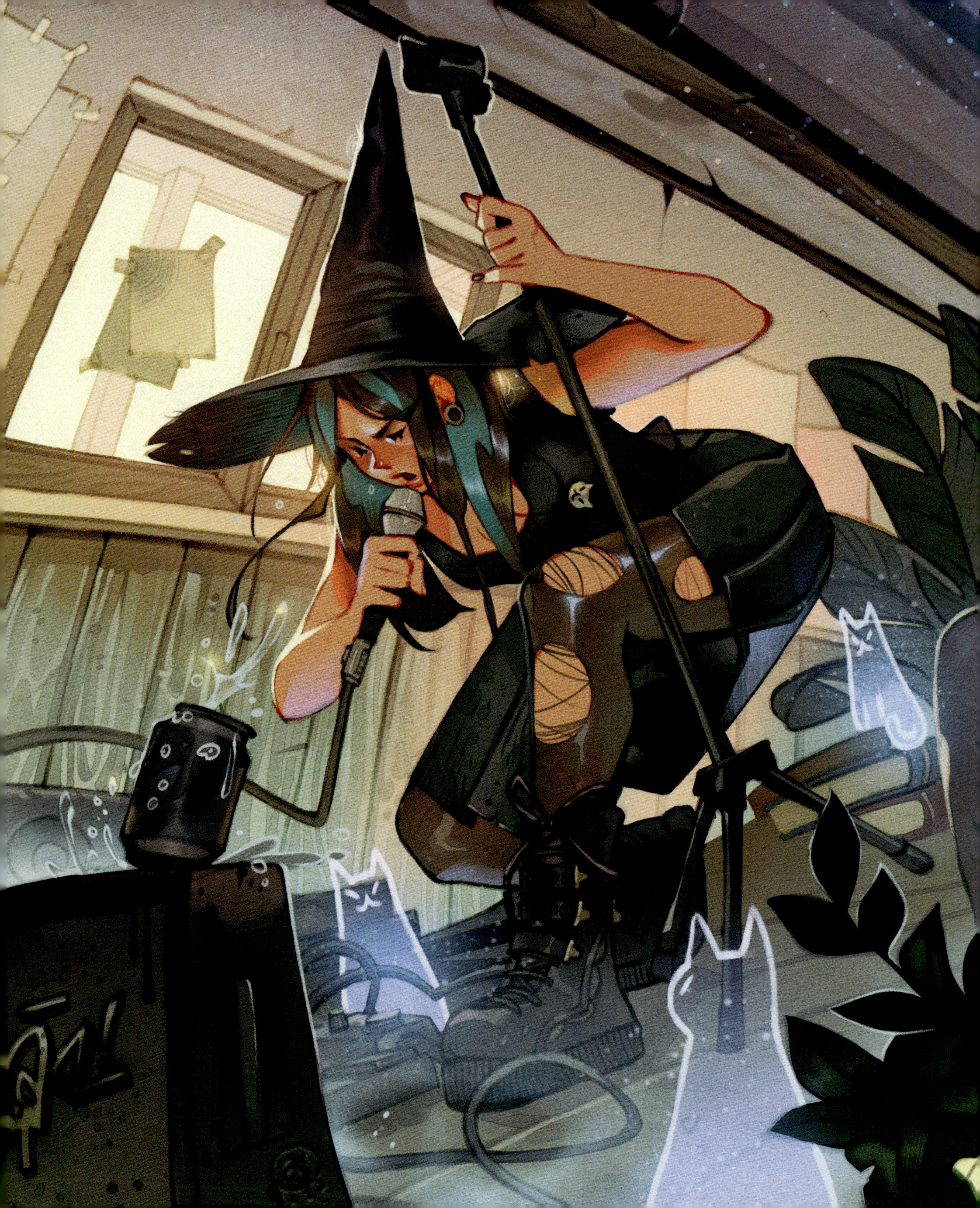

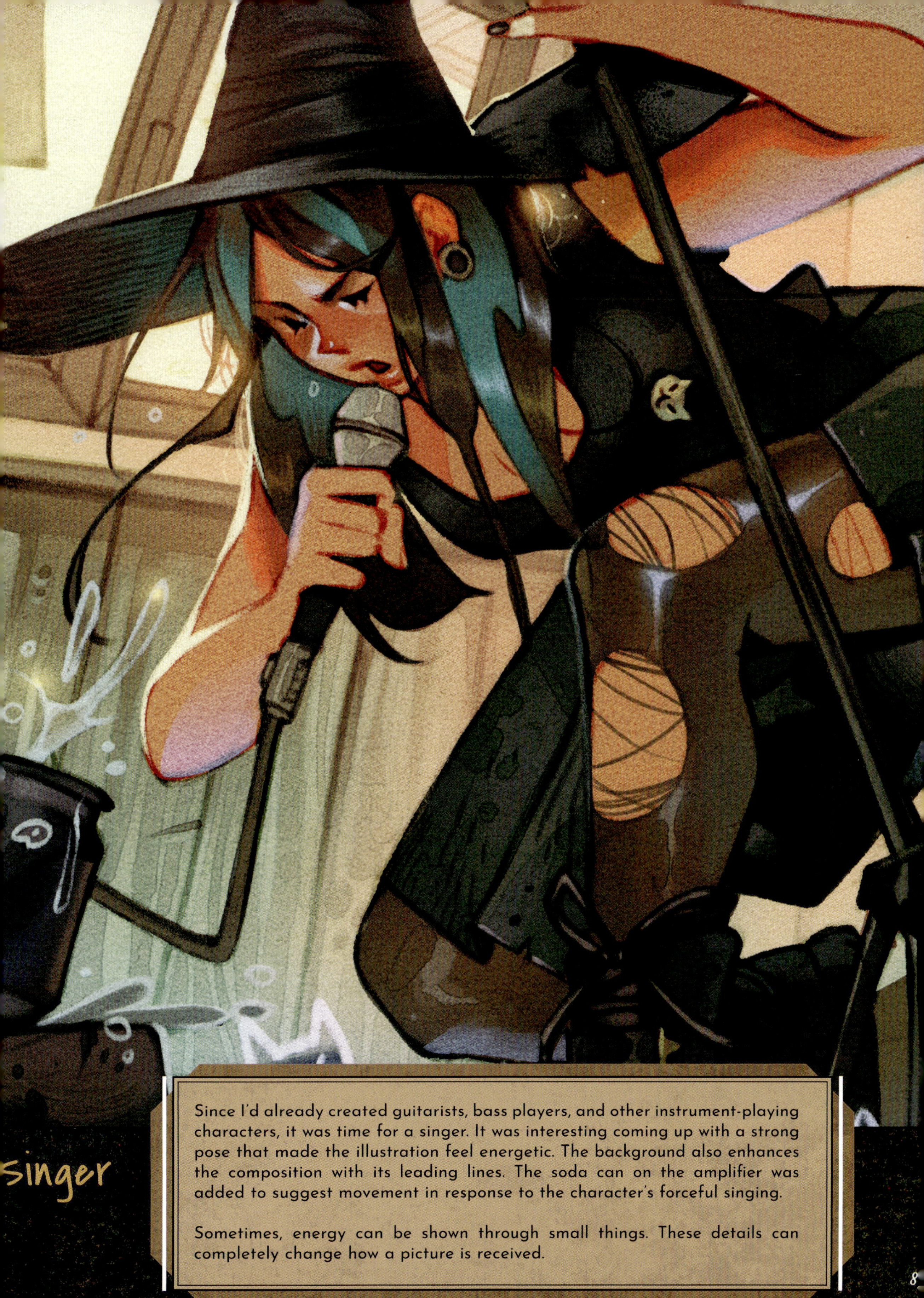

singer

Since I'd already created guitarists, bass players, and other instrument-playing characters, it was time for a singer. It was interesting coming up with a strong pose that made the illustration feel energetic. The background also enhances the composition with its leading lines. The soda can on the amplifier was added to suggest movement in response to the character's forceful singing.

Sometimes, energy can be shown through small things. These details can completely change how a picture is received.

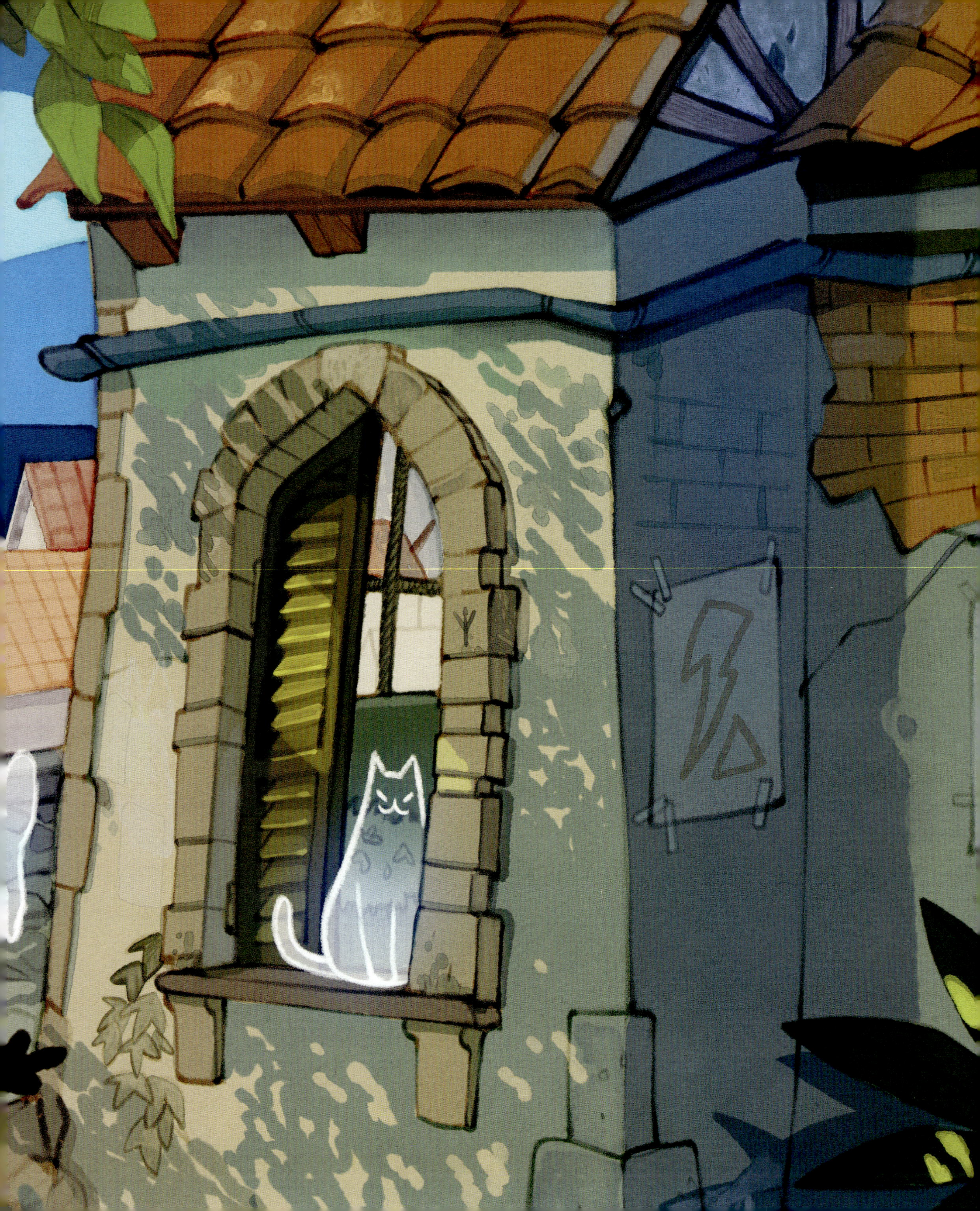

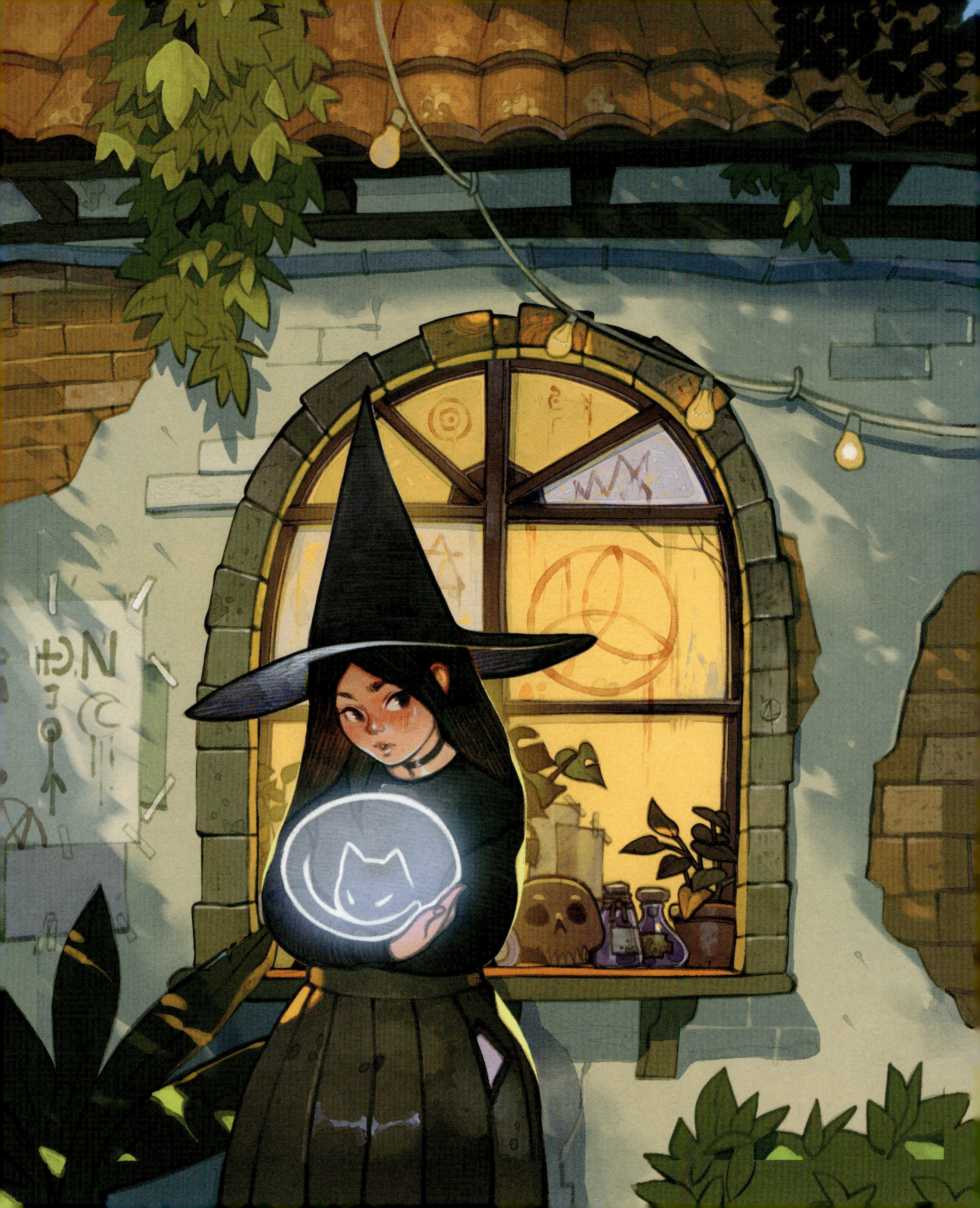

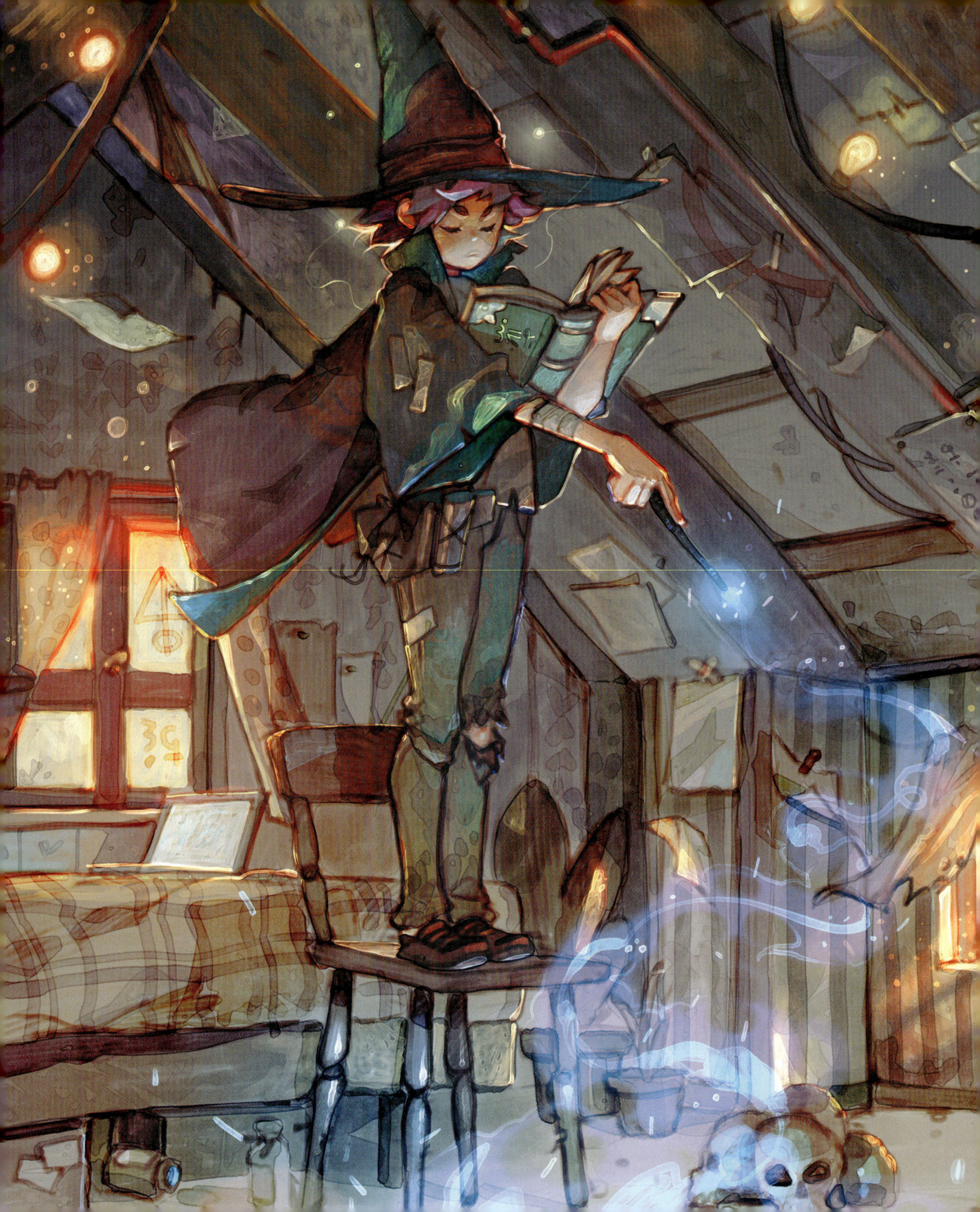

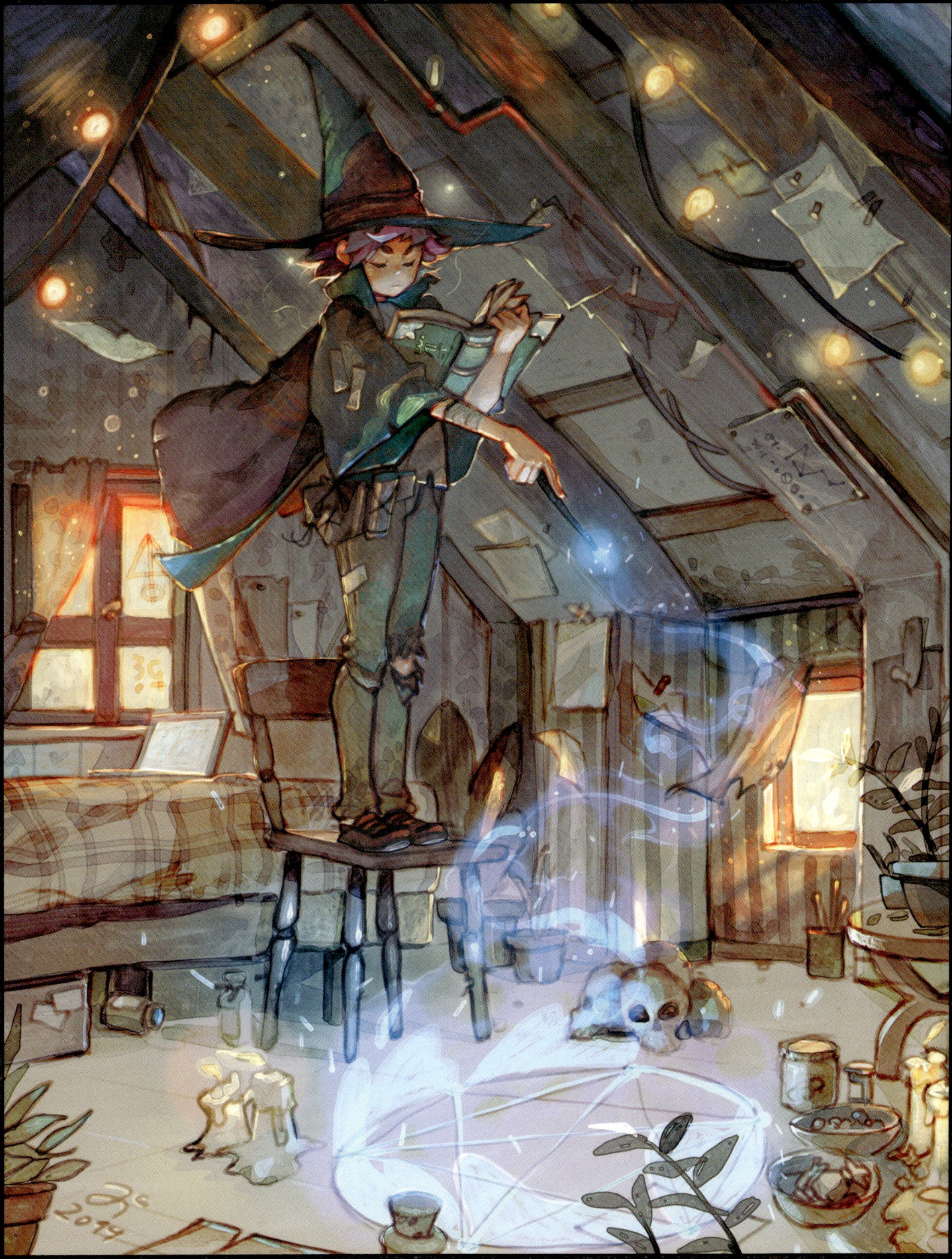

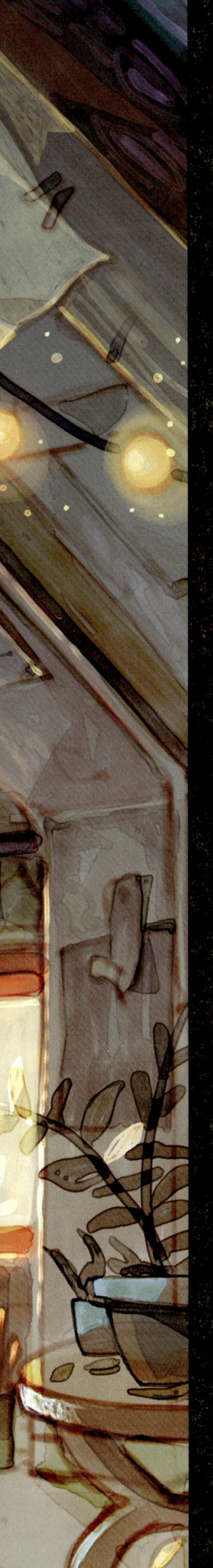

Lake

Lake and Willow are the two main characters of *Falling in the Blue*, and I created this one right after *Willow*. In fact, on Instagram, I posted them at the same time and they have the same exact aesthetic process.

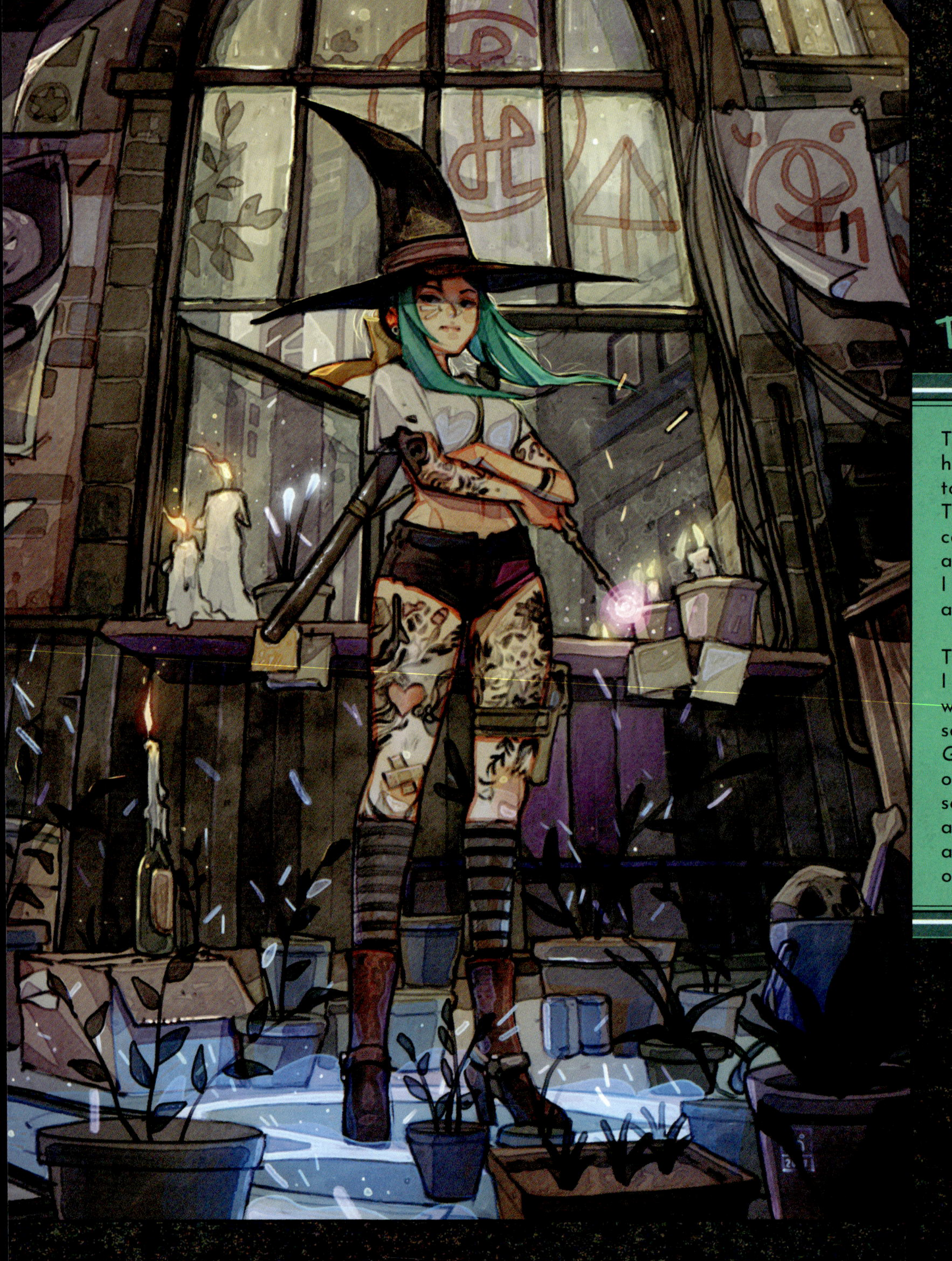

The Ritual

The technique you see here has more effects compared to what I produce nowadays. The base of the picture was completely grey before I applied the colour, but today I use a paper-like page, then add the colour onto it.

This is one of the first pieces I made with the theme of witches, along with the scenarios used in my series *Ghost Cats and Tea* and other illustrations. You can see the candles, magic circles, and a character with a punk aesthetic. There's also a mix of modern and medieval.

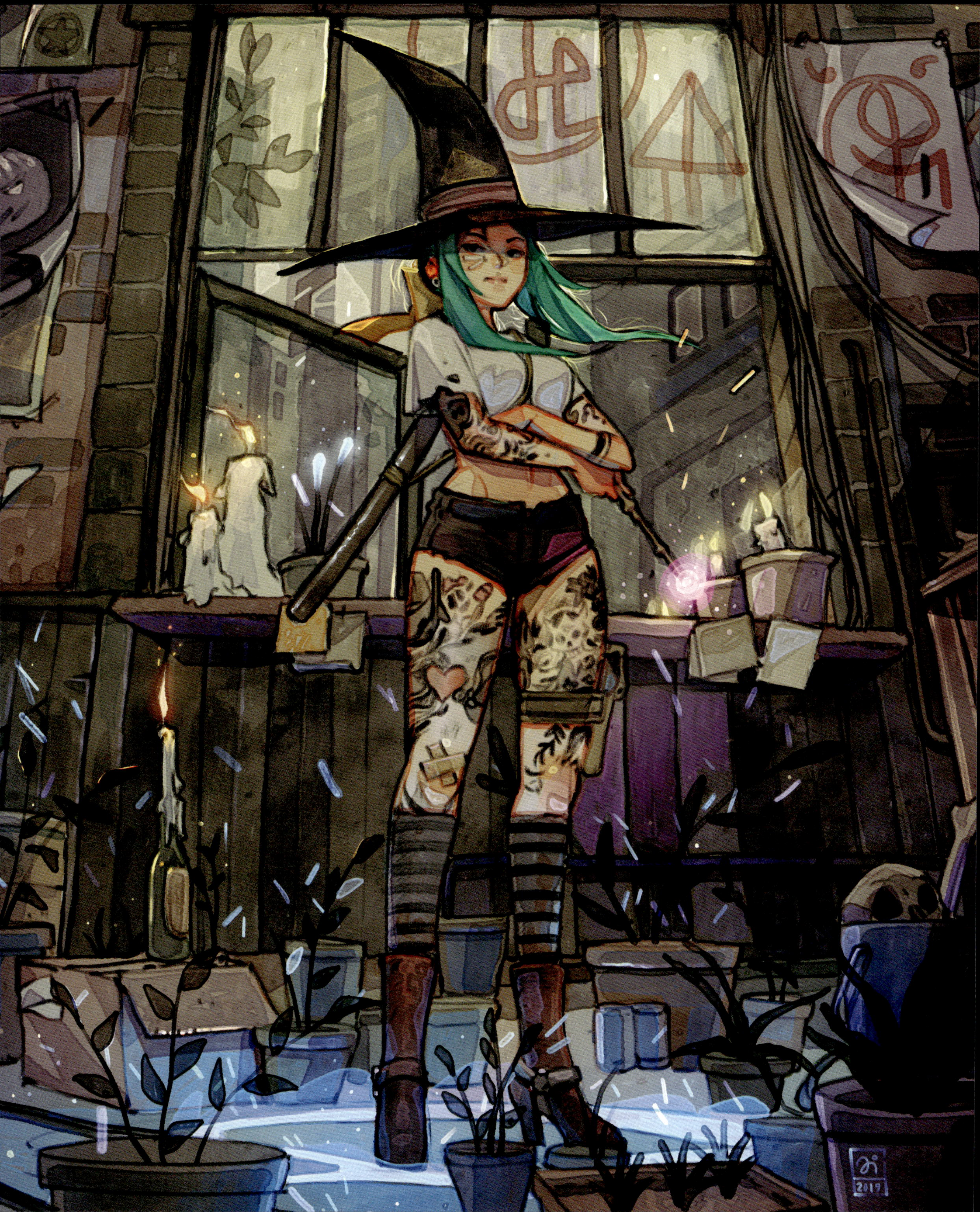

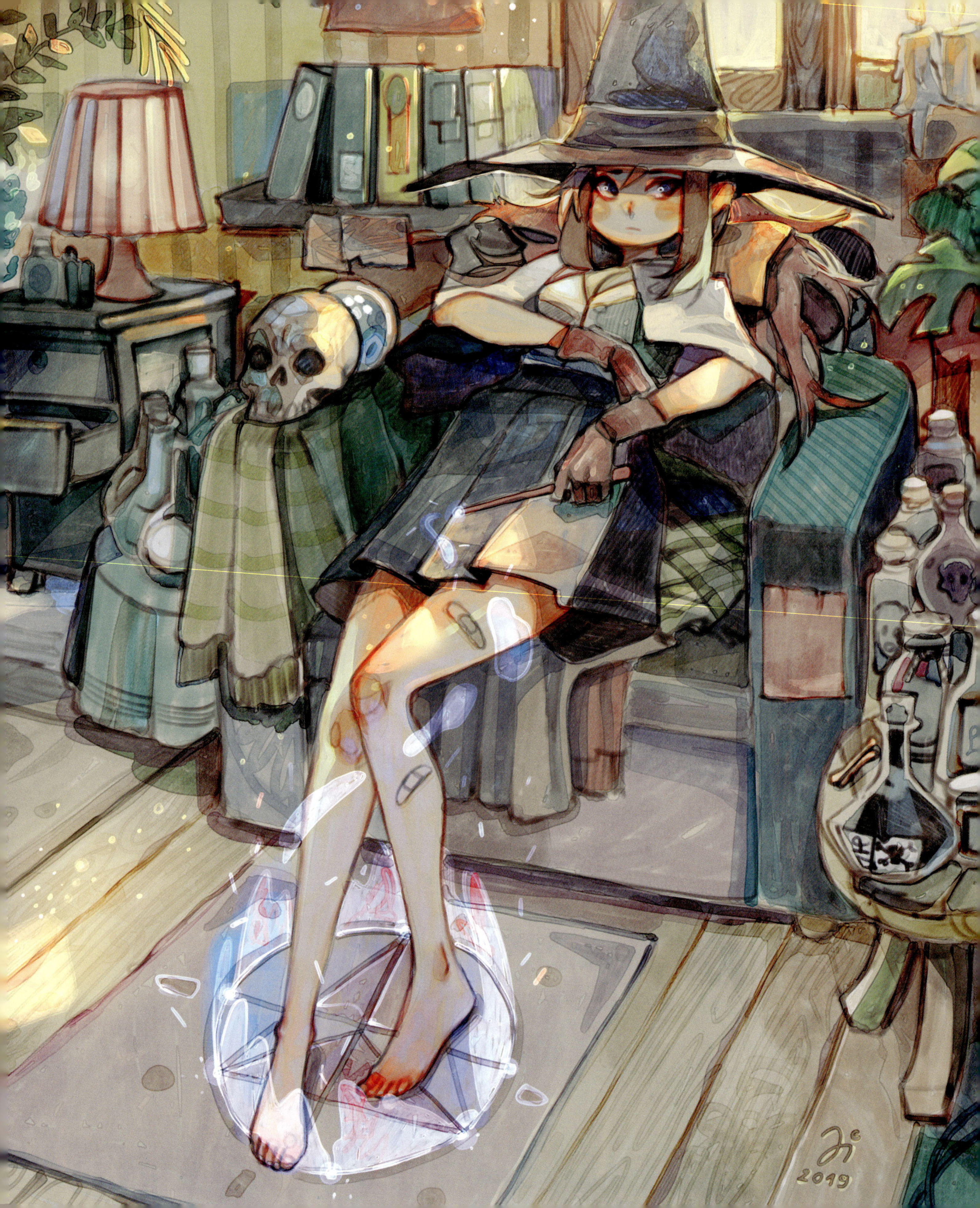
2019

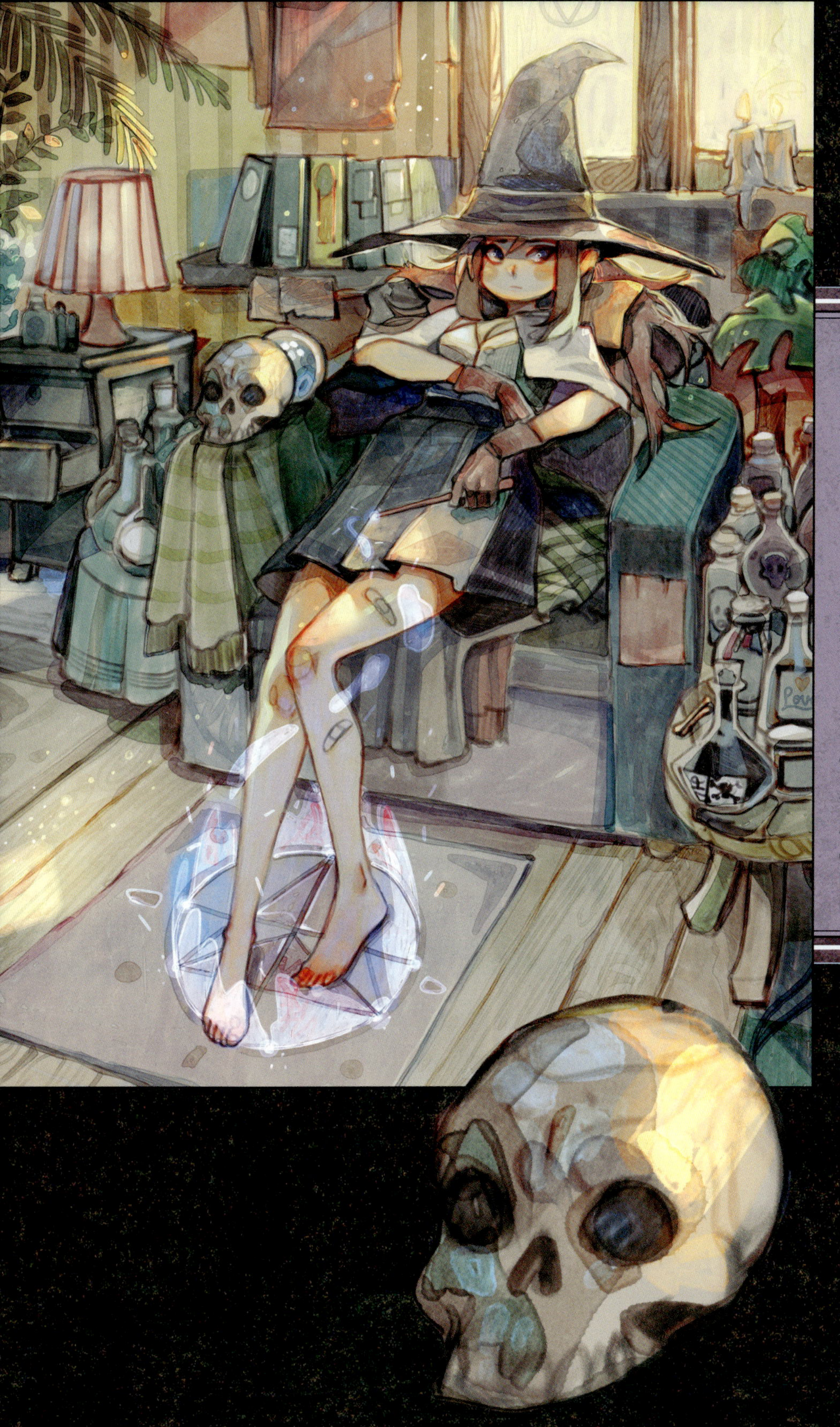

Willow

This image came before *The Ritual* and it was very off-the-book. I don't use many of the techniques used in this piece because they are very painterly, and as you can see, the line work is less visible. It's more about stacking colour on top of colour – it's more digital paint instead of watercolour-style digital paint. There's also a lot of effects like Bloom and colour-fusion methods that give strong highlights and super saturated colours.

It's titled after the main character in *Falling in the Blue*, as I was working on that Webtoon series at the time. It's an example of how I blended a previous project with new ideas that turned out to be the new project.

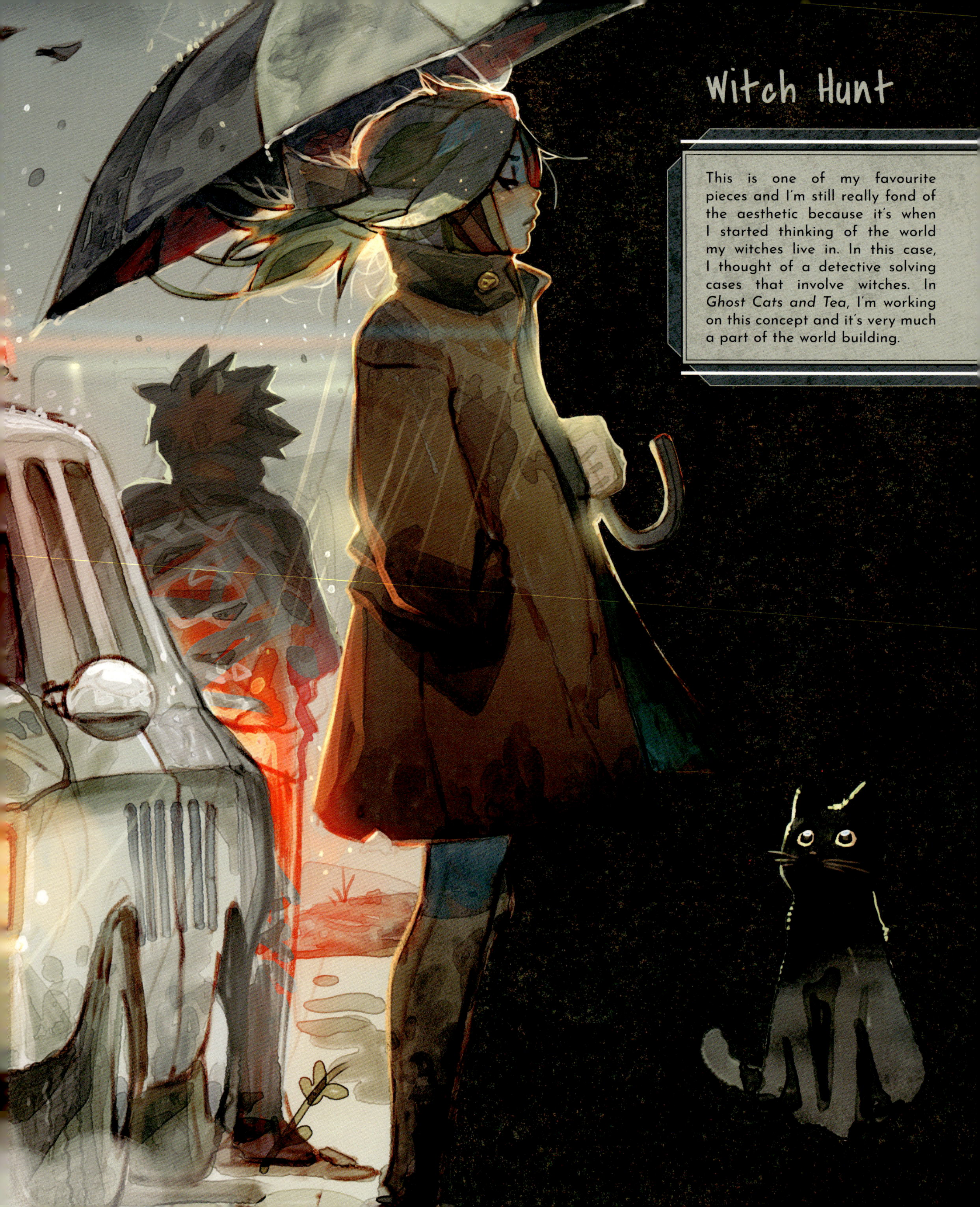

Witch Hunt

This is one of my favourite pieces and I'm still really fond of the aesthetic because it's when I started thinking of the world my witches live in. In this case, I thought of a detective solving cases that involve witches. In *Ghost Cats and Tea*, I'm working on this concept and it's very much a part of the world building.

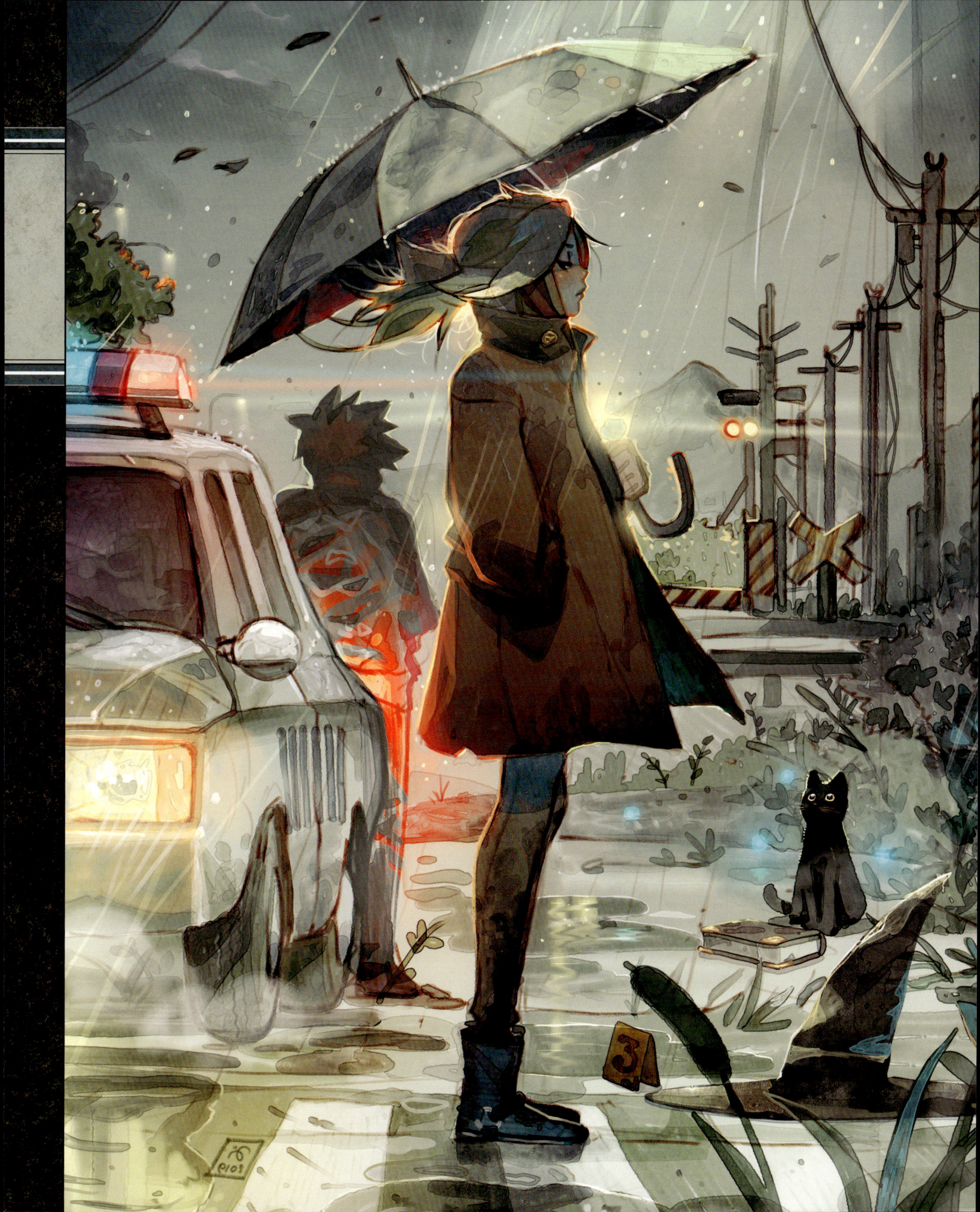

Bass and Candles

In this series, I really liked the idea of fostering a strong connection between magic, technology, and music. I used a specific warped perspective for this image, and fashioned it as an overall accessory for the mood, aesthetic, and themes of this project.

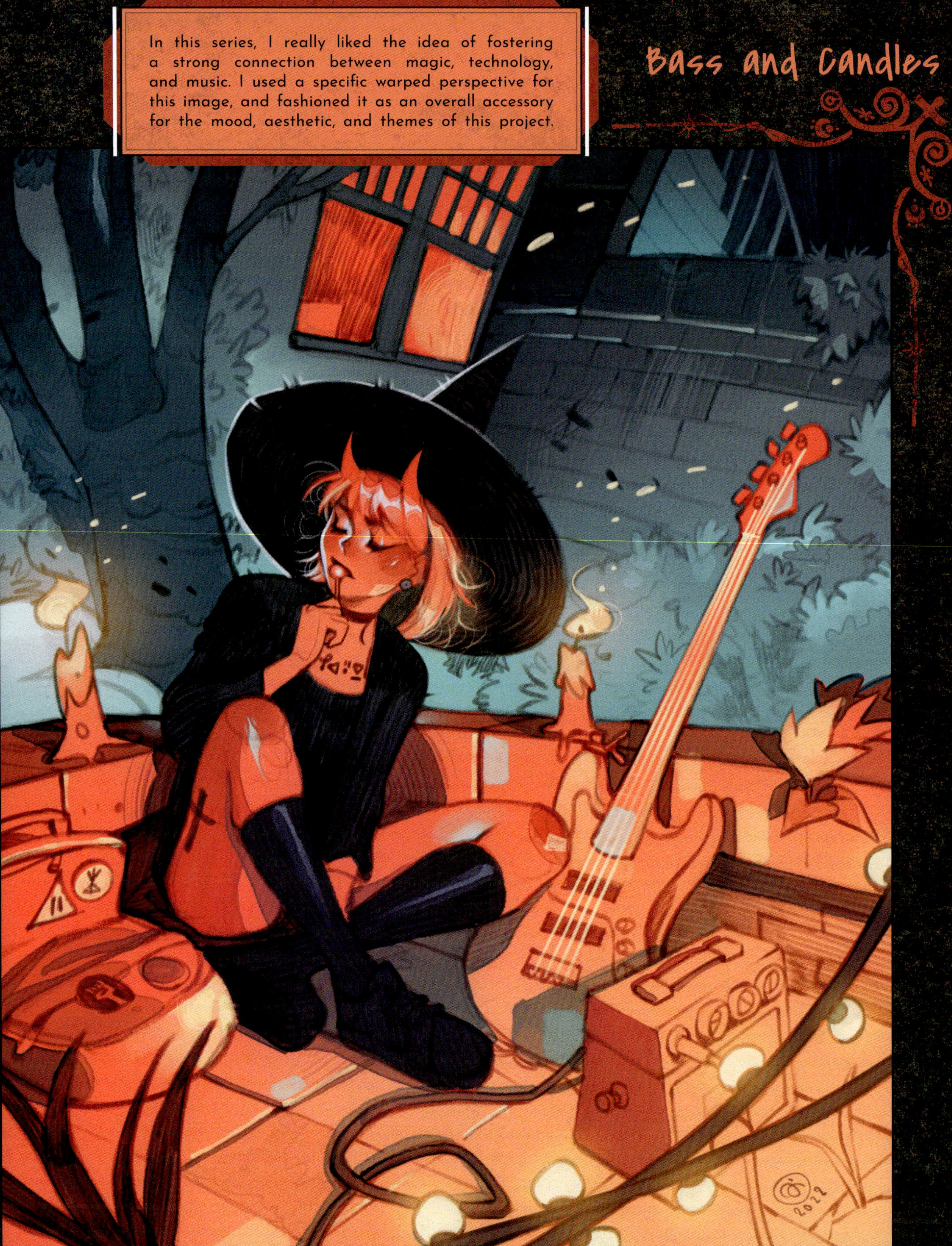

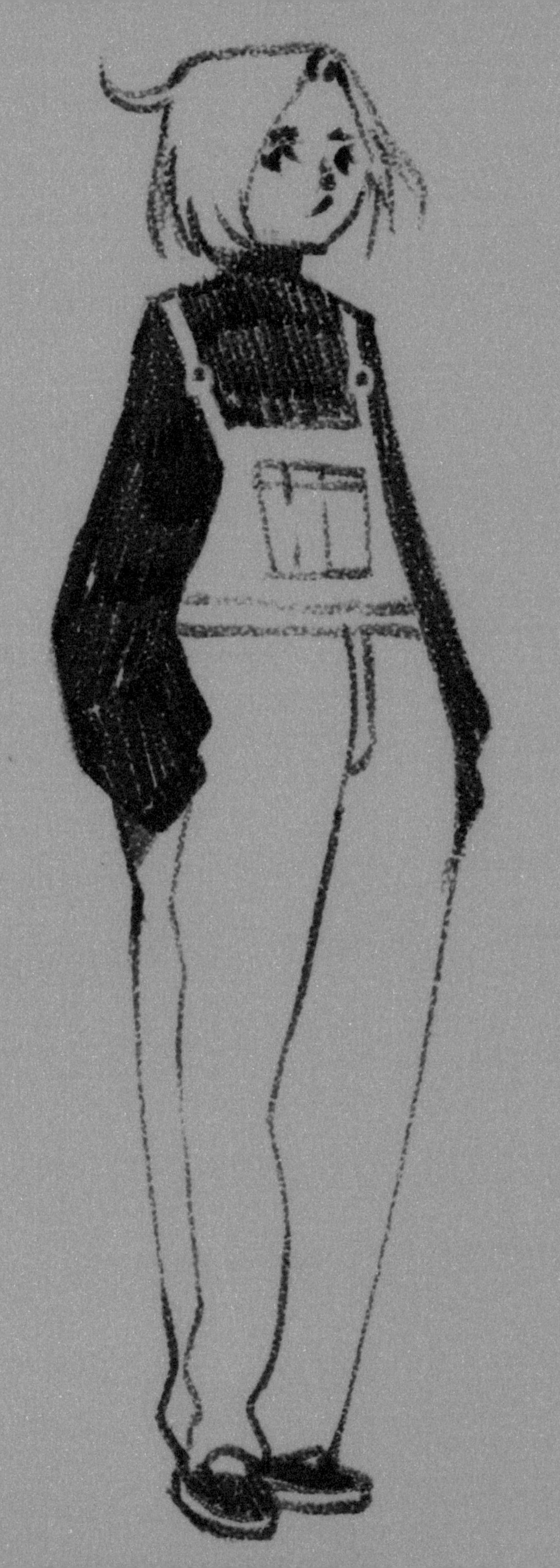

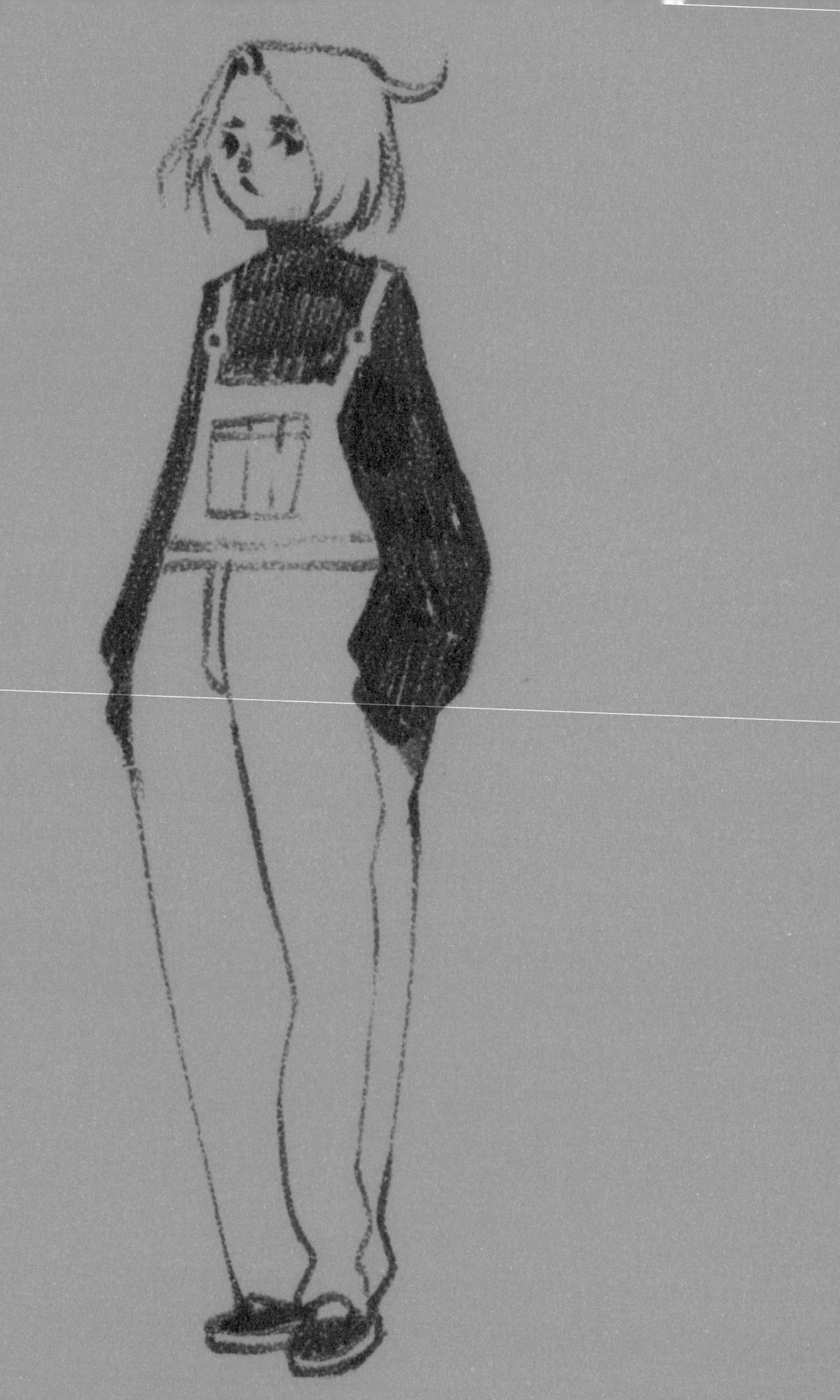

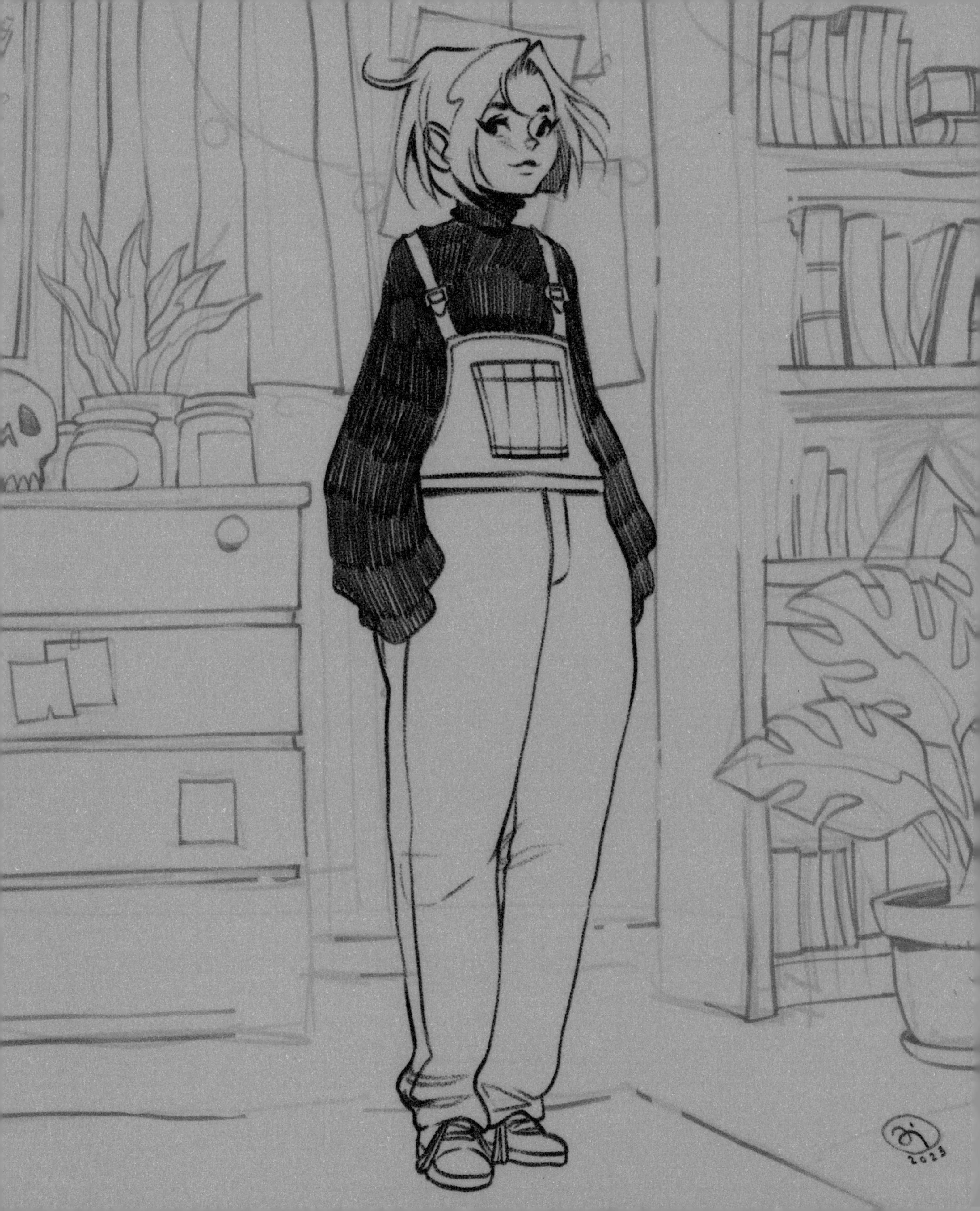
2023

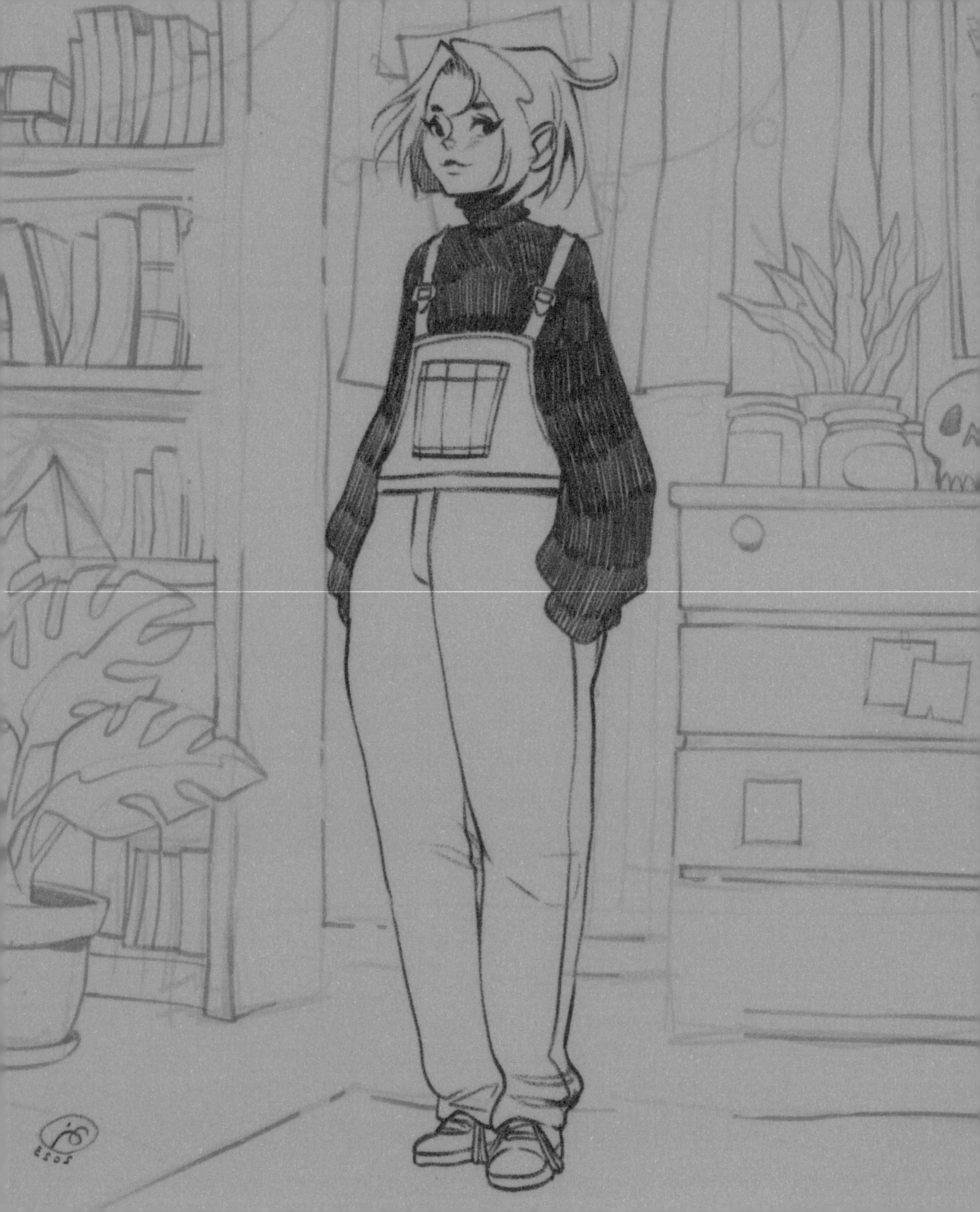

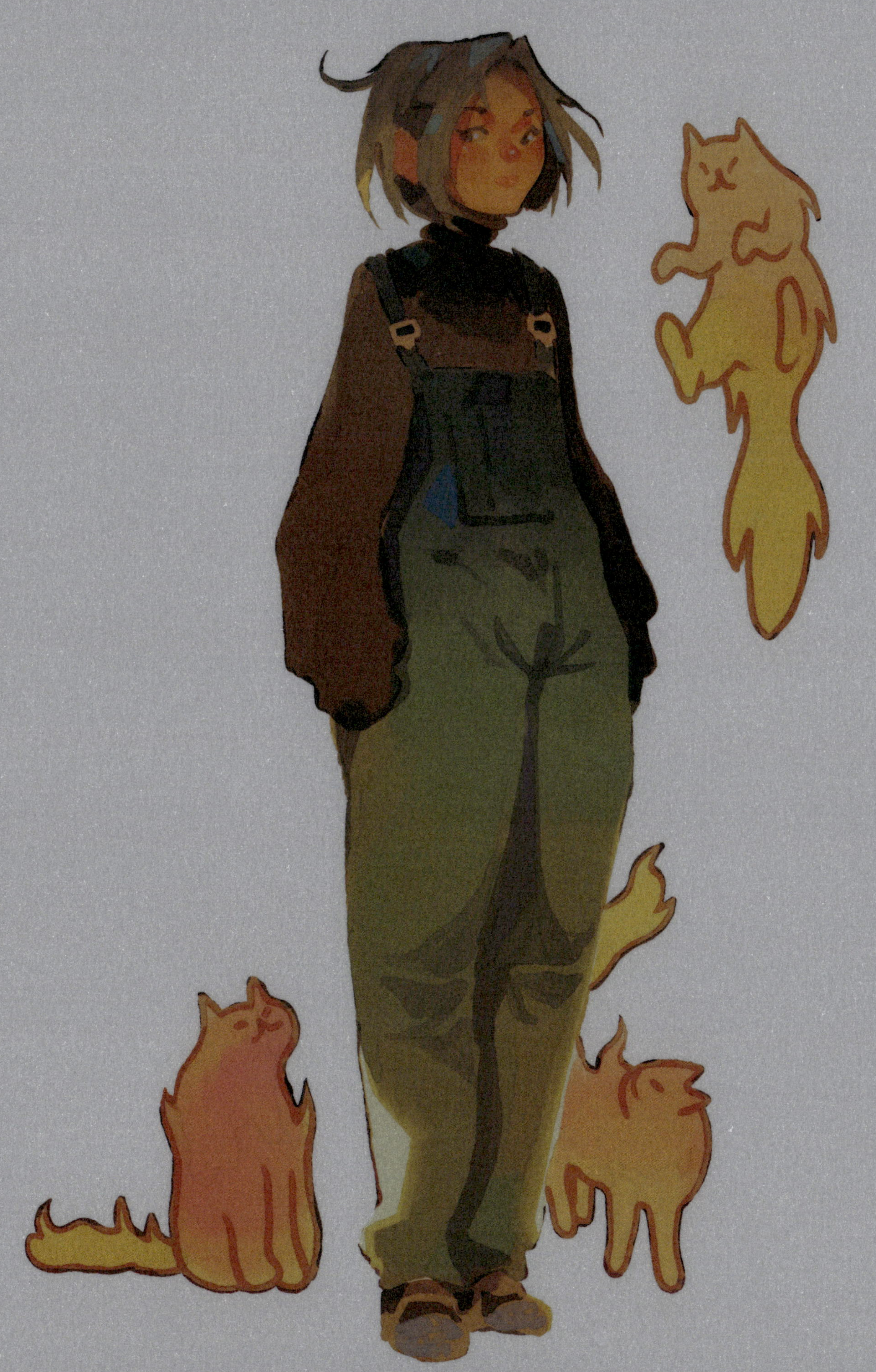

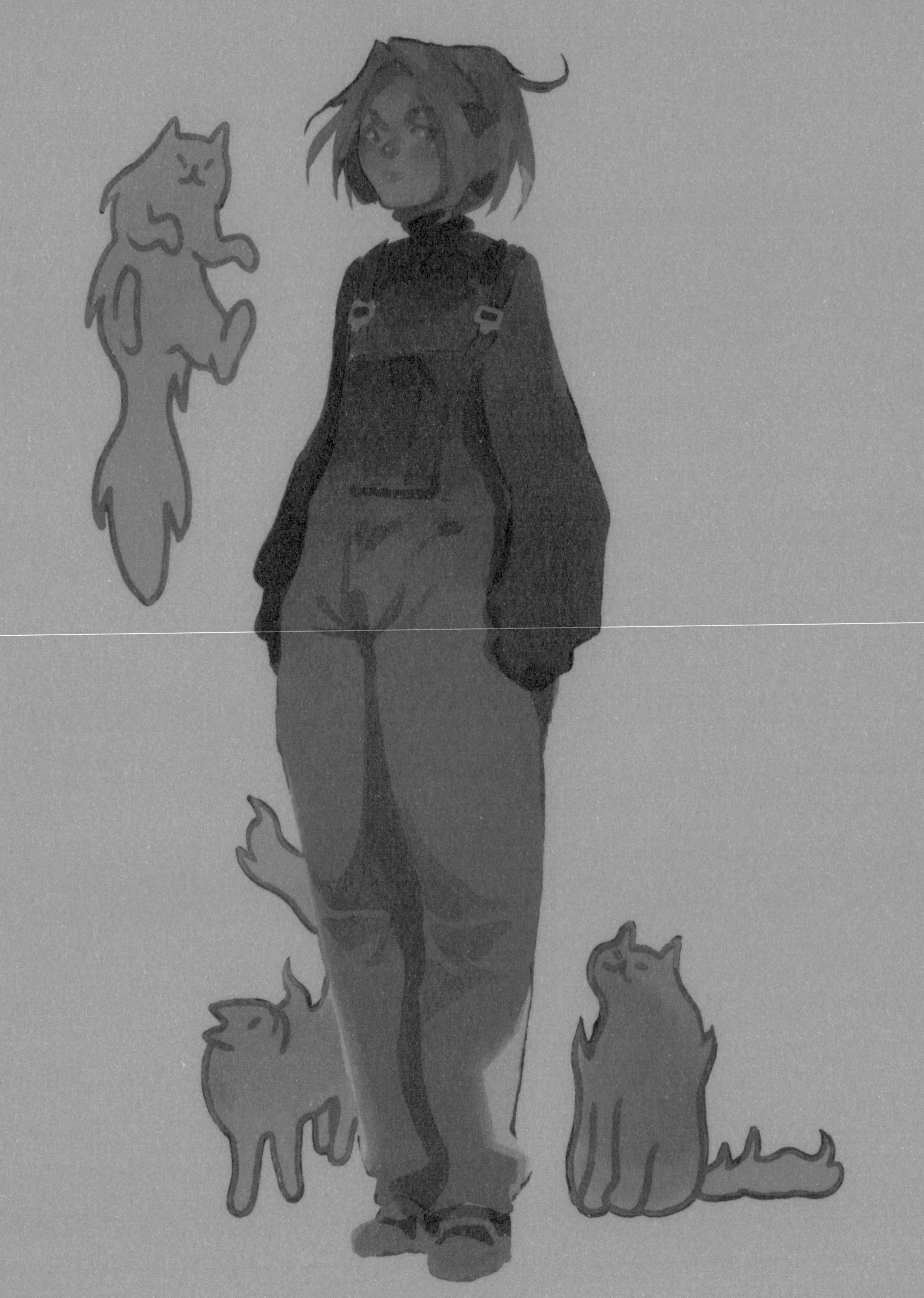

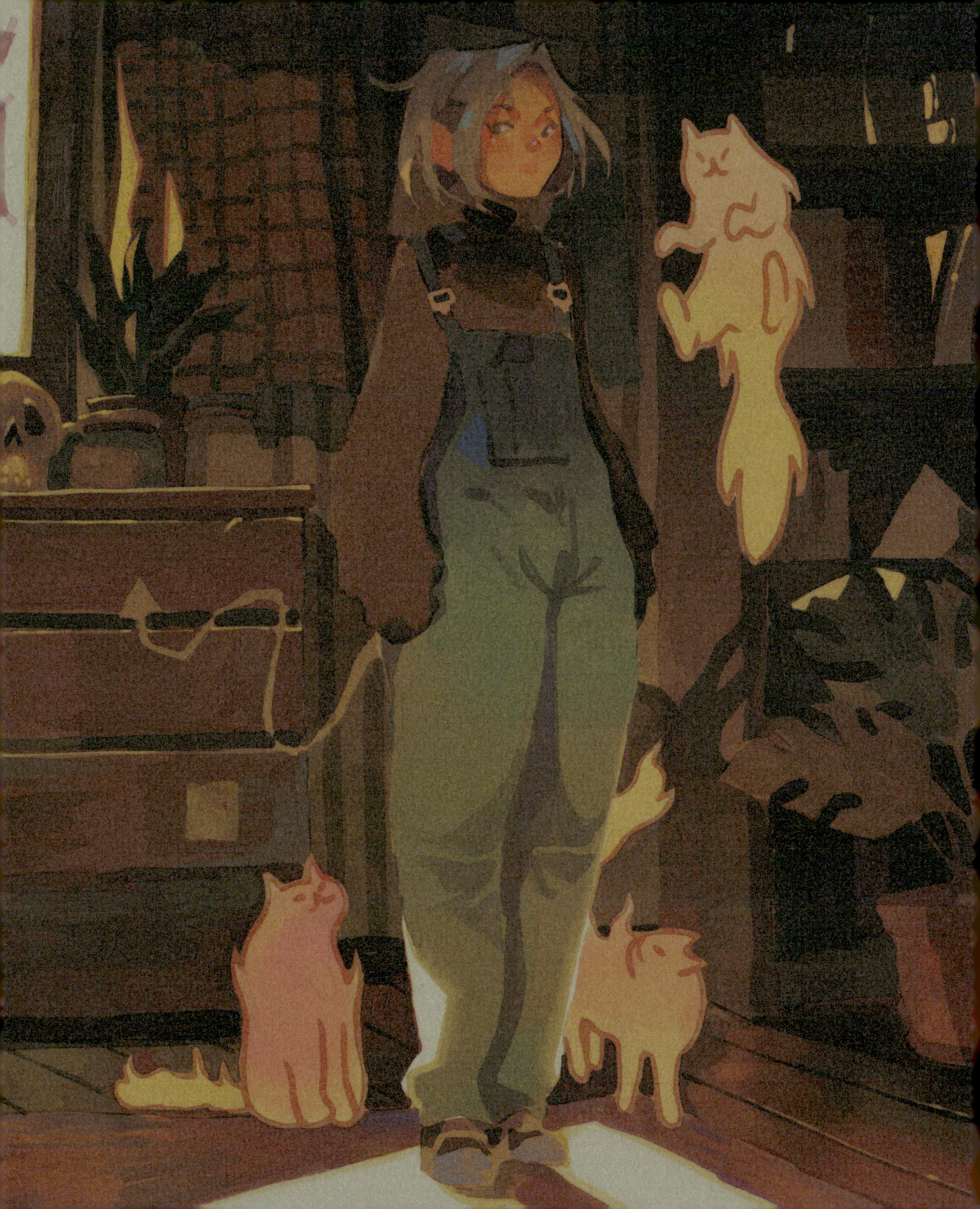

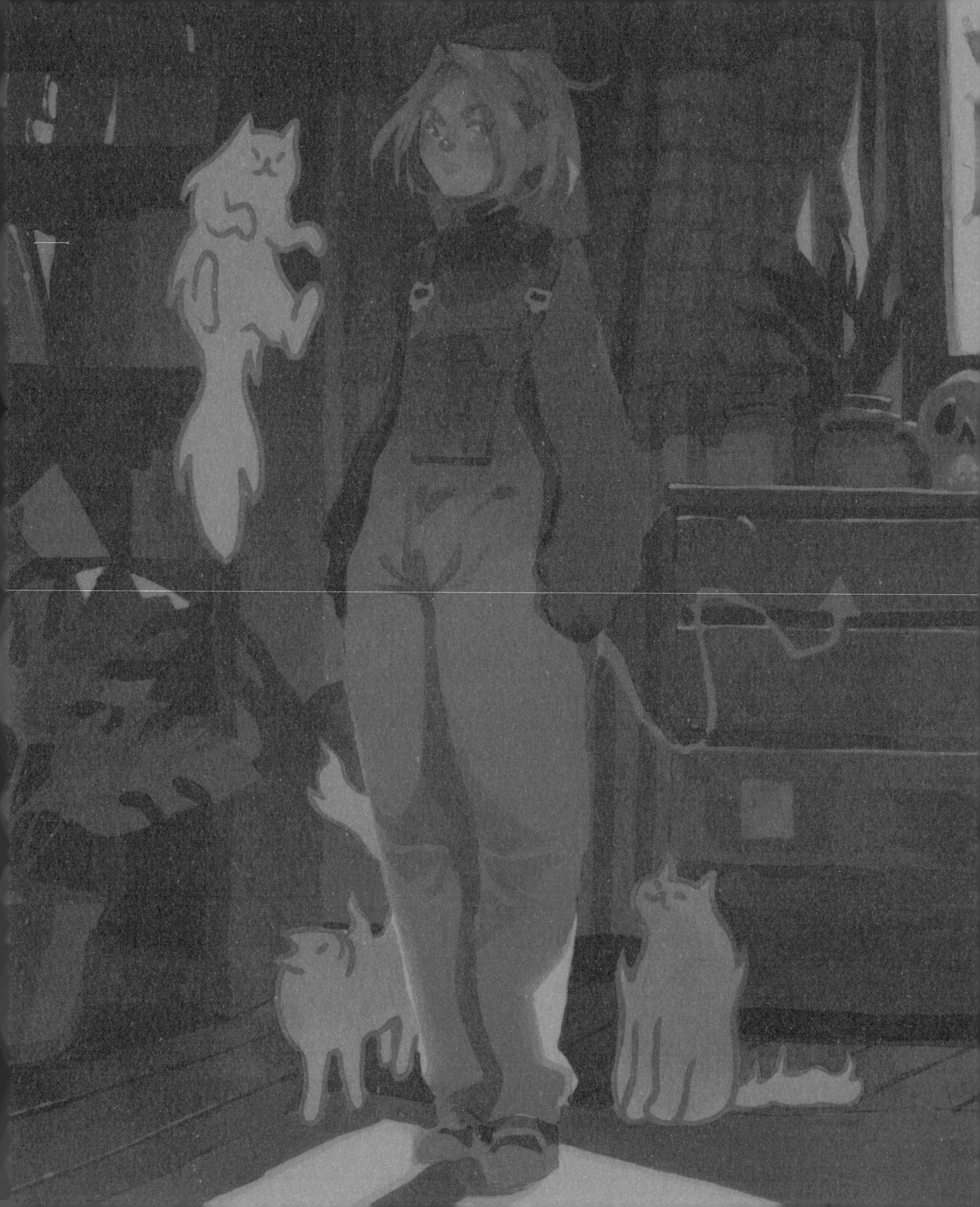

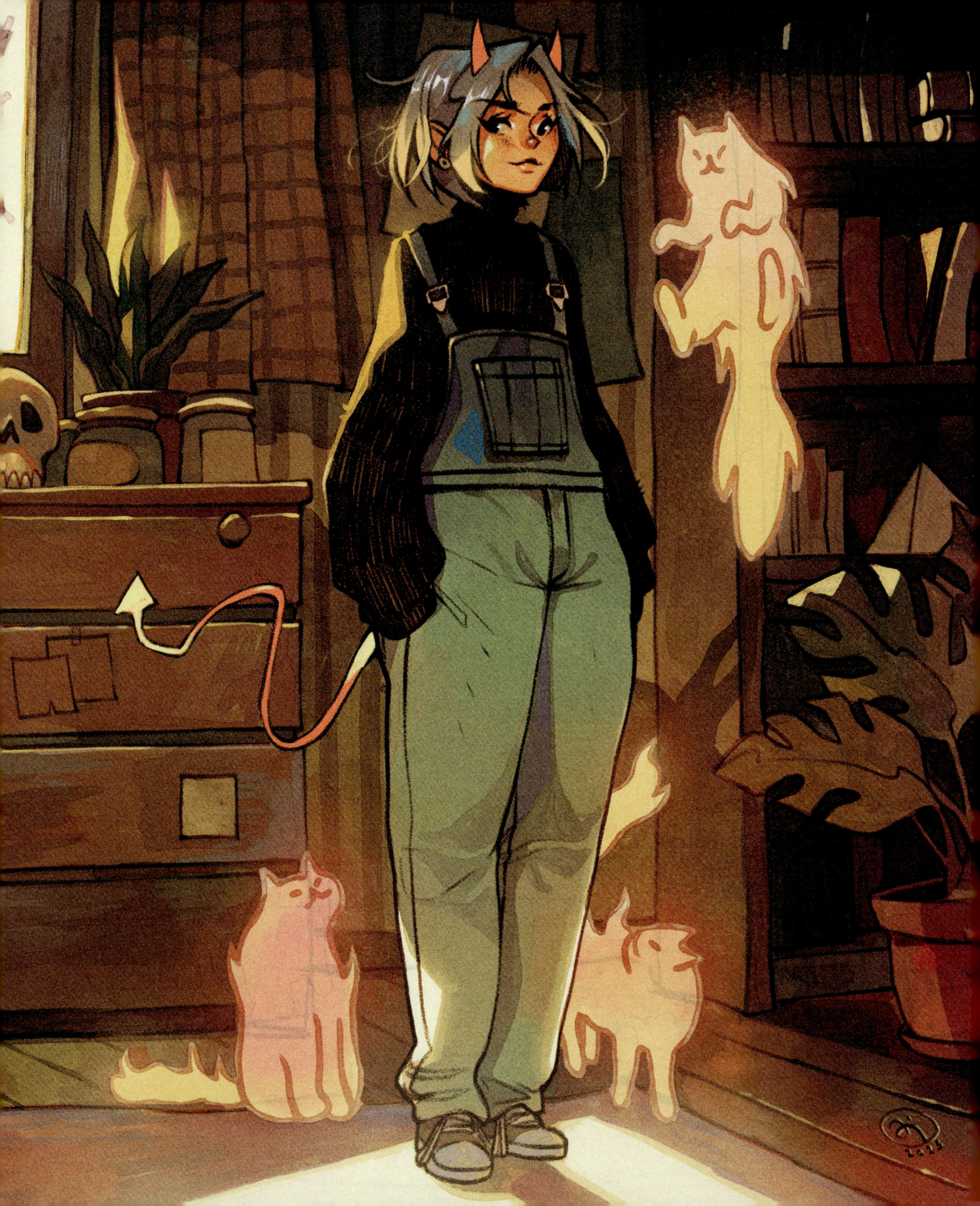

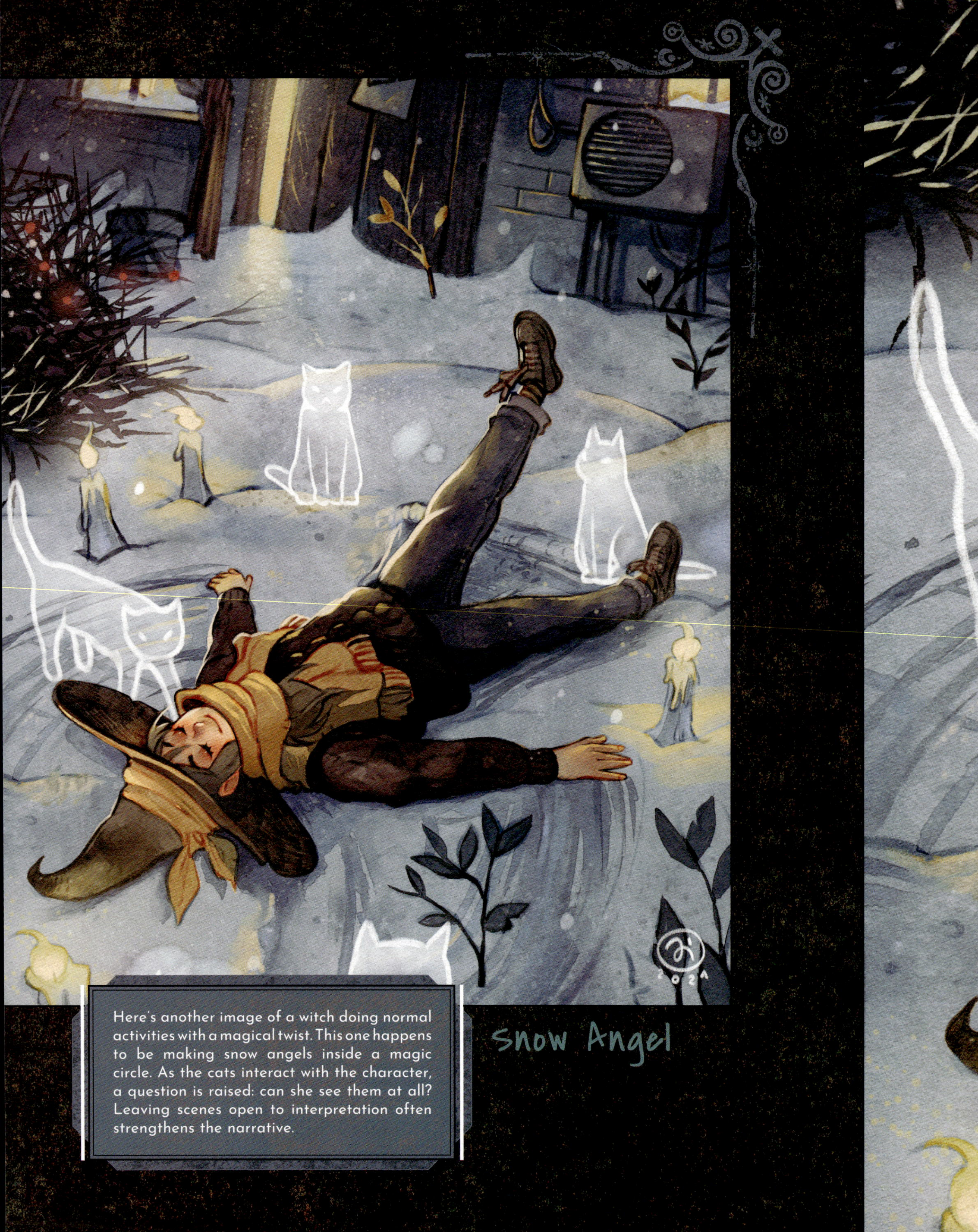

Here's another image of a witch doing normal activities with a magical twist. This one happens to be making snow angels inside a magic circle. As the cats interact with the character, a question is raised: can she see them at all? Leaving scenes open to interpretation often strengthens the narrative.

Snow Angel

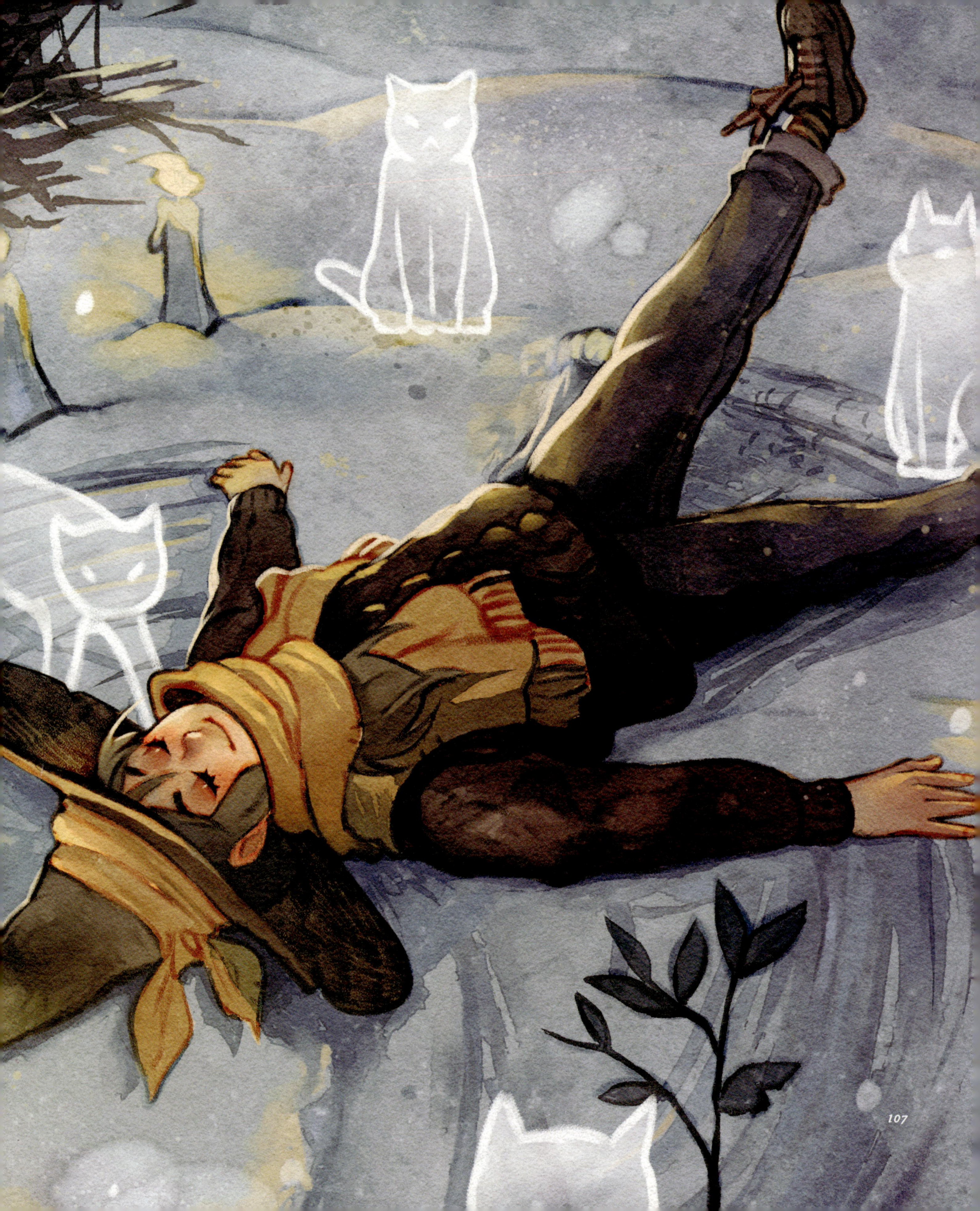

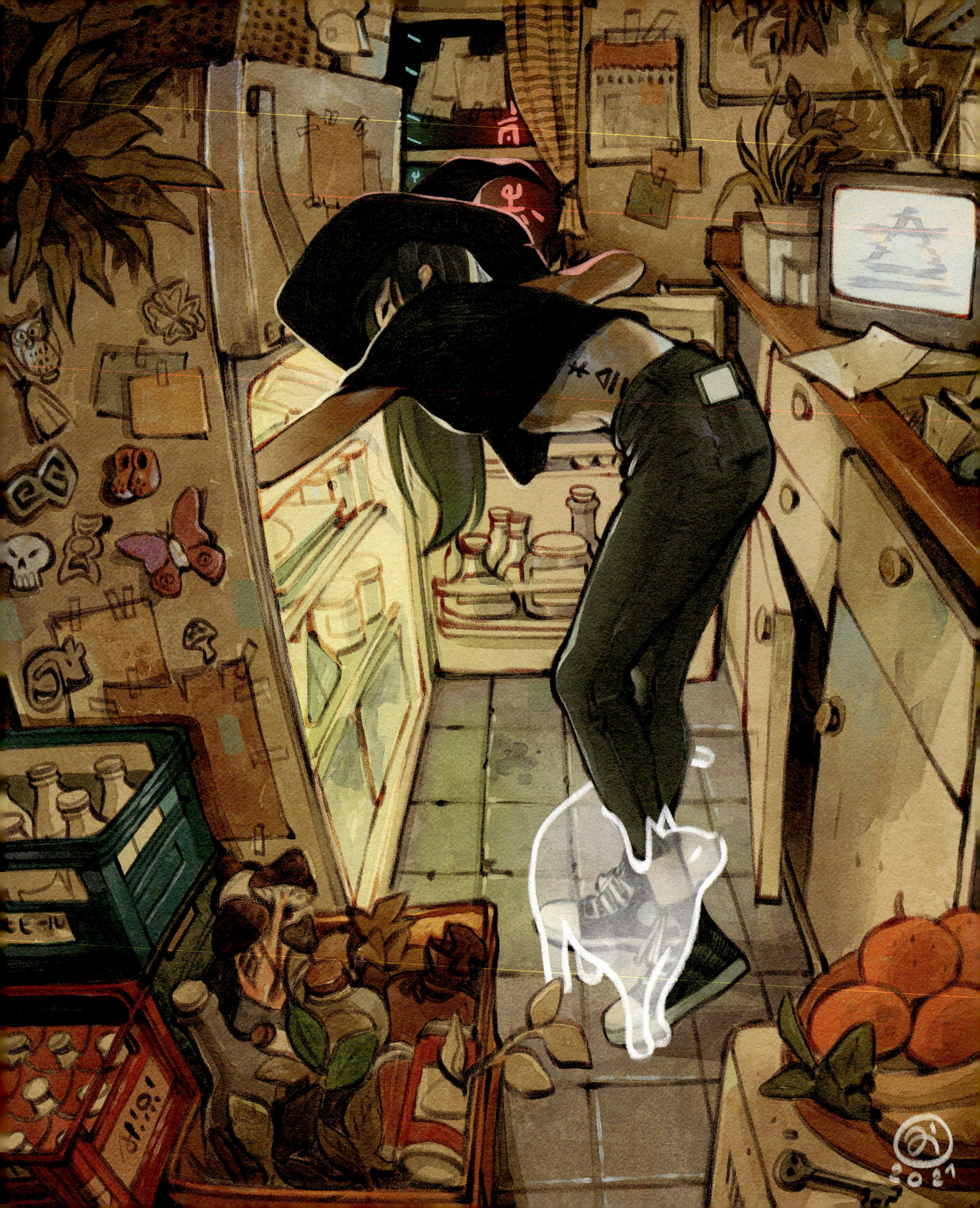

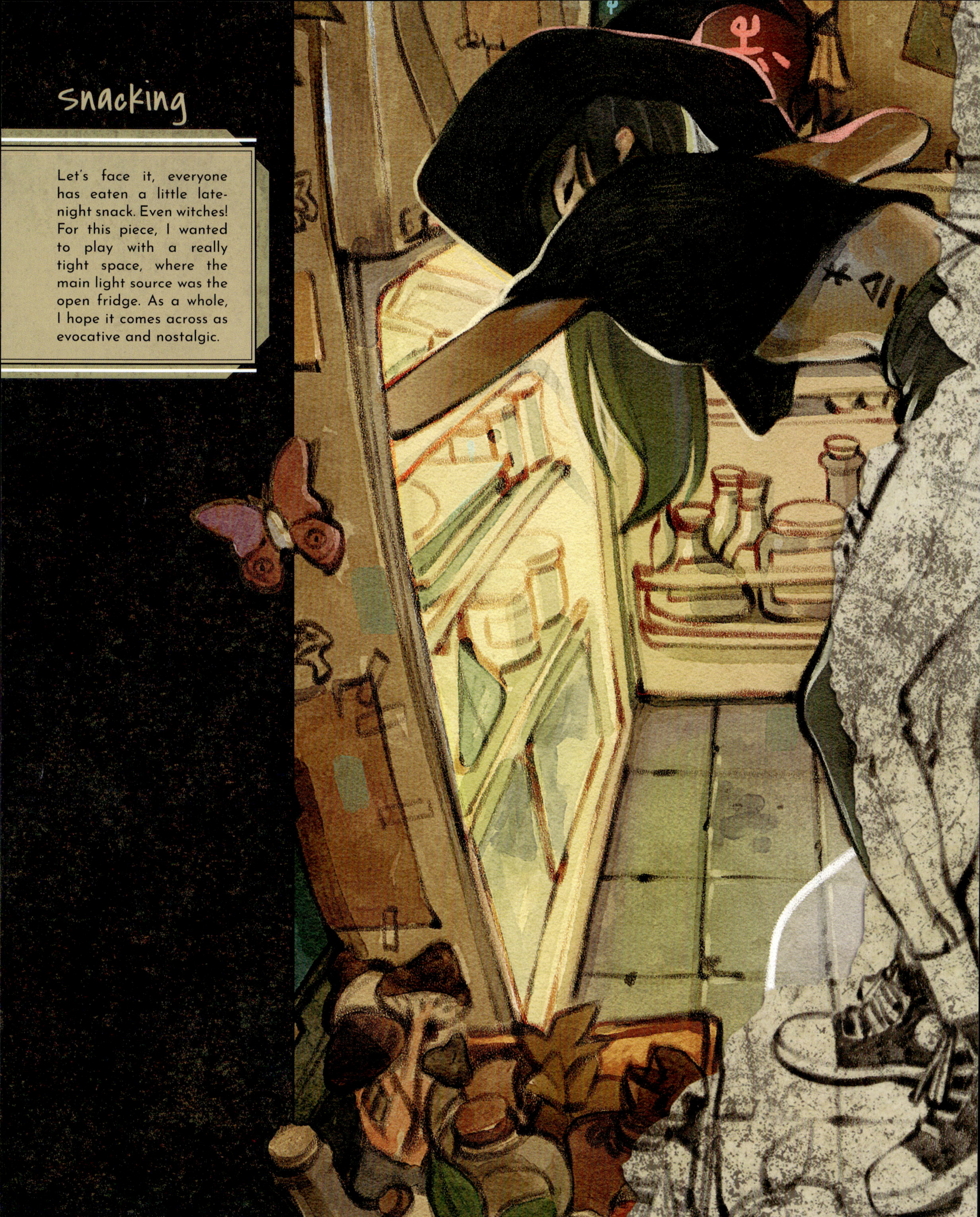

snacking

Let's face it, everyone has eaten a little late-night snack. Even witches! For this piece, I wanted to play with a really tight space, where the main light source was the open fridge. As a whole, I hope it comes across as evocative and nostalgic.

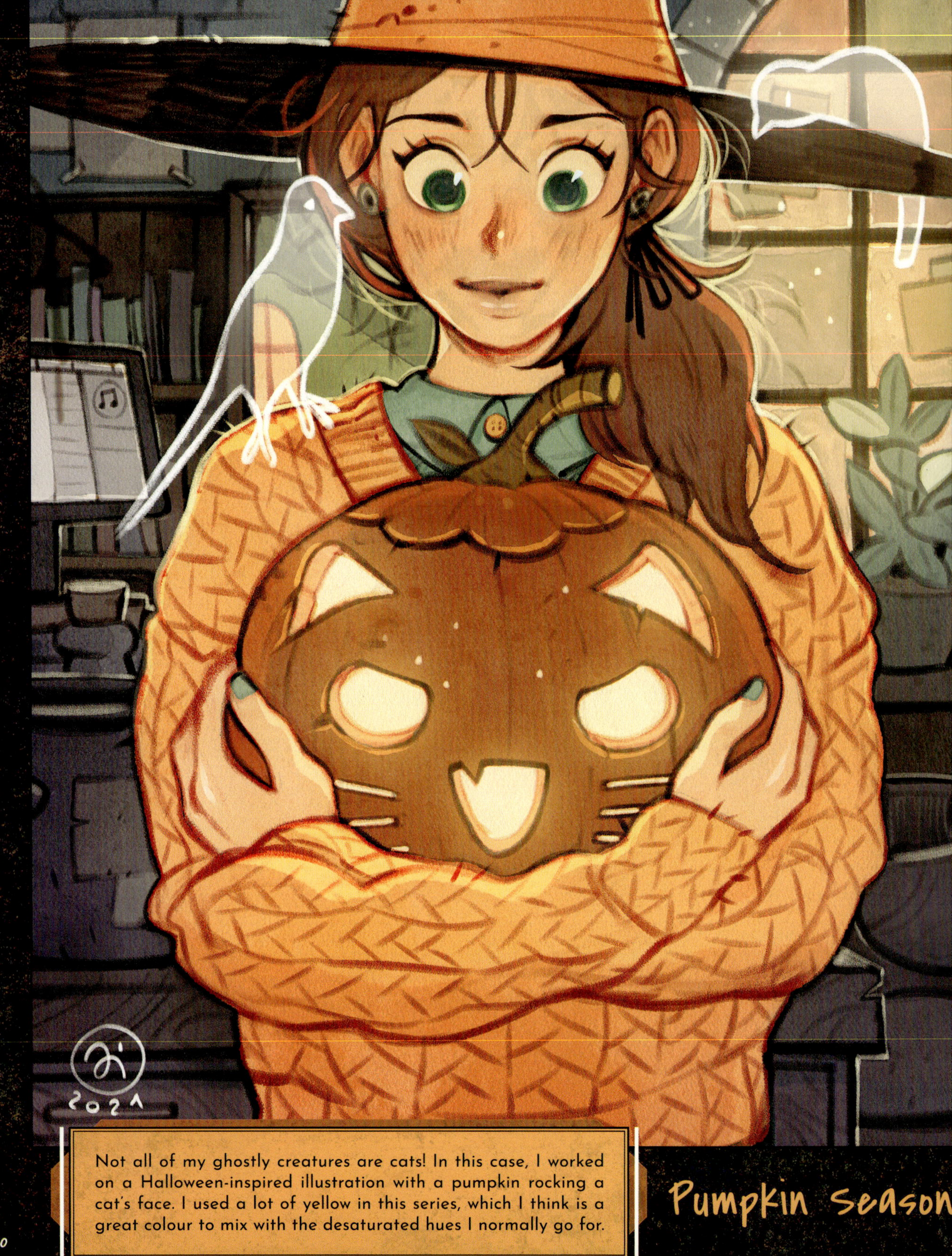

Pumpkin Season

Not all of my ghostly creatures are cats! In this case, I worked on a Halloween-inspired illustration with a pumpkin rocking a cat's face. I used a lot of yellow in this series, which I think is a great colour to mix with the desaturated hues I normally go for.

Resting on the Balcony

When I was a kid, I always sat like this while staring at the sky. As you can see, line work and cross-hatching helps me create a sense of direction. For example, the lines on the witch's hat are radial and converge towards her face, making things look unfinished and handmade, which is the look I'm after.

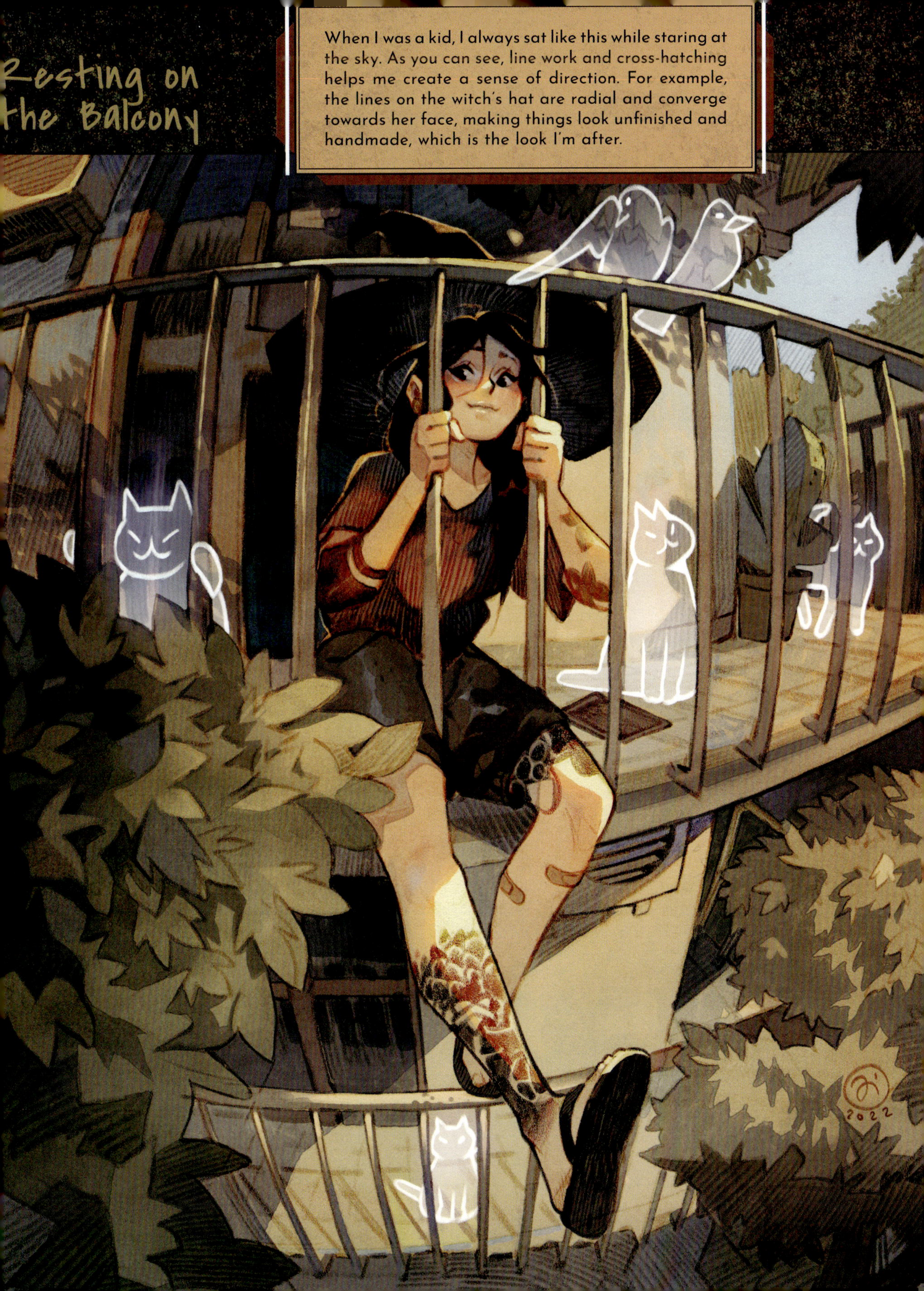

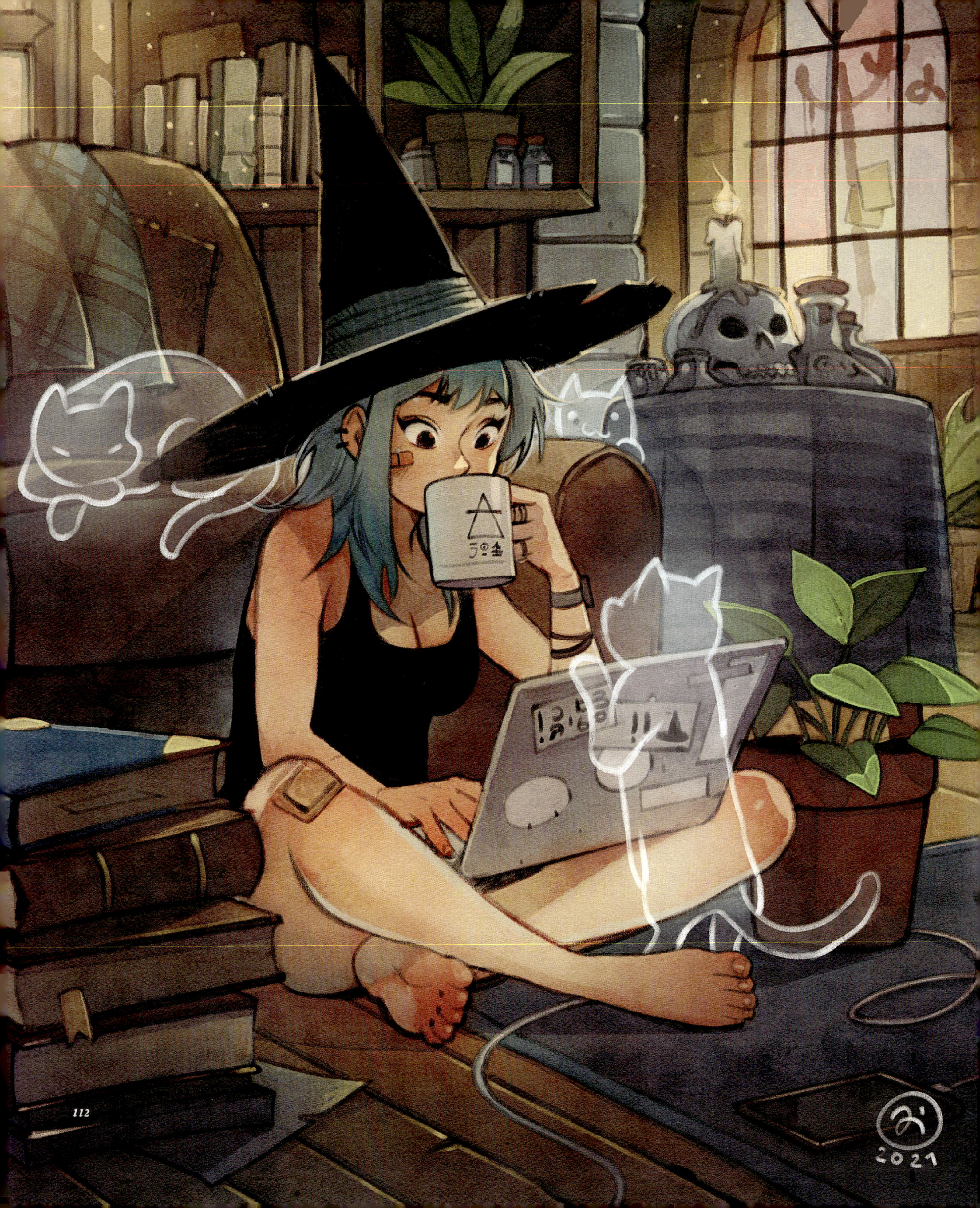

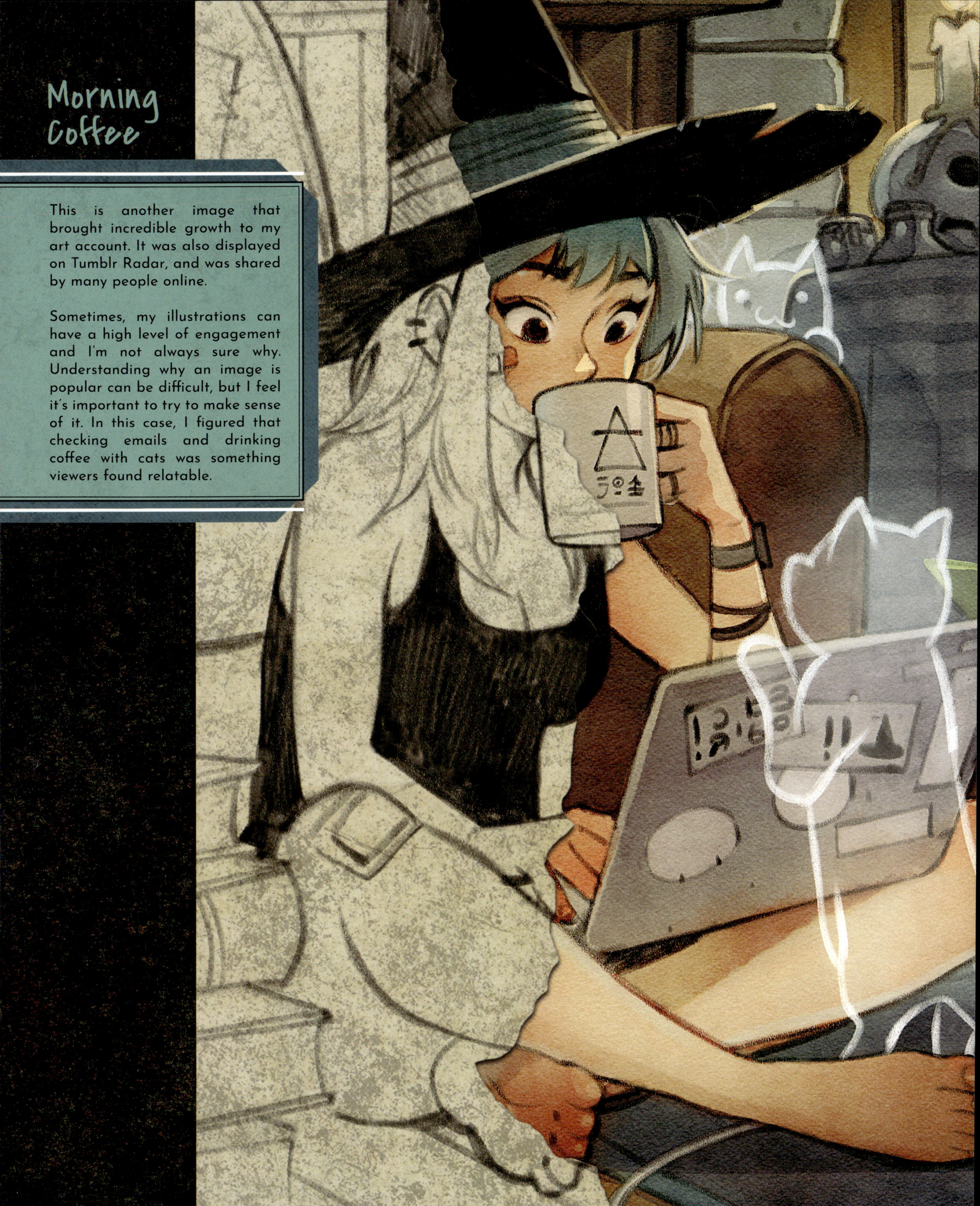

Morning Coffee

This is another image that brought incredible growth to my art account. It was also displayed on Tumblr Radar, and was shared by many people online.

Sometimes, my illustrations can have a high level of engagement and I'm not always sure why. Understanding why an image is popular can be difficult, but I feel it's important to try to make sense of it. In this case, I figured that checking emails and drinking coffee with cats was something viewers found relatable.

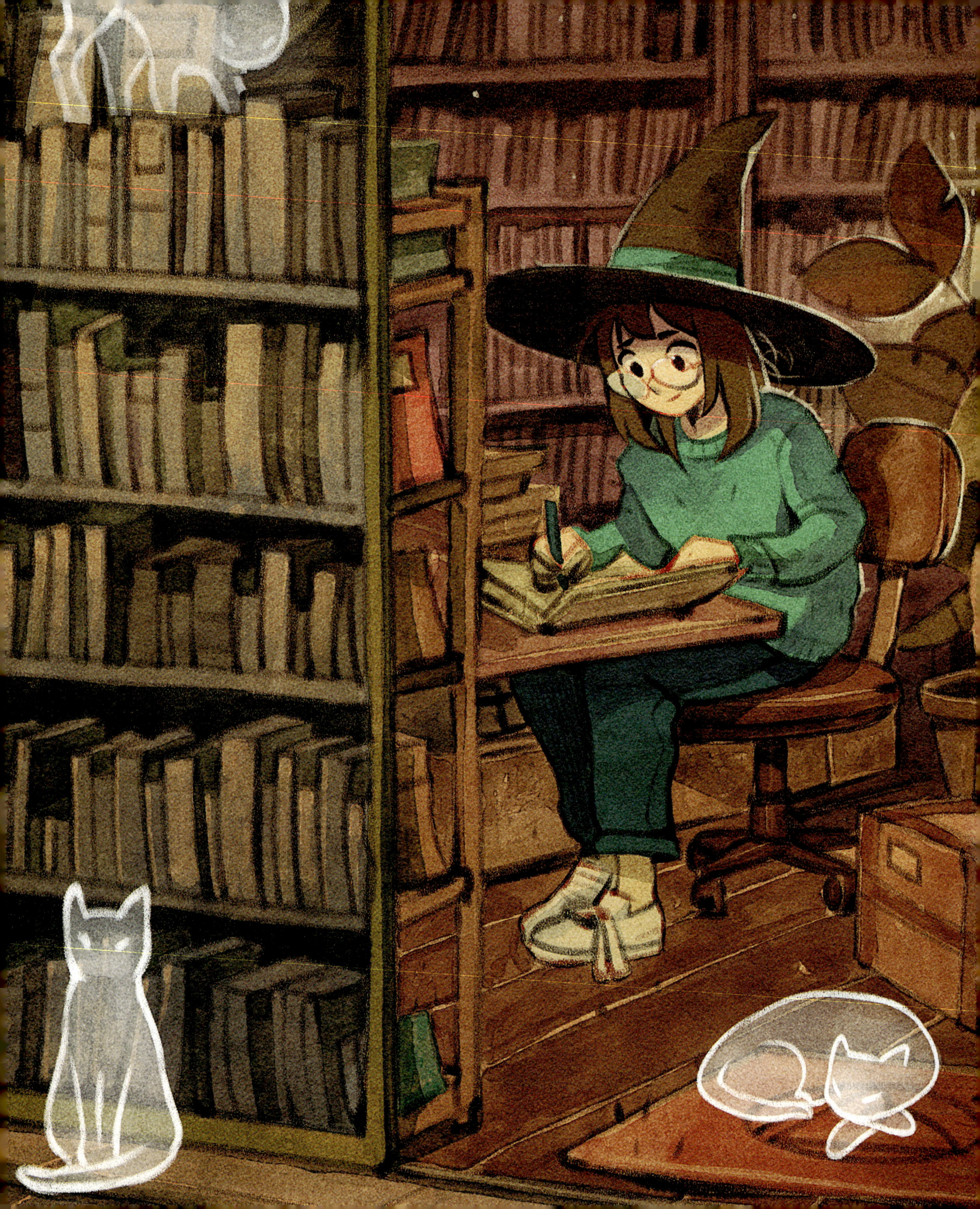

Staying at the Library

In this series, you'll see lots of reading, writing, and drawing. To create a mystical vibe, I added light mist in the background and let the ghost cats pop out of the canvas, as if they're breaking the atmosphere and palette with their presence.

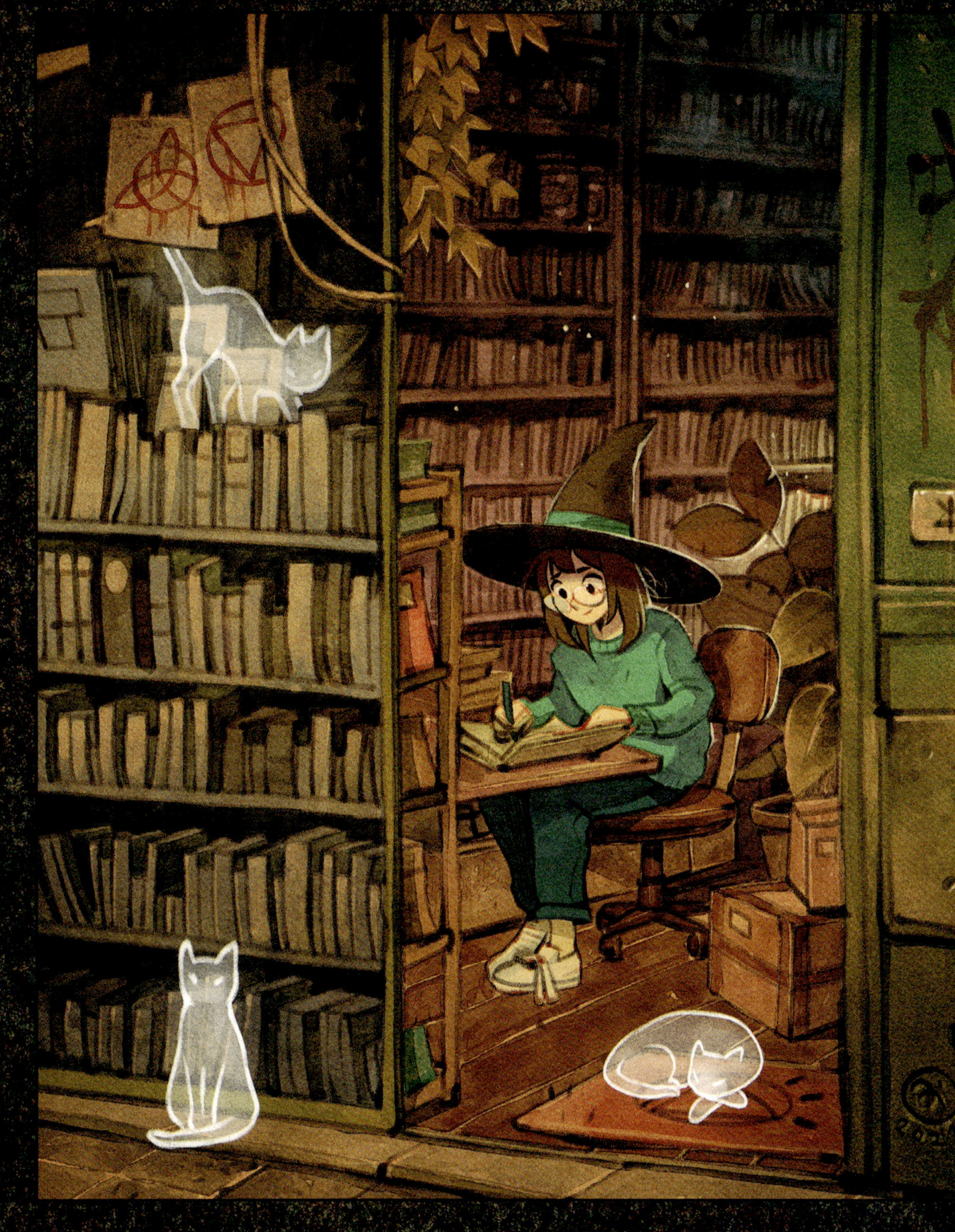

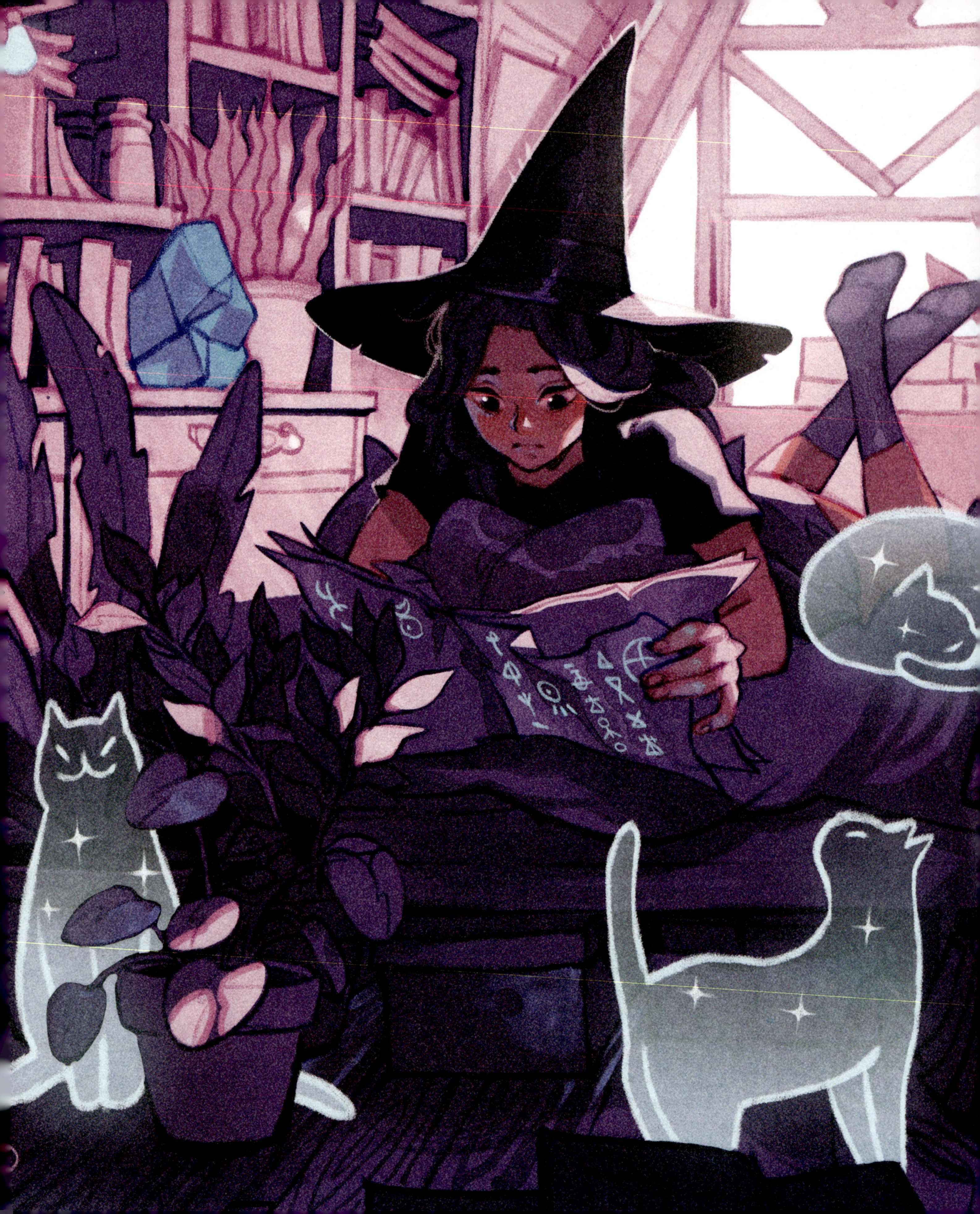

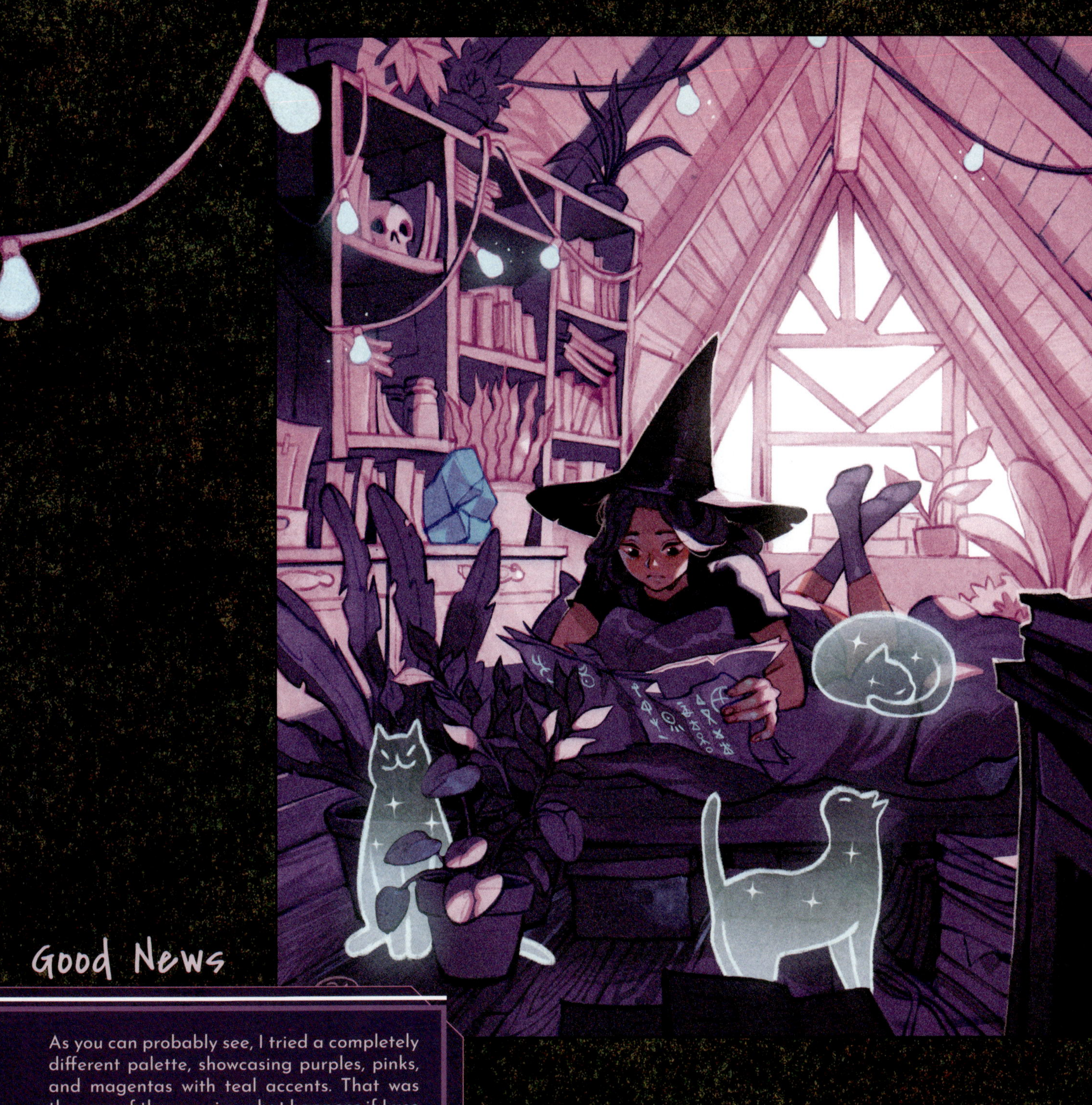

Good News

As you can probably see, I tried a completely different palette, showcasing purples, pinks, and magentas with teal accents. That was the crux of the exercise: what happens if I use different tones on a picture? How would I handle it? What would the results look like? There's still a limited palette, but I'm pushing my boundaries in terms of colour.

Coven Cafe

This picture inspired the name of my community! I really like the idea of a cafe run by witches. I wanted to create a strong contrast between the cold outdoor colours (blues, greens, and purples) and the warmer inside tones (cadmium yellow, orange, and red).

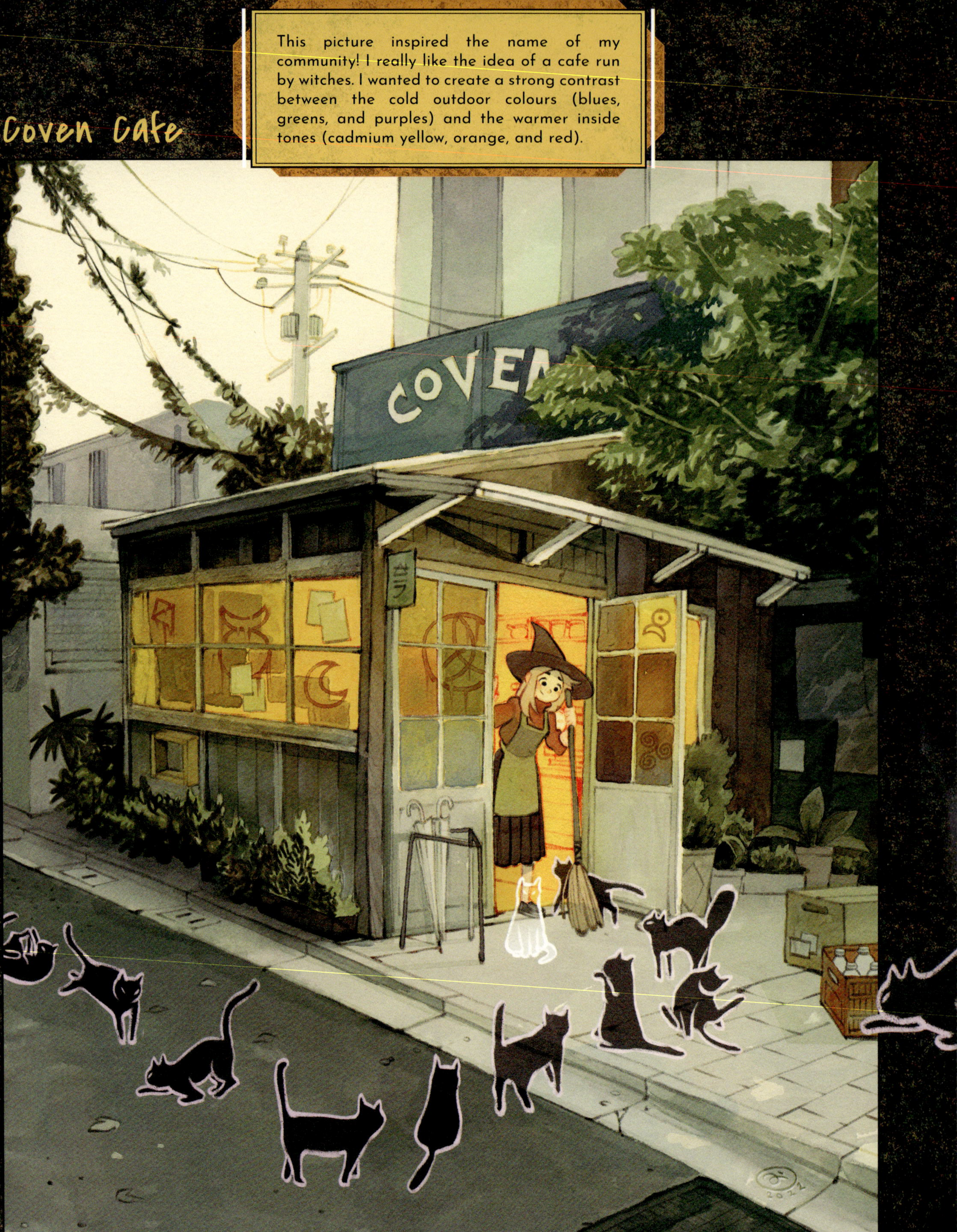

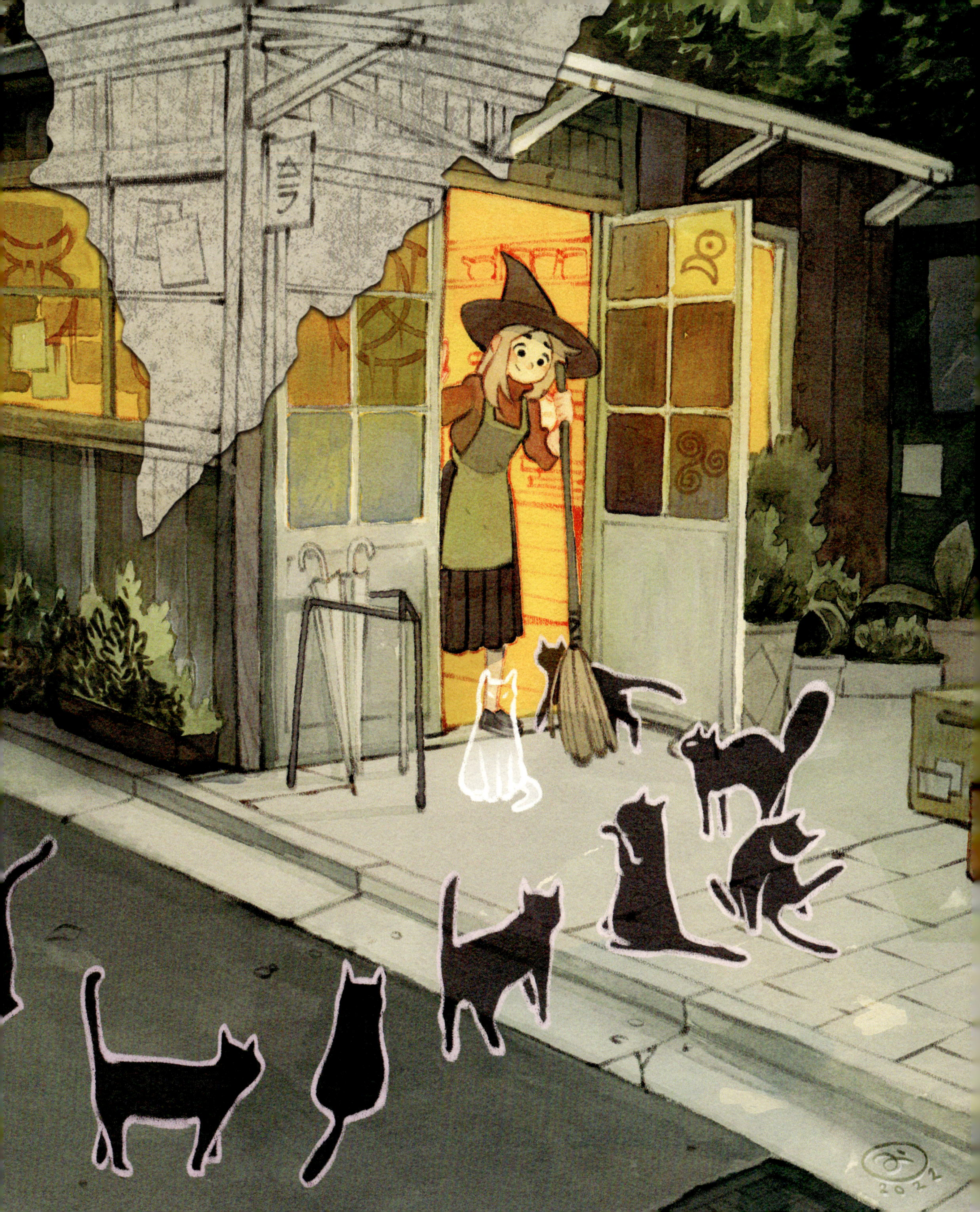

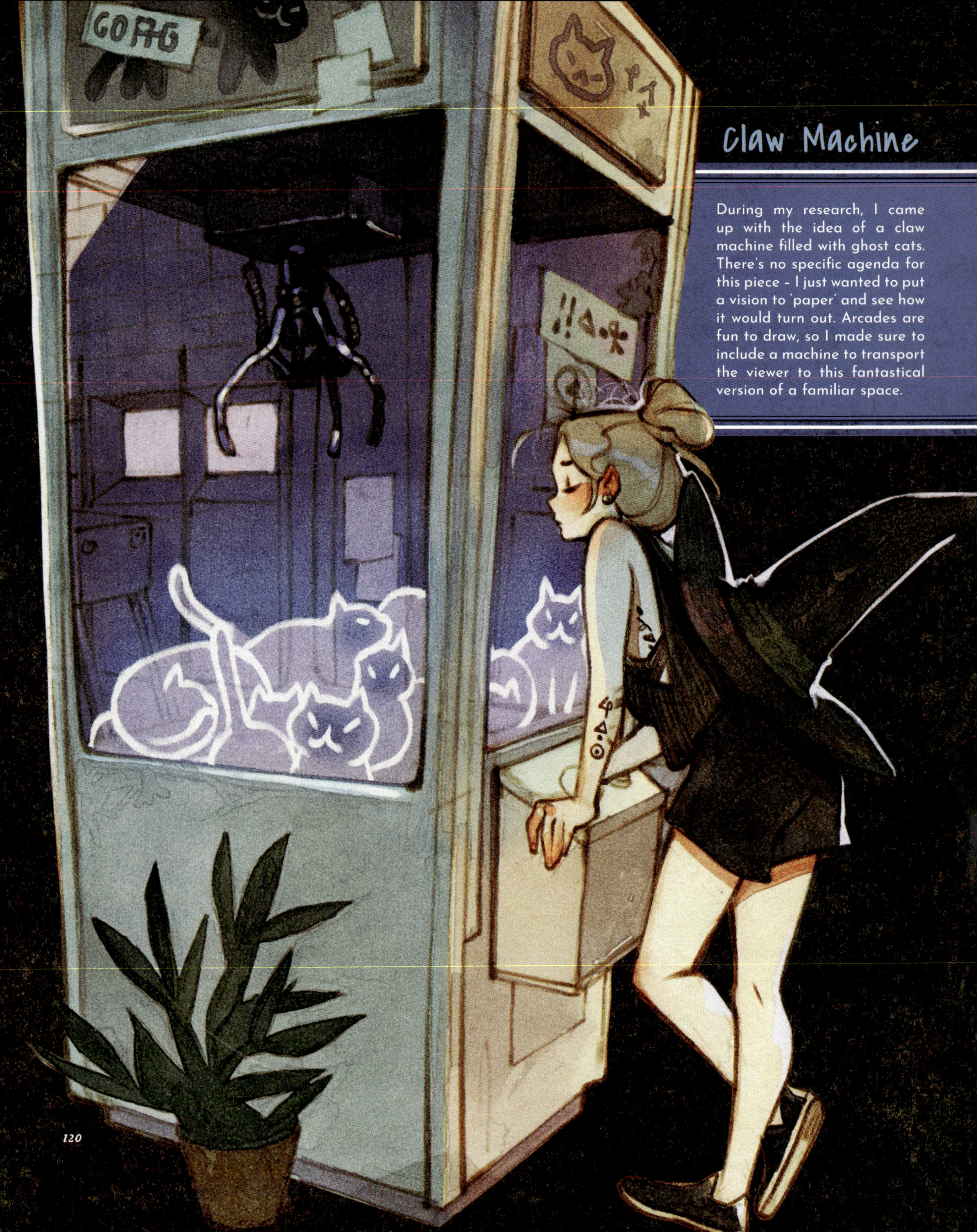

Claw Machine

During my research, I came up with the idea of a claw machine filled with ghost cats. There's no specific agenda for this piece – I just wanted to put a vision to 'paper' and see how it would turn out. Arcades are fun to draw, so I made sure to include a machine to transport the viewer to this fantastical version of a familiar space.

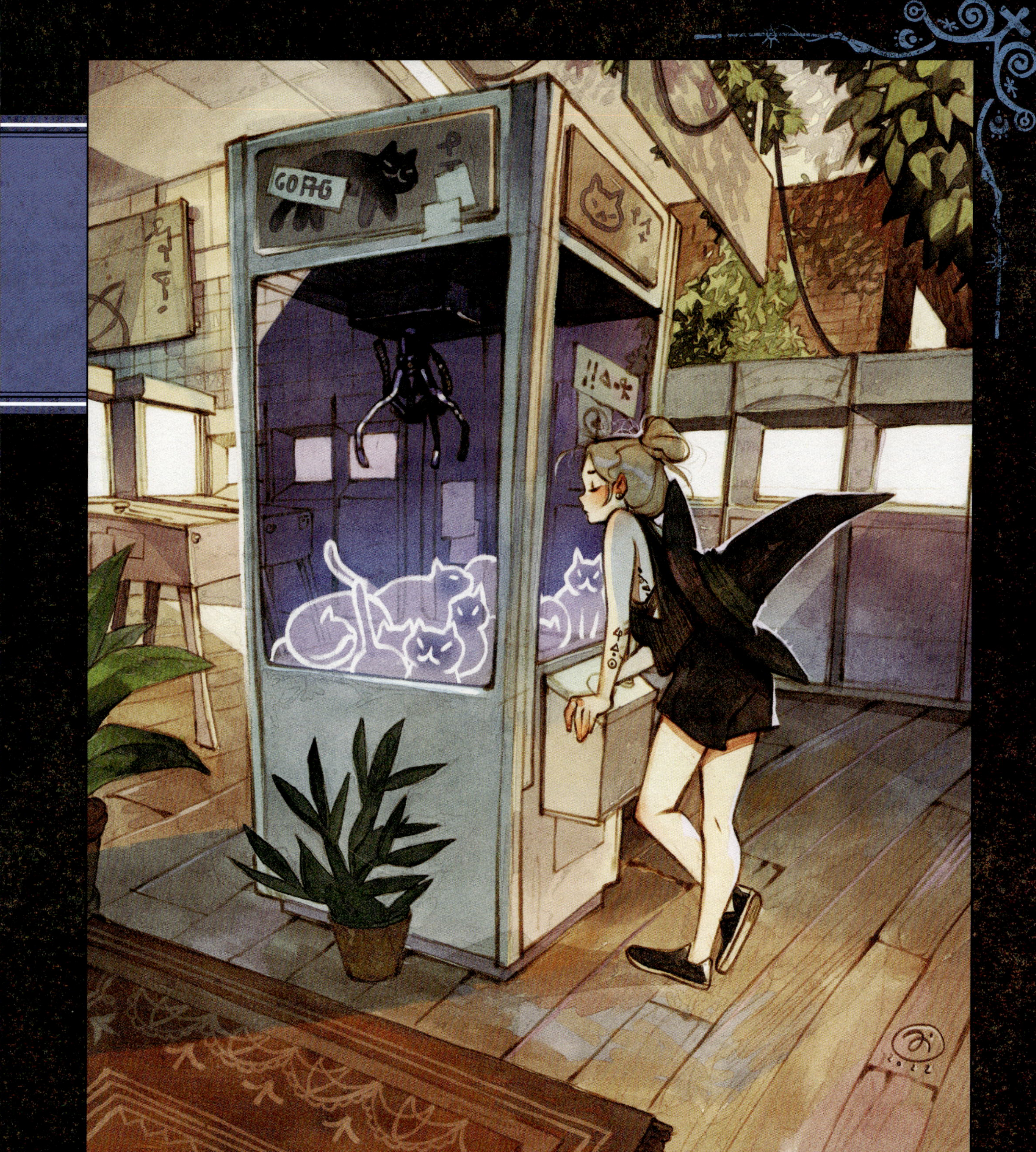

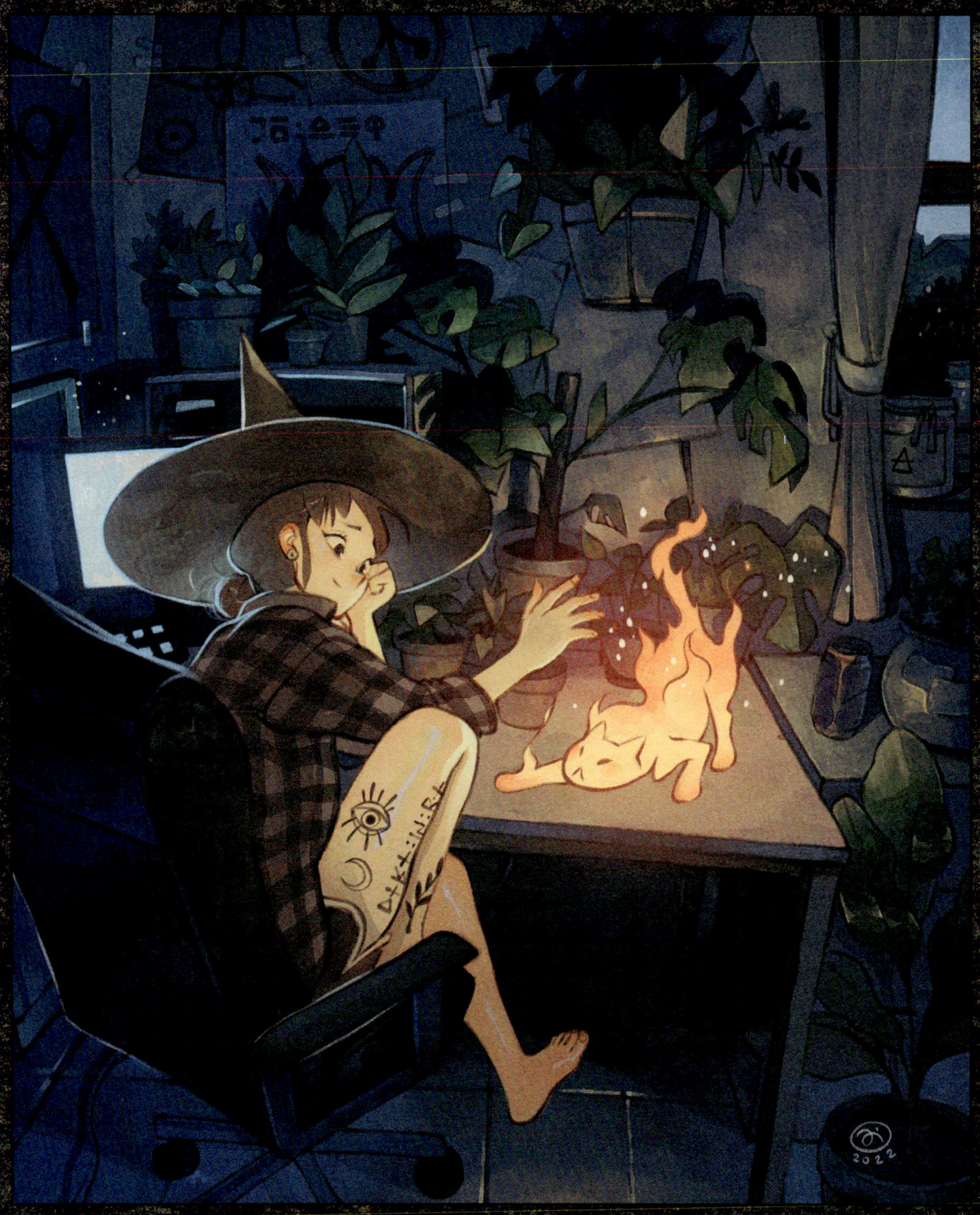

This is one of the most-liked pictures in my gallery. After deciding I wanted to draw a fire kitty, I decided to set the tones to blue and grey in order to make it feel 'warm'. This enhanced the contrast. I also decided to add a screen behind the main character's head to balance the lighting. Narrative elements like the evening sky and suburban backdrop enhance the composition.

Fire Kitty

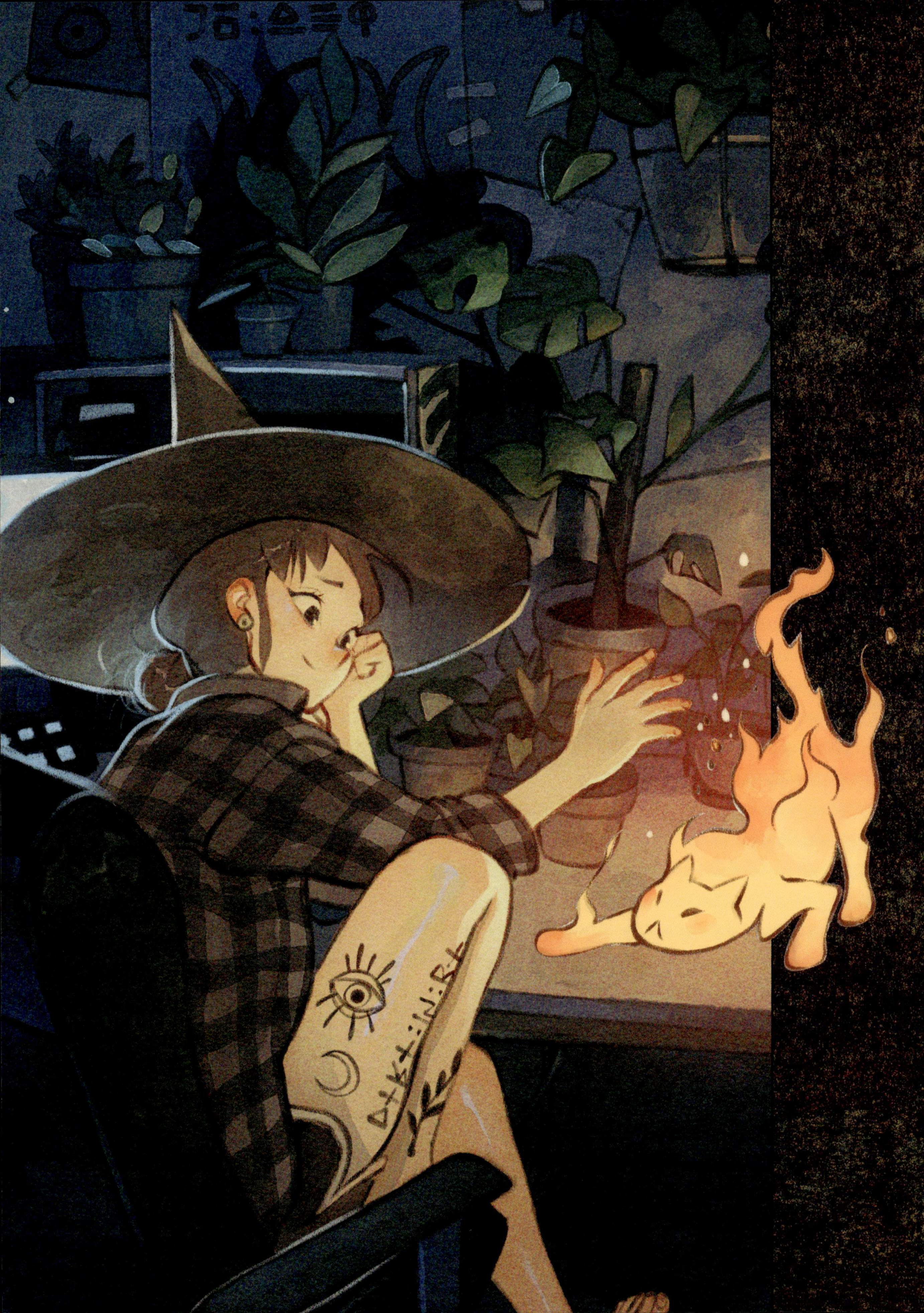

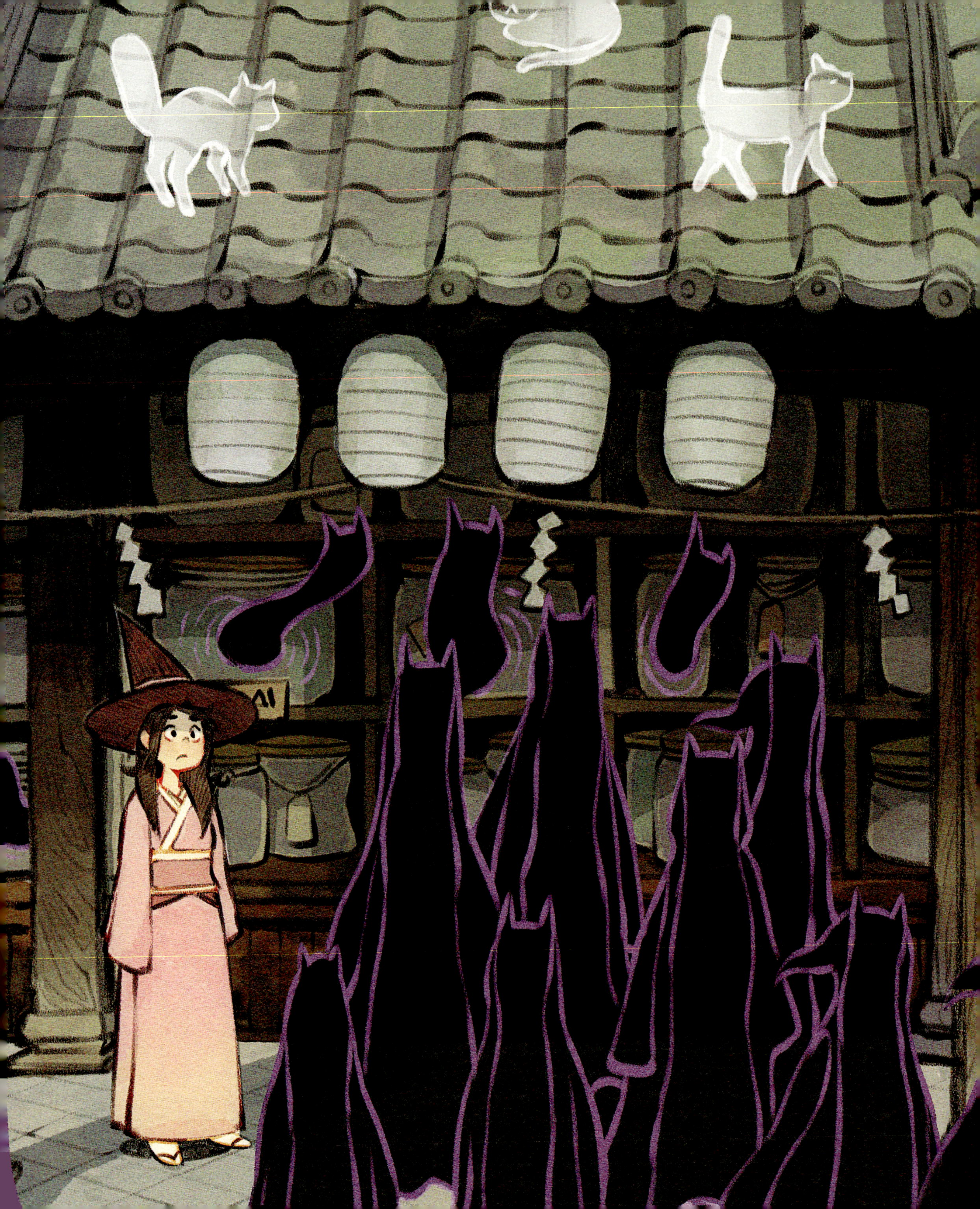

Parade

I really like the ghostly characters in their black cloaks and purple outlines. They're a sort of antagonist or counterbalance to the cute and carefree cats. I'm still toying with this idea and it might change in the future, but I enjoyed the process. The setting is a typical Japanese temple, and the main character is wearing a kimono. It's been really fun finding references for these elements!

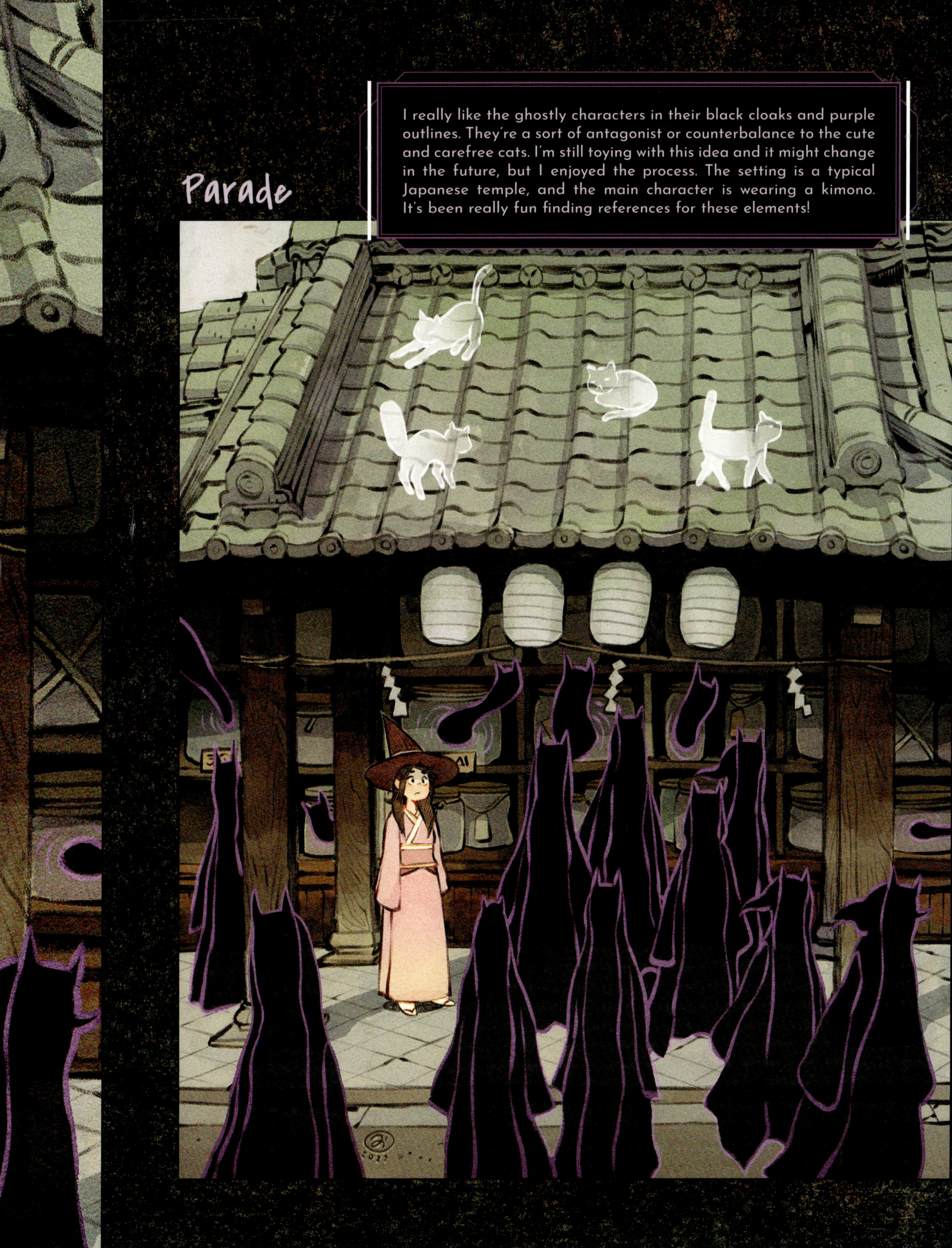

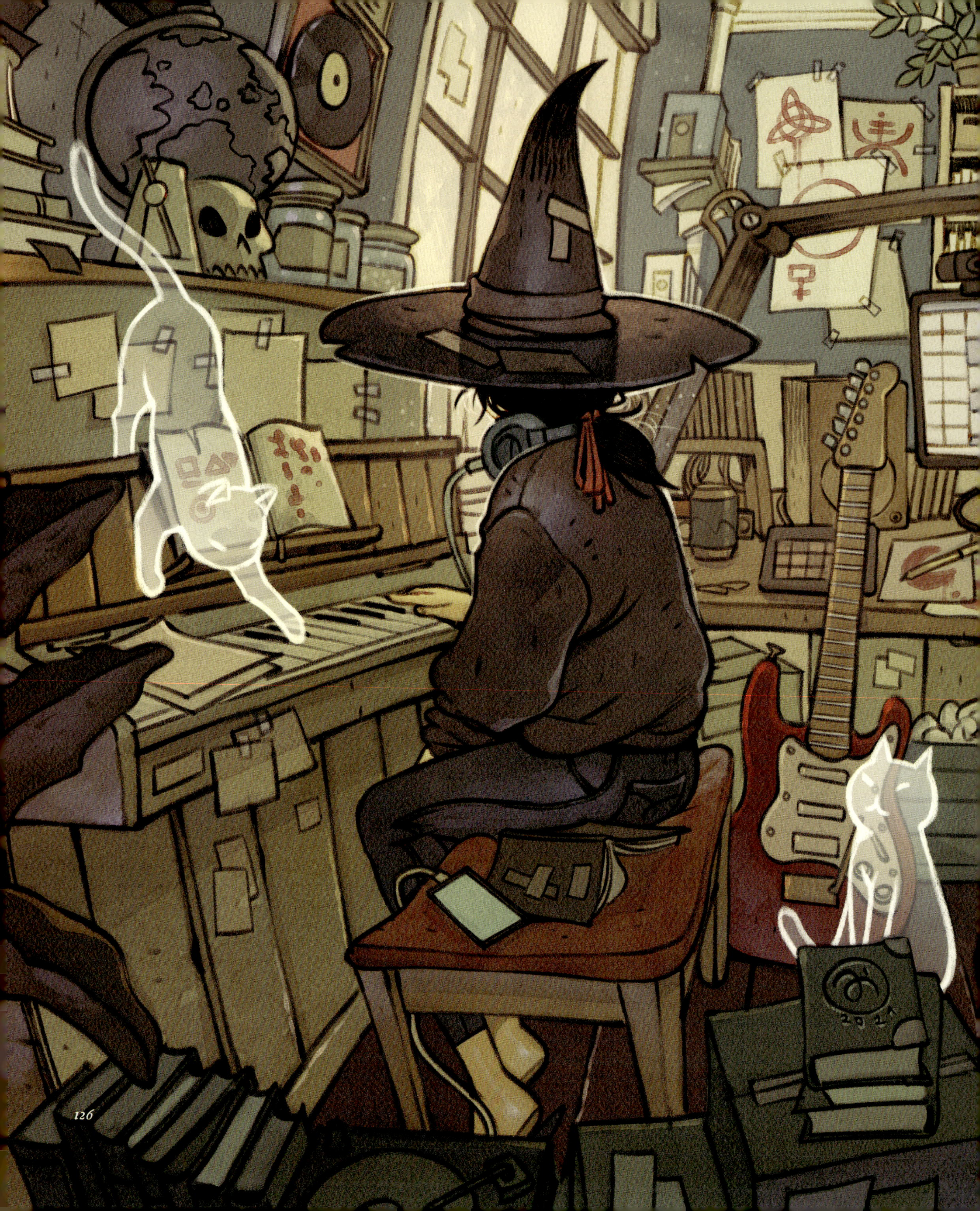

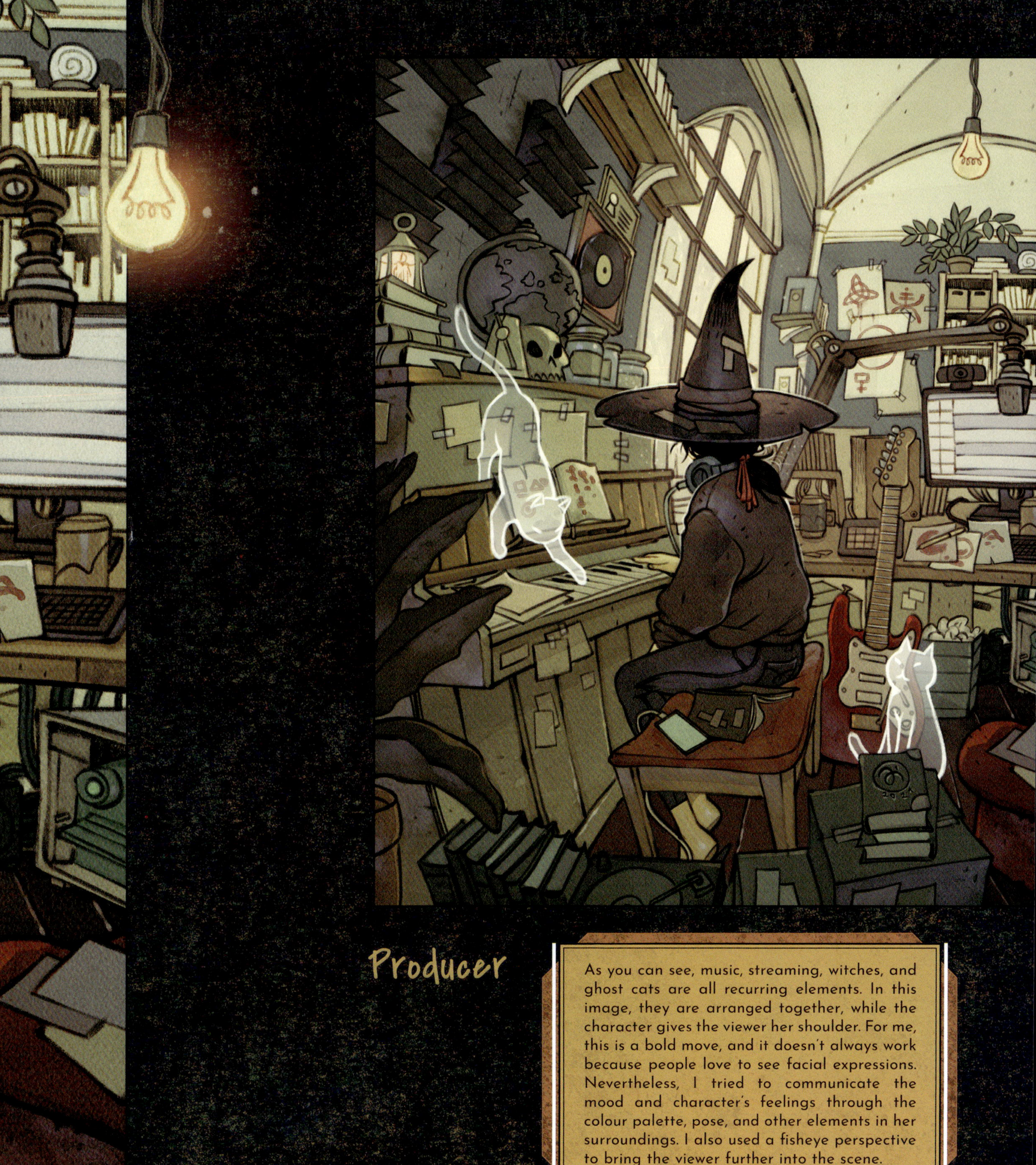

Producer

As you can see, music, streaming, witches, and ghost cats are all recurring elements. In this image, they are arranged together, while the character gives the viewer her shoulder. For me, this is a bold move, and it doesn't always work because people love to see facial expressions. Nevertheless, I tried to communicate the mood and character's feelings through the colour palette, pose, and other elements in her surroundings. I also used a fisheye perspective to bring the viewer further into the scene.

Visitors

This is one of the first images where I introduced the spectral characters in their black cloaks. For me, the one detail that makes this scene work is the scared black cat and the confused main character. When creating pictures where the situation isn't clear, it's important to make the viewer wonder about the outcome. I want them to ask questions about the series lore, as this can lead to new ideas!

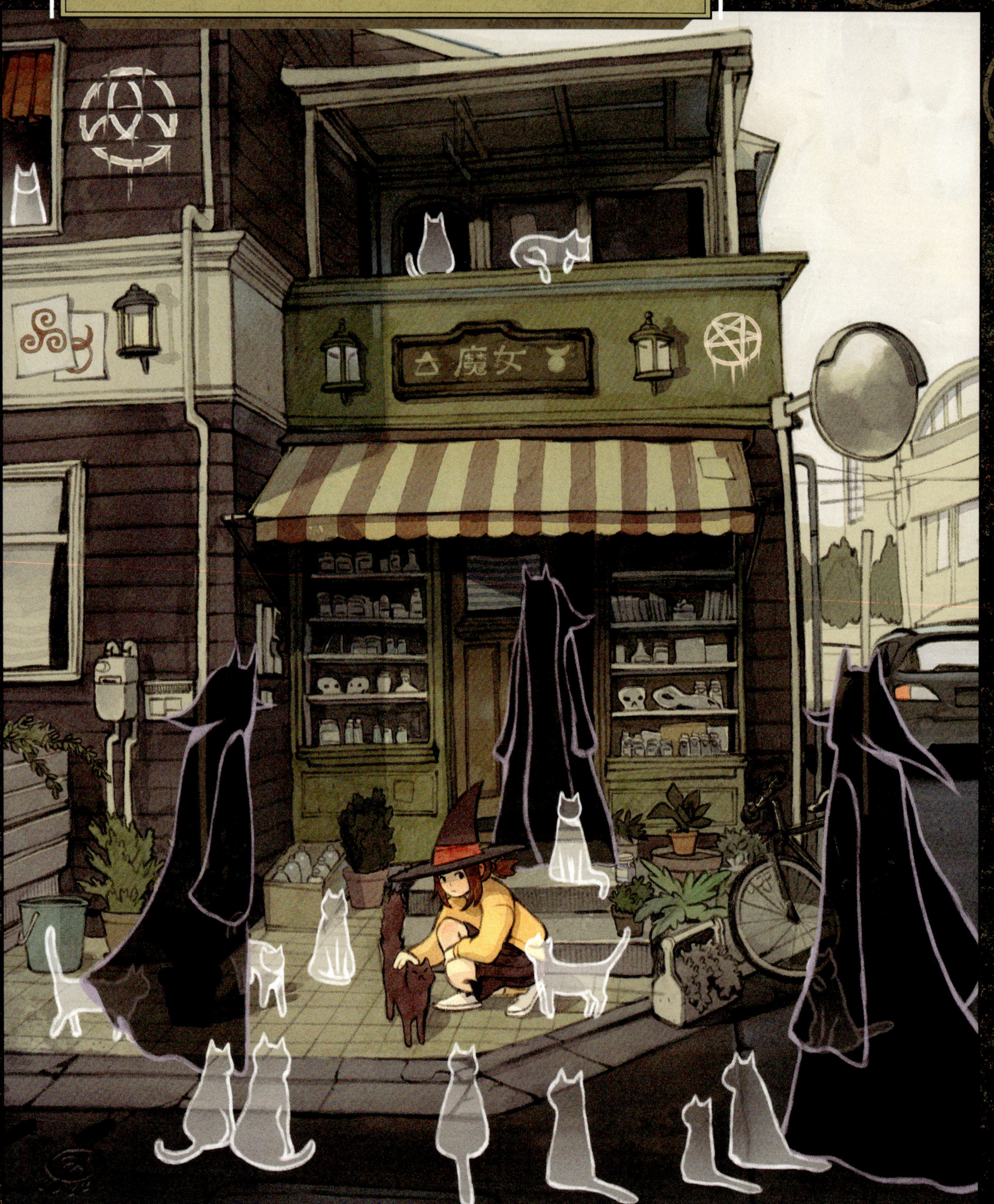

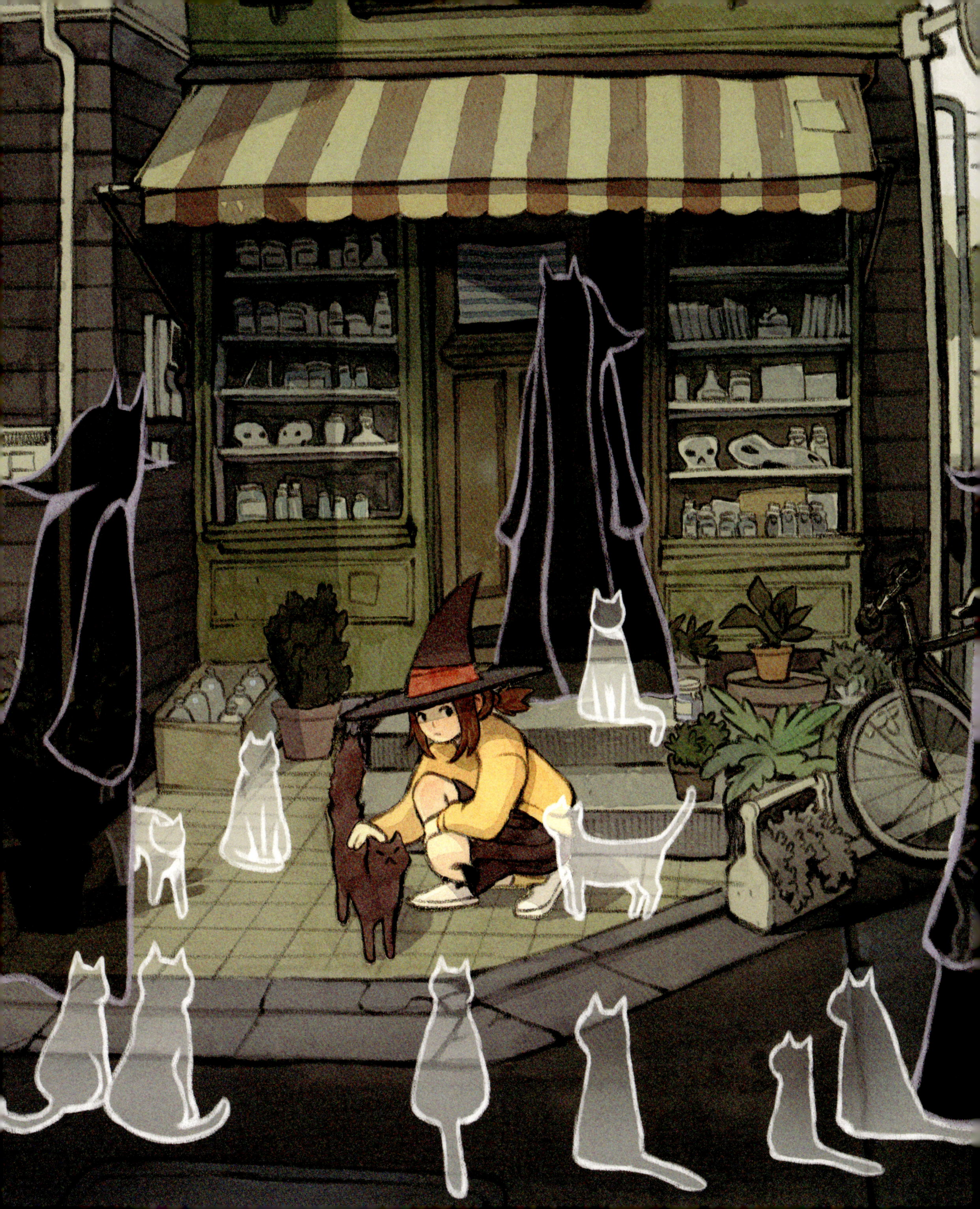

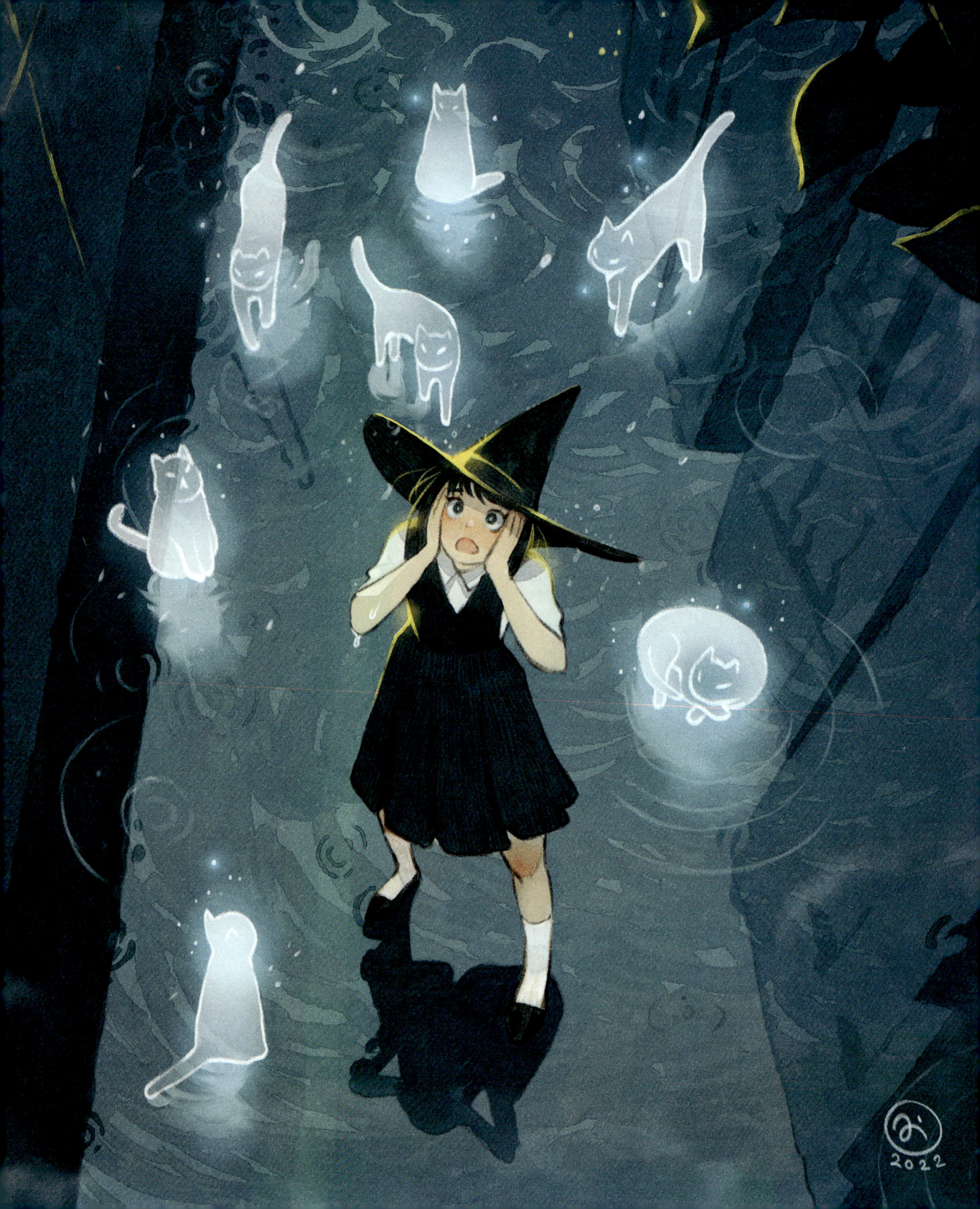

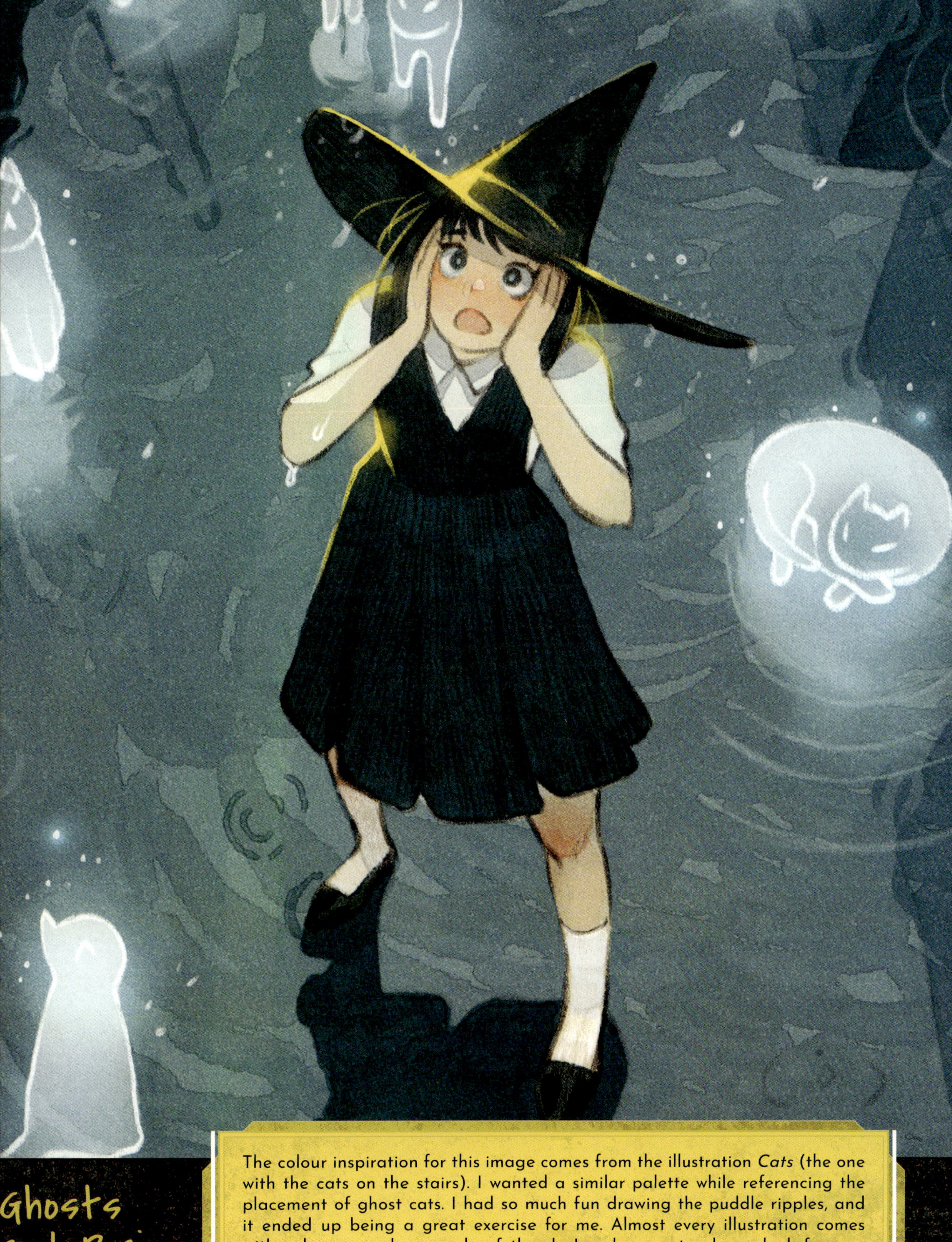

Ghosts and Rain

The colour inspiration for this image comes from the illustration *Cats* (the one with the cats on the stairs). I wanted a similar palette while referencing the placement of ghost cats. I had so much fun drawing the puddle ripples, and it ended up being a great exercise for me. Almost every illustration comes with a lesson, and as a rule of thumb, I make sure to always look for new ways to learn about my projects or workflow. It helps me avoid stagnation.

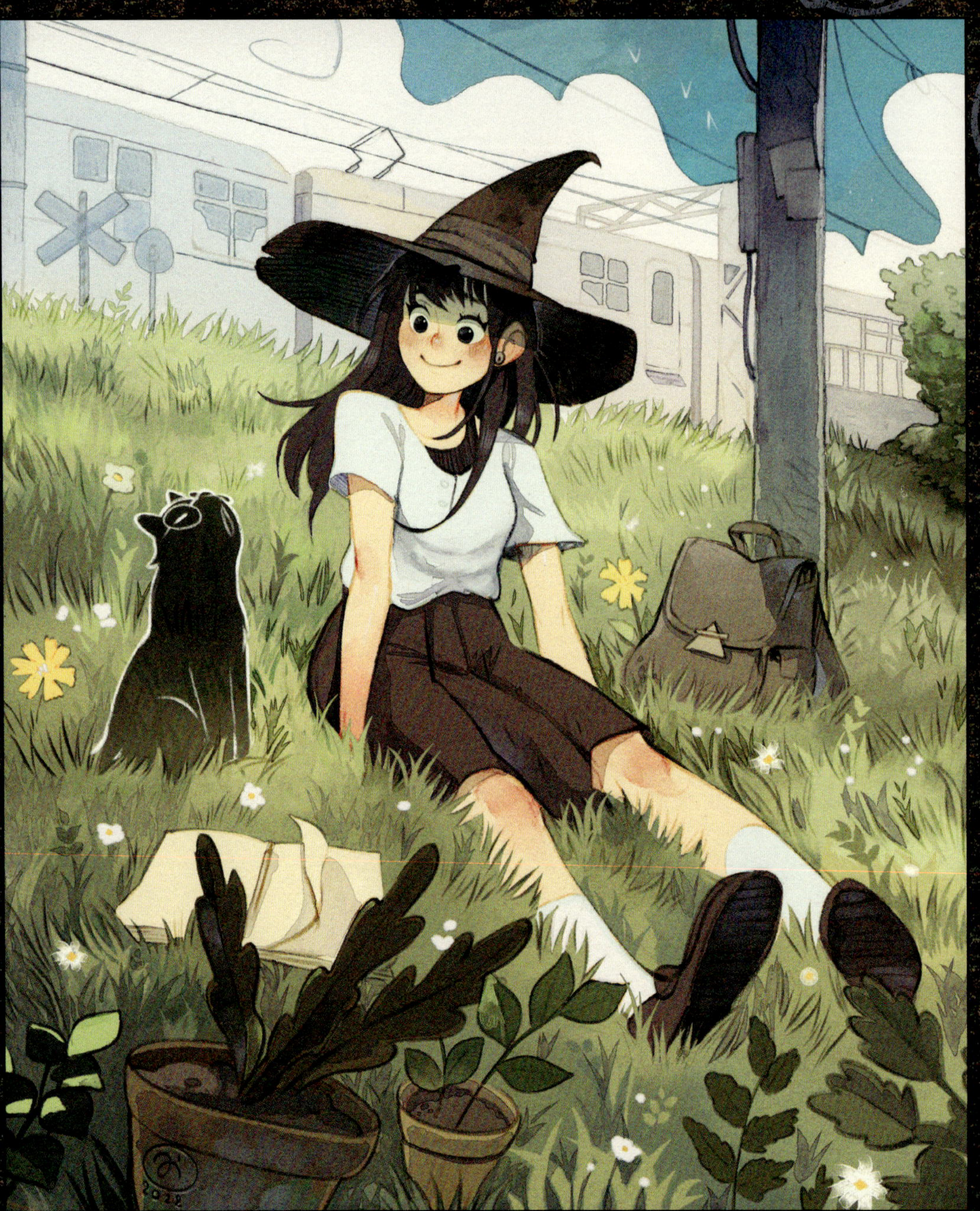

Hill

In contrast to my many night-based illustrations, this scene shows a bright blue morning sky. Sometimes, I like to try out scenes I don't usually lean towards and see how I perform in terms of consistency. Experimenting with different aspects of design is what makes it interesting for me. Each new added element helps to strengthen my worldbuilding, while my style and themes become tailored to my vision.

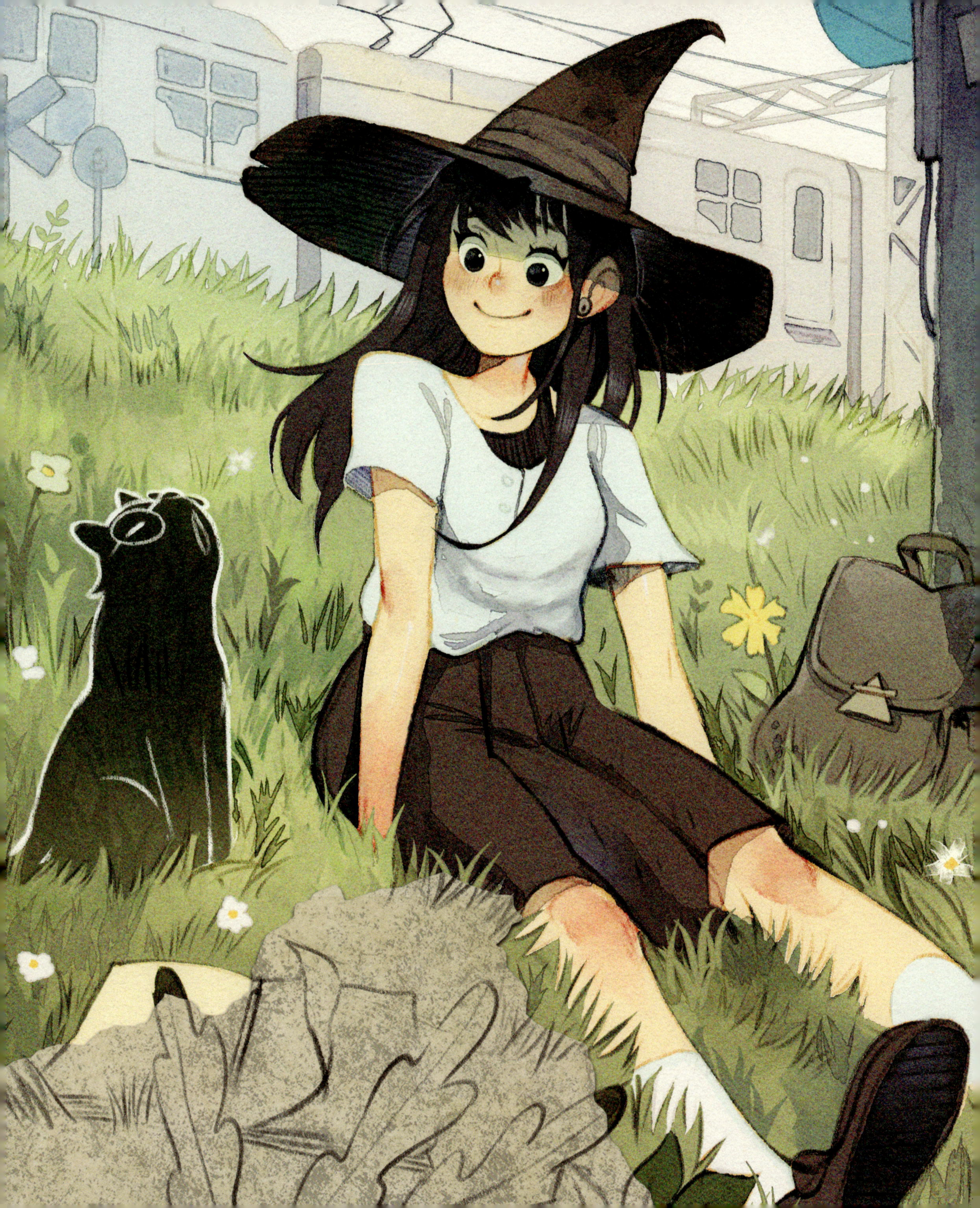

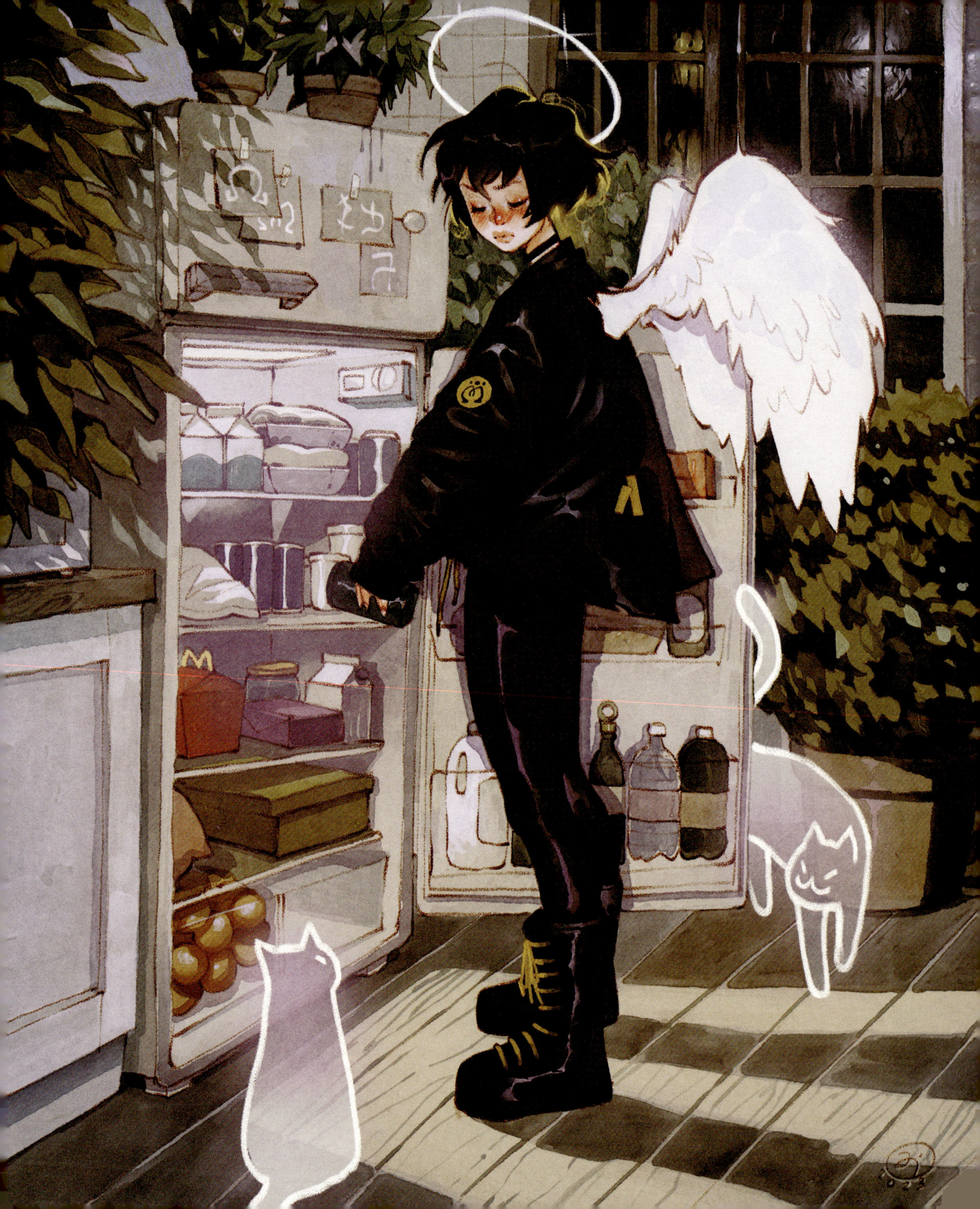

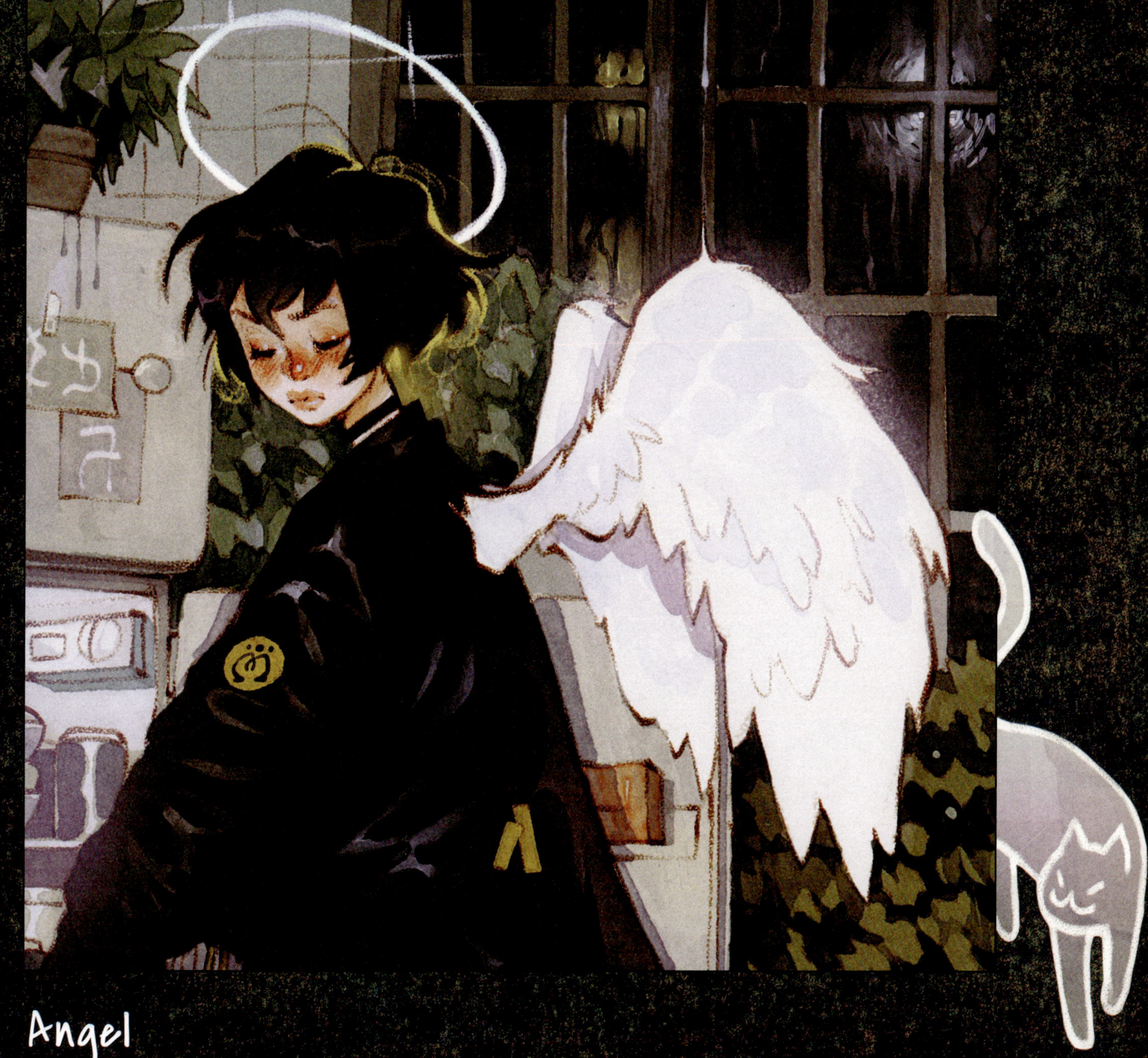

Angel

This illustration was a new concept-art test for *Ghost Cats and Tea*. I wanted to explore different characters, especially new creatures, so I decided on an angel. The image shows a slice of life in an interior space. For some juxtaposition, I chose a punk, urban look for the angel. The colours are muted towards magenta, so it was a little experimental. The light comes from a camera flash as shown in the top-right corner of the window.

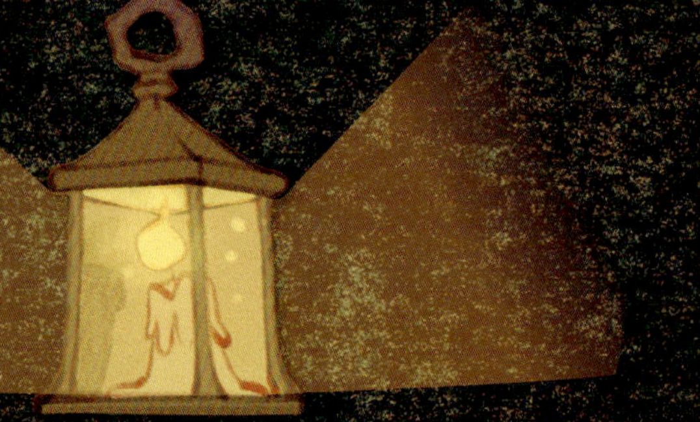

It's often said that cats can move as fluidly as water, and in this case, the cat is a literal interpretation of that idea. I had a lot of fun creating this one – overall, enjoying the process is what matters the most to me.

The orange colours from the pumpkins make the scene feel warm and cosy, while the water cat's blue hues create a strong contrast. The character's expression implies that they didn't expect this event to happen, and as a result, the lore develops further. Rome wasn't built in a day, and neither was this series.

Water Bottle

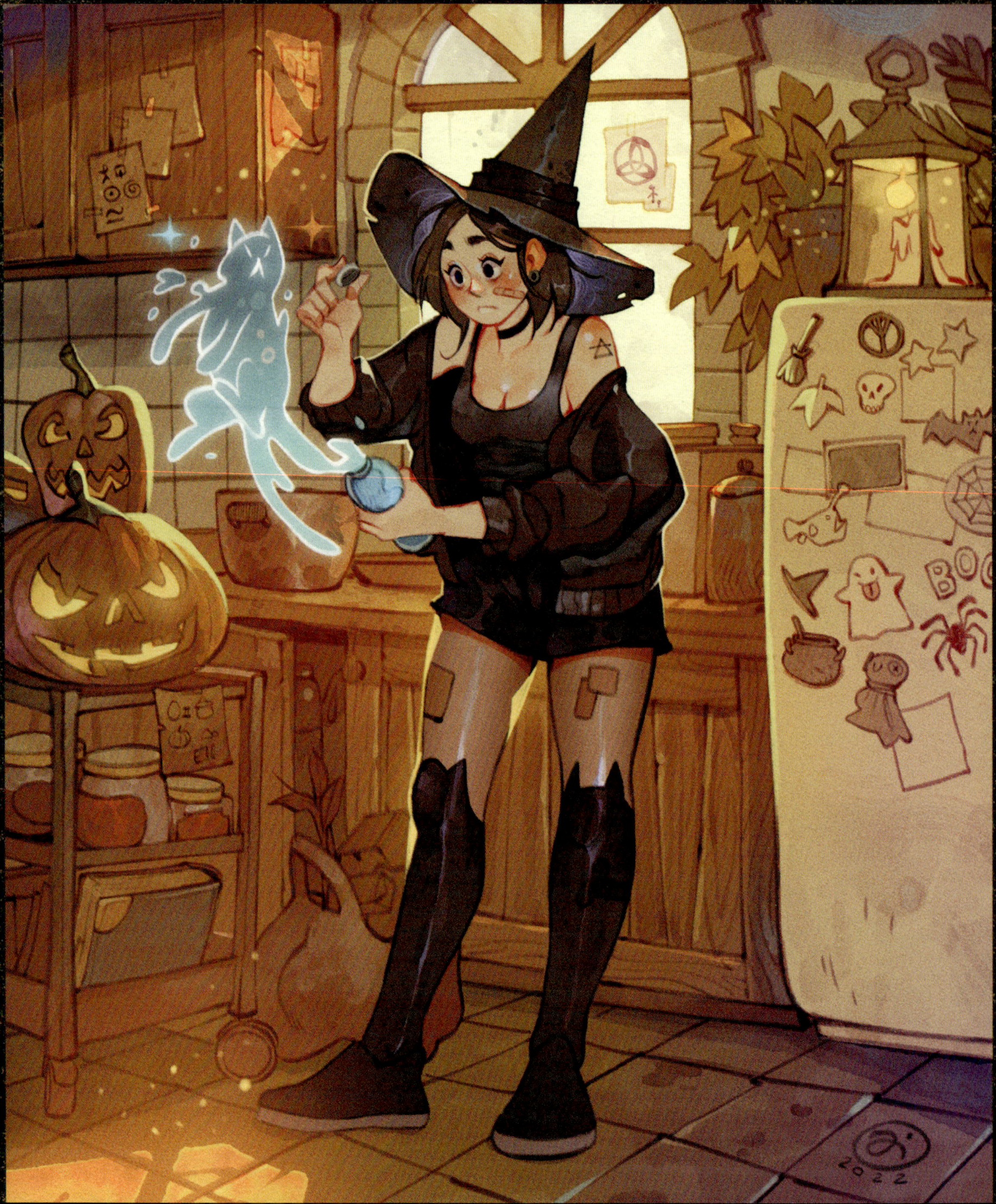

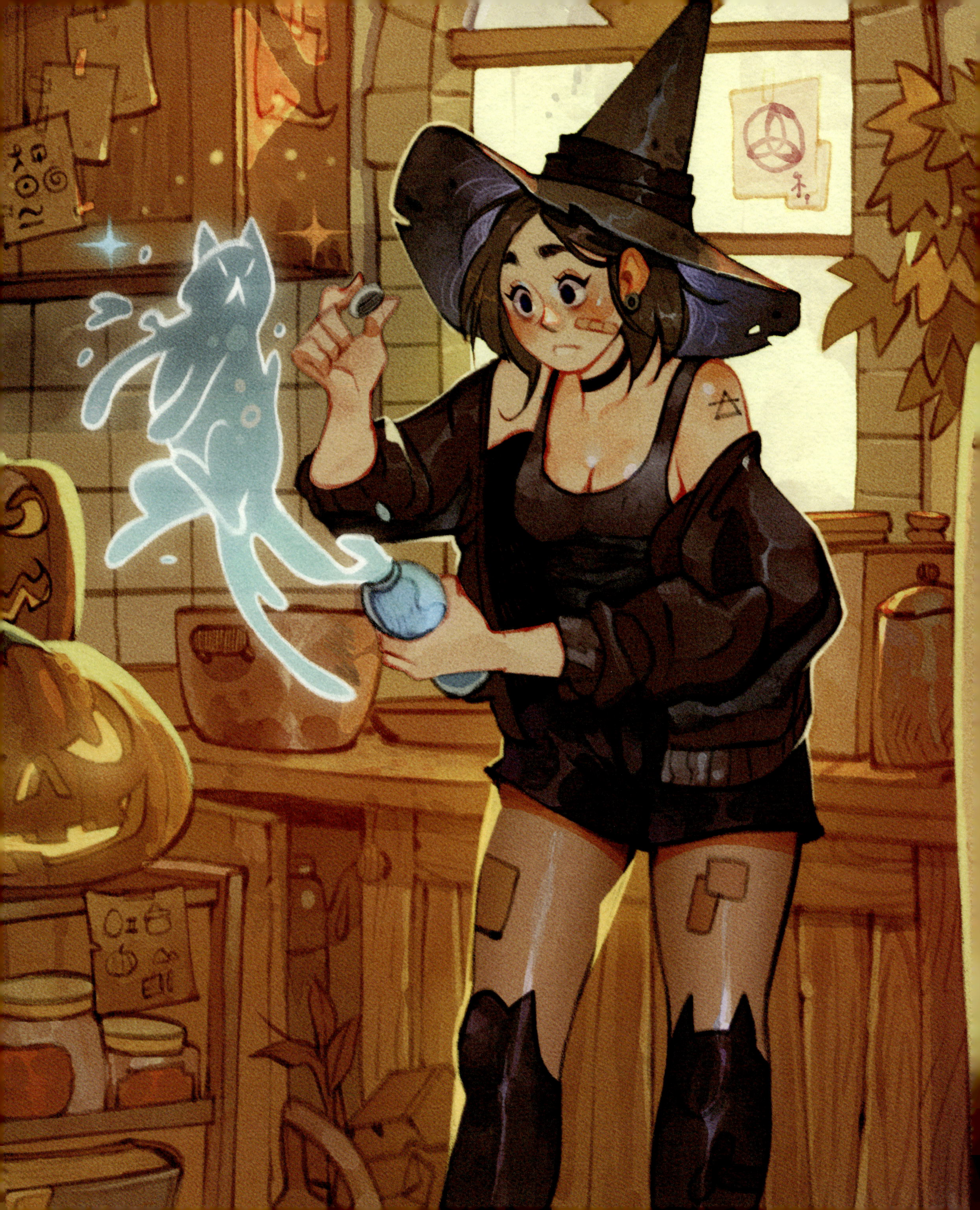

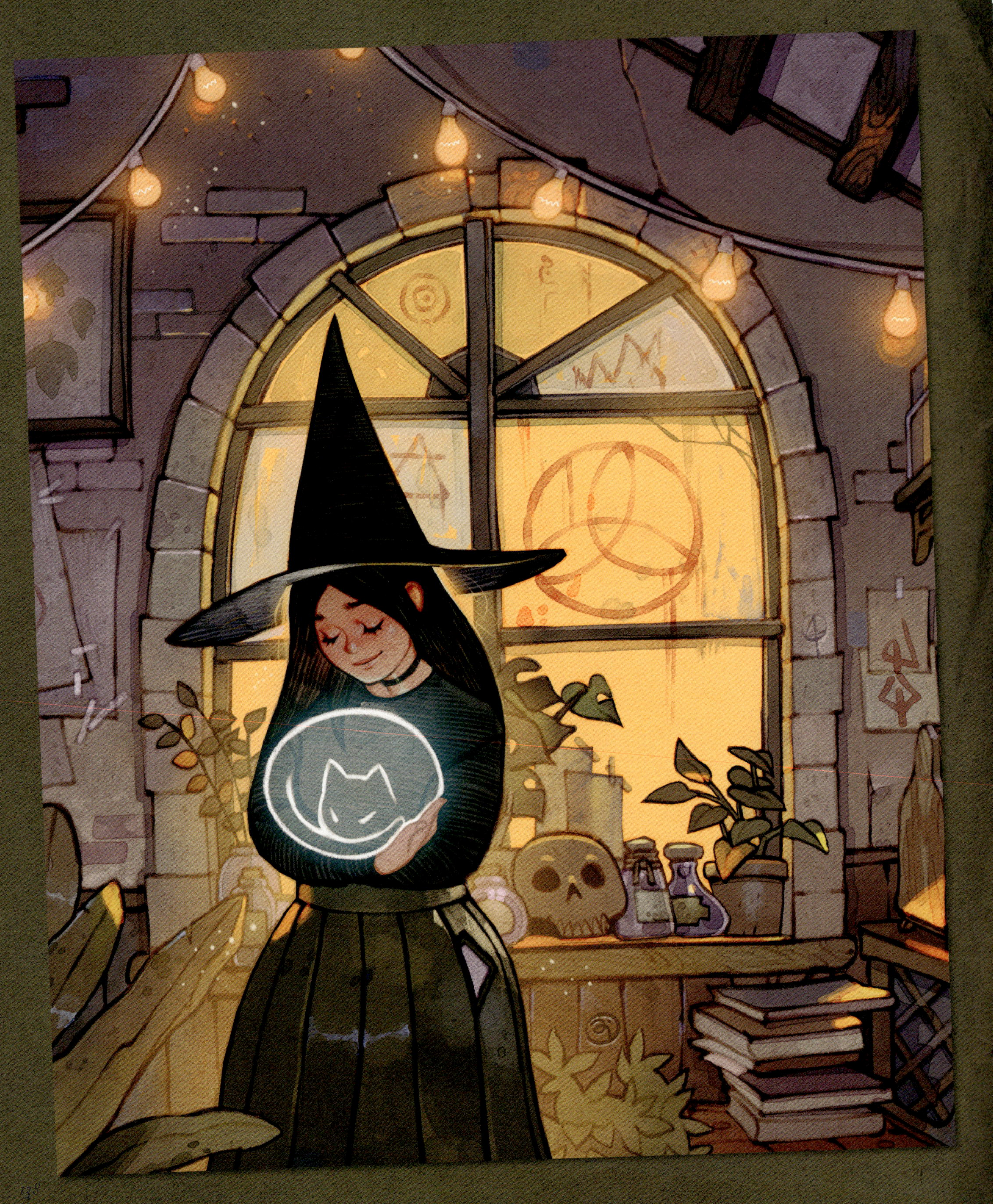

COVER TUTORIAL

I created a new piece of art specifically for the cover of this book, and in this tutorial I'll show you how! I approached the design in the most personal way possible by incorporating most of the elements I normally use, such as witches, ghost cats, and spooky symbols. It was important for this cover to represent me and my current aesthetic.

The scene itself is not too complex. I created four initial thumbnails, making sure they all had present, relatable characters that are well known in my artwork. In the chosen image, the triangular shapes of the witch's hat and skirt are sturdy, balanced style choices, while the setting is deliberately calm and relaxing.

It's very important to keep thinking of ideas, even after you've come up with one or two designs. This is especially true when considering important projects like book covers. In all four of my options, I tried to think of concepts that were very much tied to me. That way, instead of attempting to make them look perfect, I made them mine. Even if there were mistakes or something looked unbalanced, I needed the artwork to represent me. Trying to make things look perfect doesn't make sense to me because there is no perfect – it's all relative.

Think of how you can make your artwork unique and personal, and don't sweat the small stuff. Let's get started!

01: Thumbs

This step isn't necessarily shown in many tutorials, but I wanted to share my four preliminary options. I don't always begin with a bunch of alternatives, but I do if I need to bounce ideas around with a client or someone involved in the creative process. It's always good to have variety.

I wanted four broad character variations: a half-bust, a portrait, a character behind a counter, and a character in a dynamic pose. I chose the first image because the window allowed for fun dust-jacket details while also showcasing the setting.

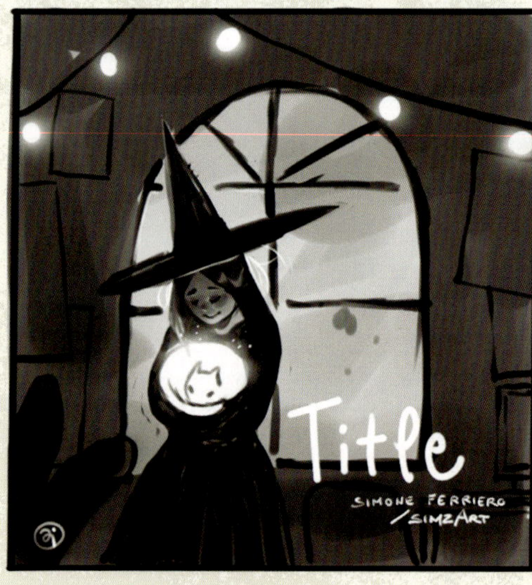

1.
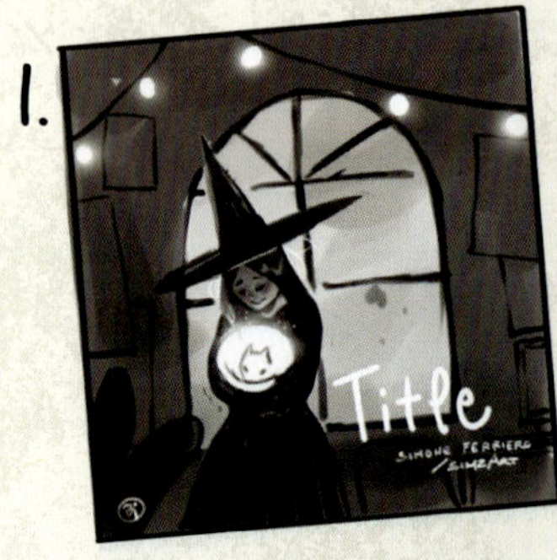

2.
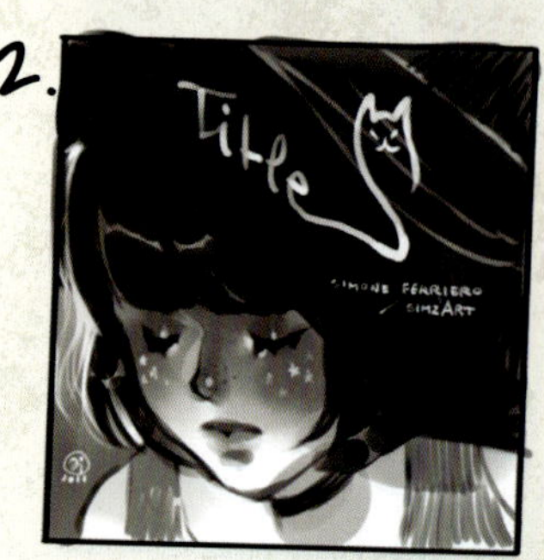

3.
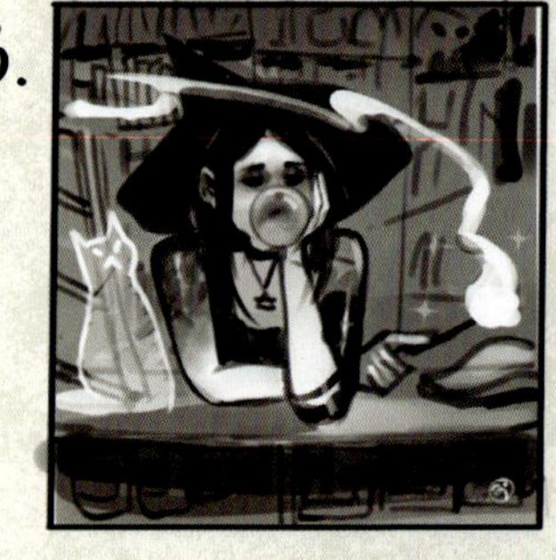

4.
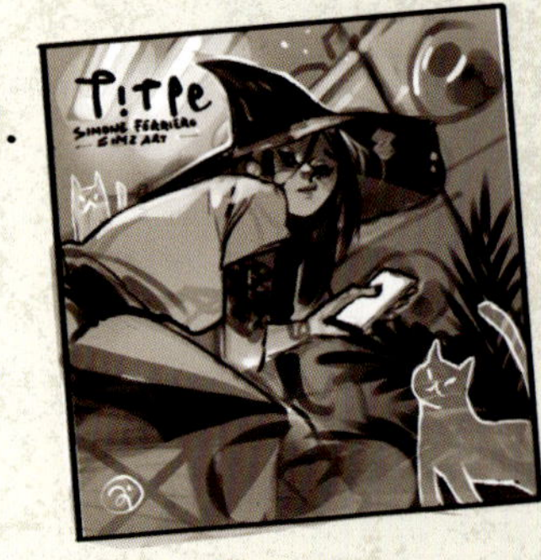

02: Line art

During the sketch phase, I like to use cross-hatching to establish midtones. I'm really fond of that rough, 'handwrought' style, where colours don't fully cover the line work, and it appears as though it's been traditionally painted. That's very important for the aesthetic and mood of my artwork. It can't look too polished.

For now, the cat in the character's arms is just a figment of her imagination, as I'll add it on a separate layer in the following step.

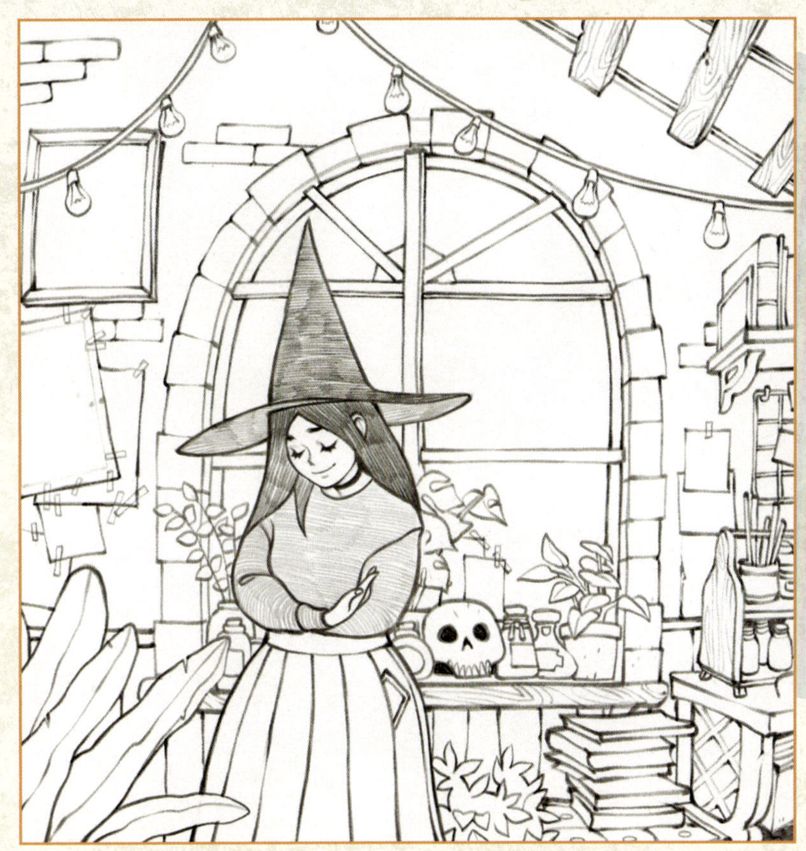

Loosen up

Don't let the idea of perfection negatively affect your line art. Usually, when an artist is pressured to make great art right from the get-go, their line work (and even their ideas) stiffen. It's okay to be spontaneous!

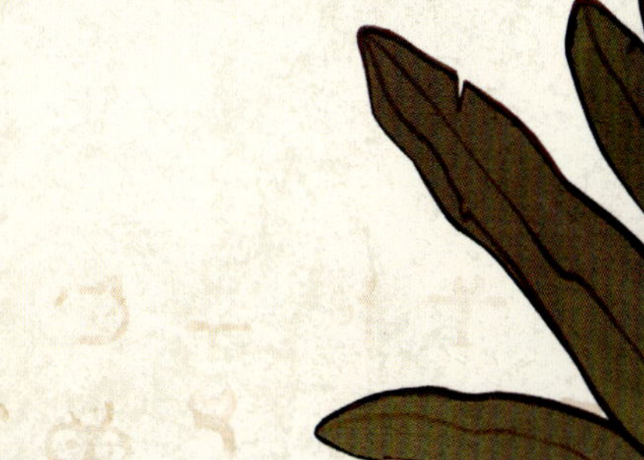

03: Setting main values

The next thing I do is separate the current line art into four layers: one with the cat, one with the character, one with the background, and one for the areas that I'll be highlighting, such as the window and the overhead light bulbs.

It helps me visualize the main elements of the composition, and allows me space to revisit certain areas in detail without compromising my other progress. In a nutshell, it grants me more speed and precision.

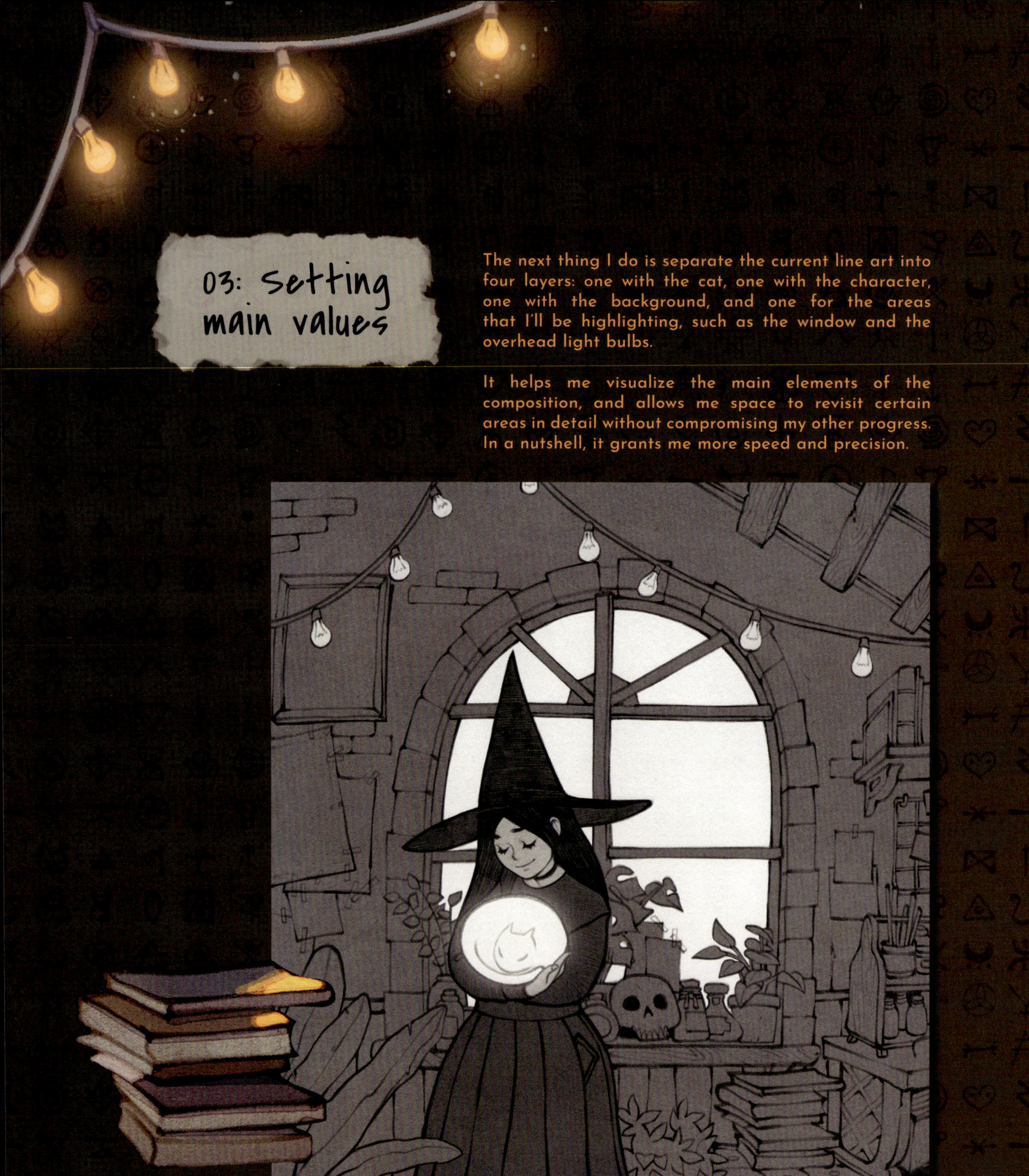

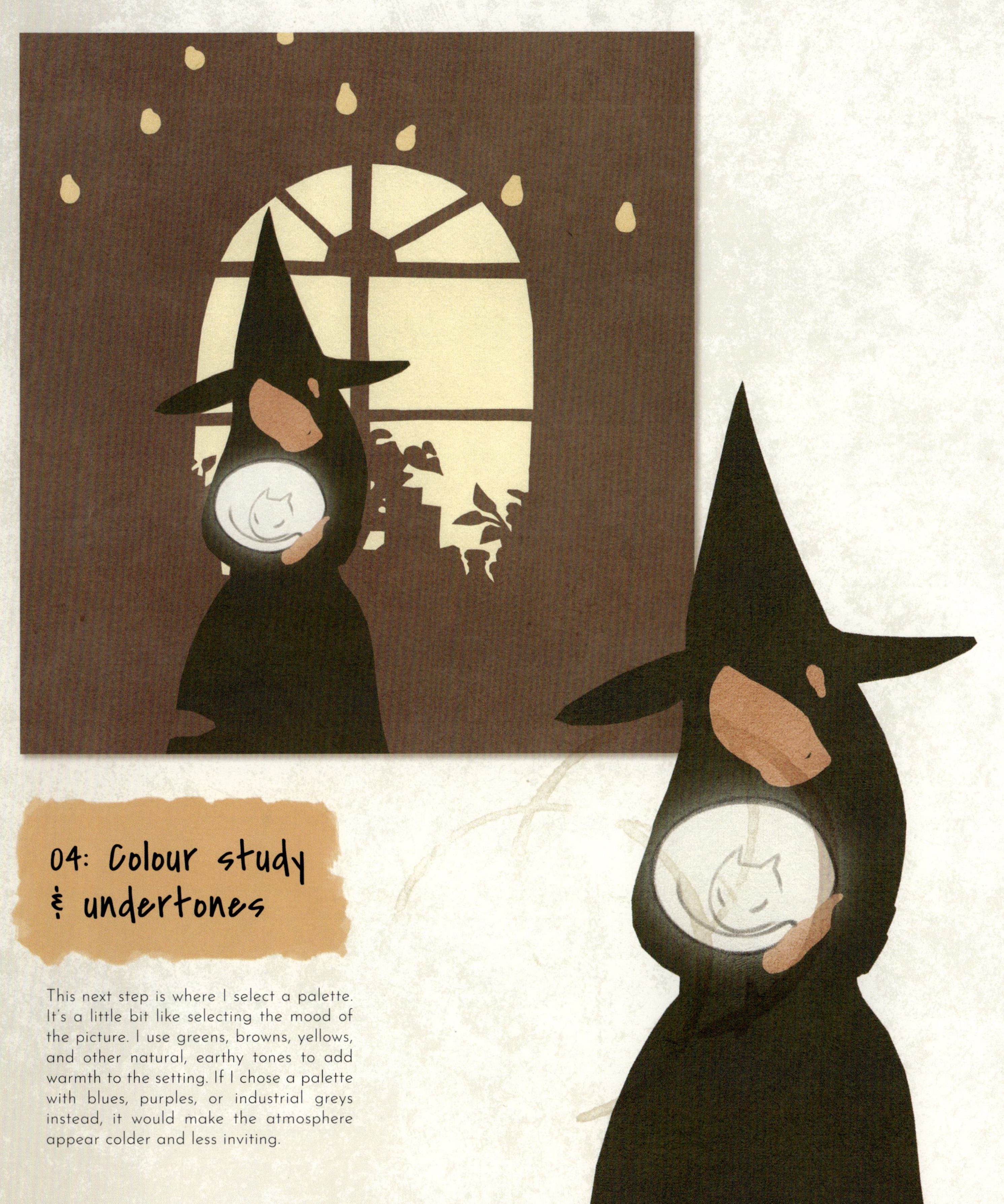

04: Colour study & undertones

This next step is where I select a palette. It's a little bit like selecting the mood of the picture. I use greens, browns, yellows, and other natural, earthy tones to add warmth to the setting. If I chose a palette with blues, purples, or industrial greys instead, it would make the atmosphere appear colder and less inviting.

05: Rendering

Can you spot the colour palette from Step 04 in the top-right corner? I want to use hues like greens, whites, and different skin tones to establish the overall colour set. I also make sure to use a limited amount of colour in the rendering stages.

At this point, I add reflections and textures. Right now, the only glowing effect is on the cat.

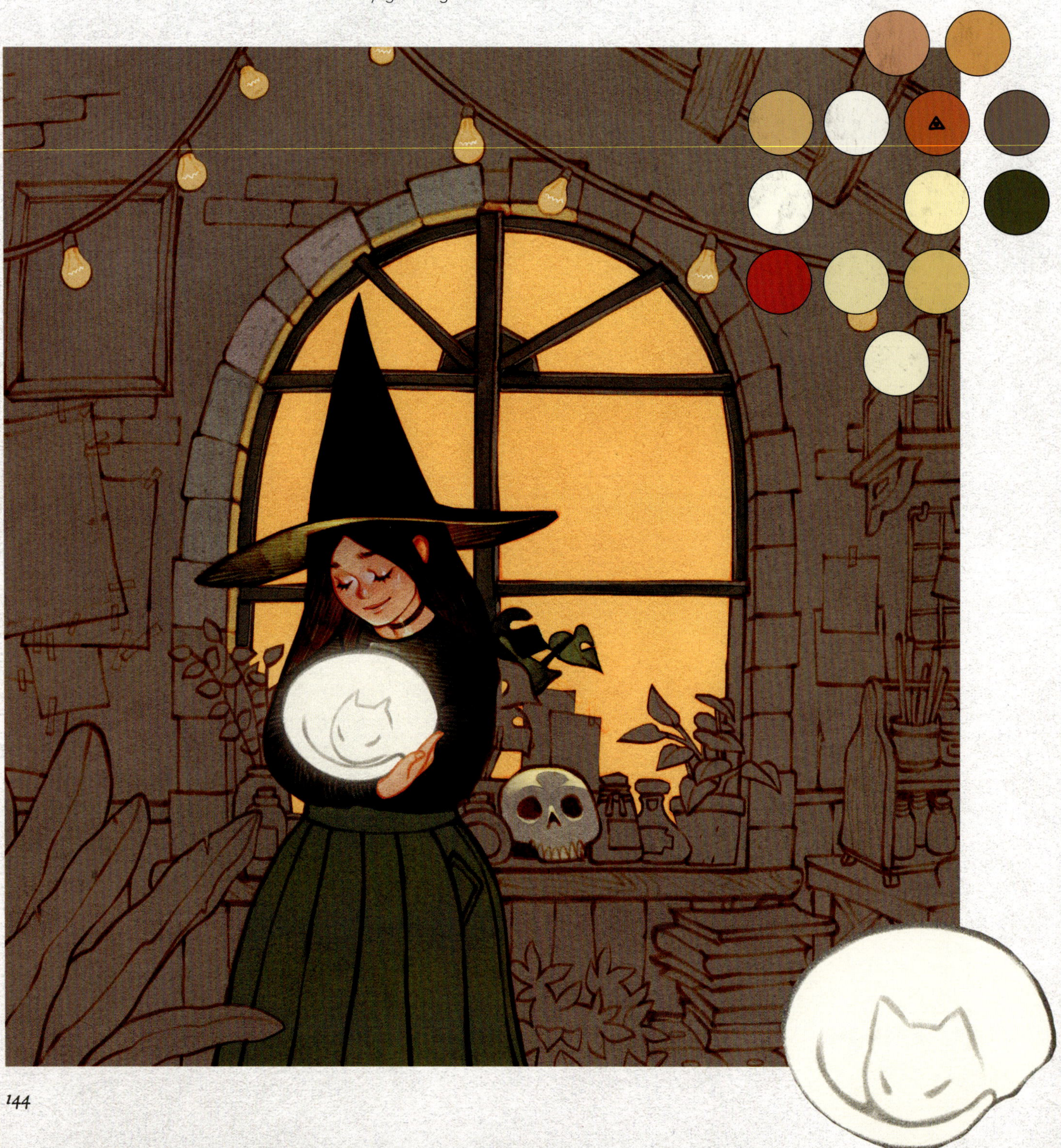

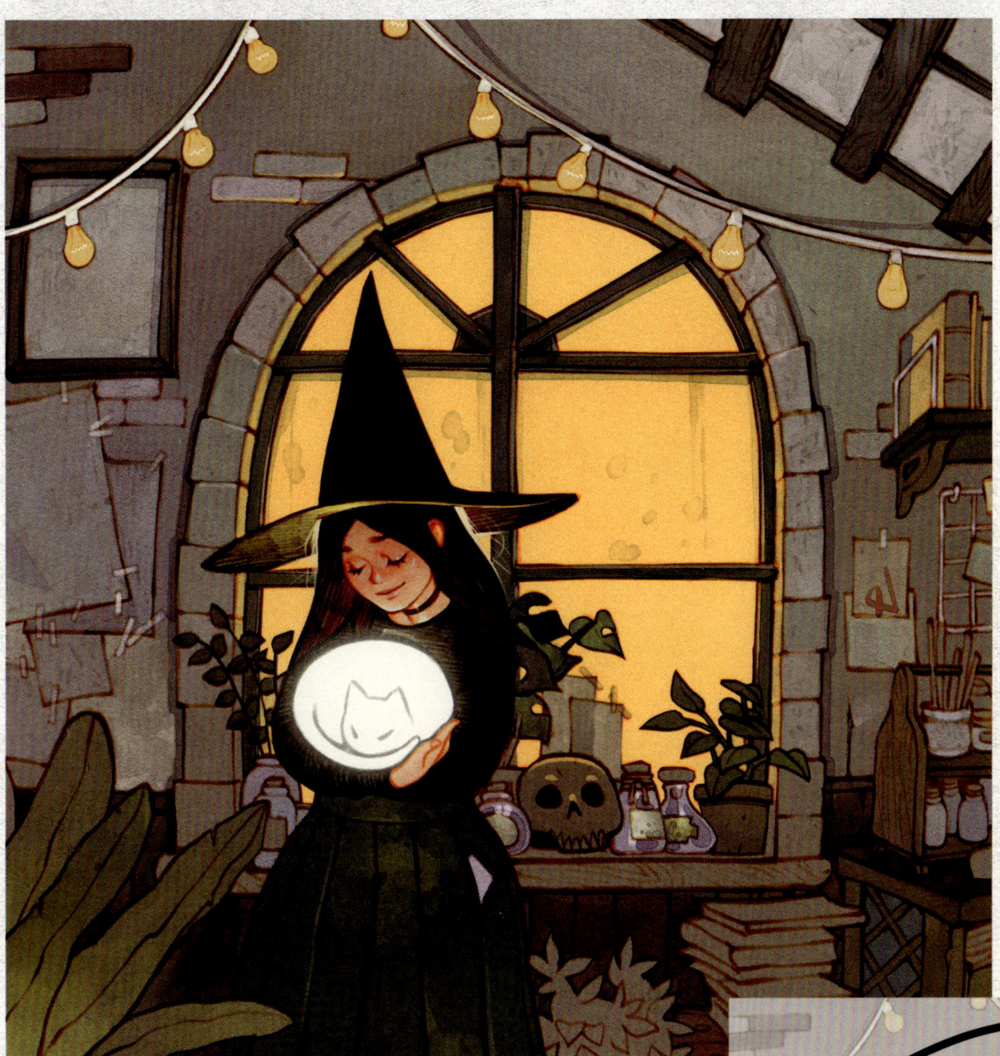

06: Adding details

When adding details, I try to follow a technique called radial development. I start from the most interesting part of the image – the character, in this case – and spiral outwards from there, sort of like a nautilus shell. The corners, or less significant areas, usually have a lower level of detail. This is to help direct the eye towards areas of interest.

As an example, I add reflections on the glass potion bottles, and smudge lines to the windows. The point is to create a fall-off effect towards areas of lower interest.

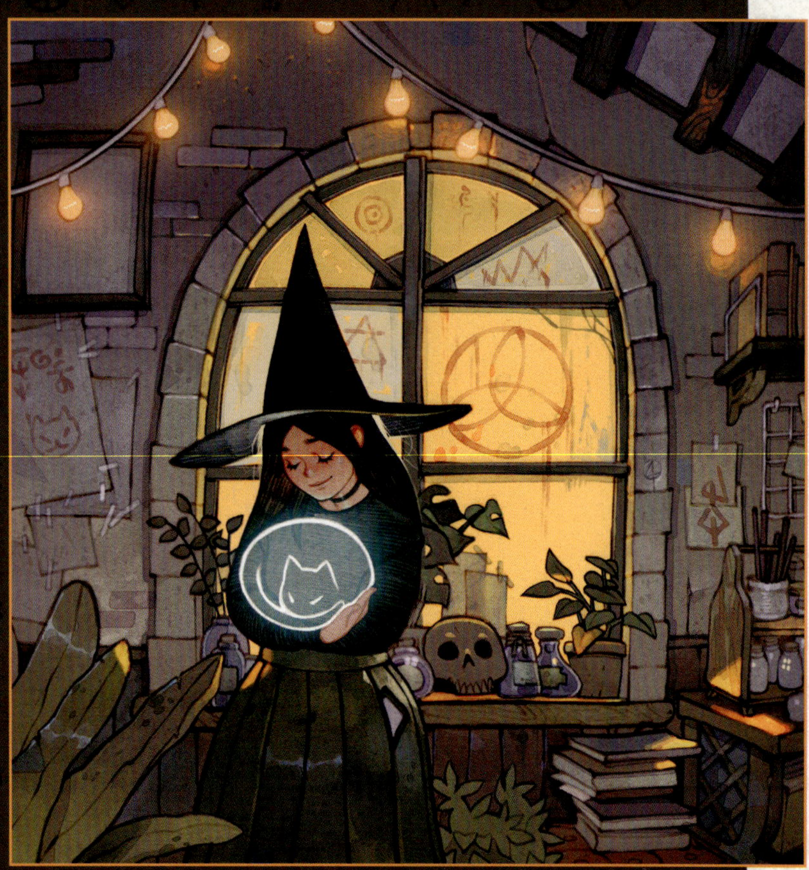

07: Glow up

Ah, this is one of my favourite parts!

In this step, I focus on creating a soft glow around the light bulbs. I also add some highlights to the bottom-right corner of the desk, and to the plant near the bottom-left. I normally save highlights for the very end, as there is certainly such a thing as 'too much'. If you're not careful, they can overpower the rest of the illustration in the same way that too much salt can ruin your dinner. To enhance your image, you just need to sprinkle a little here and there. Doing the opposite means you risk losing track of your main subject.

I had to learn to use these effects sparingly. For me, ninety-nine per cent of an image has to be traditionally rendered.

08: Here we glow again

In this final step, I take the previous concept a little further and add more glow behind the character. For me, it gives off a mystical aura. I also add details to the windows, and write text on the posters.

And there you have it! The cover for my first art book is complete! I hope you enjoyed following along.

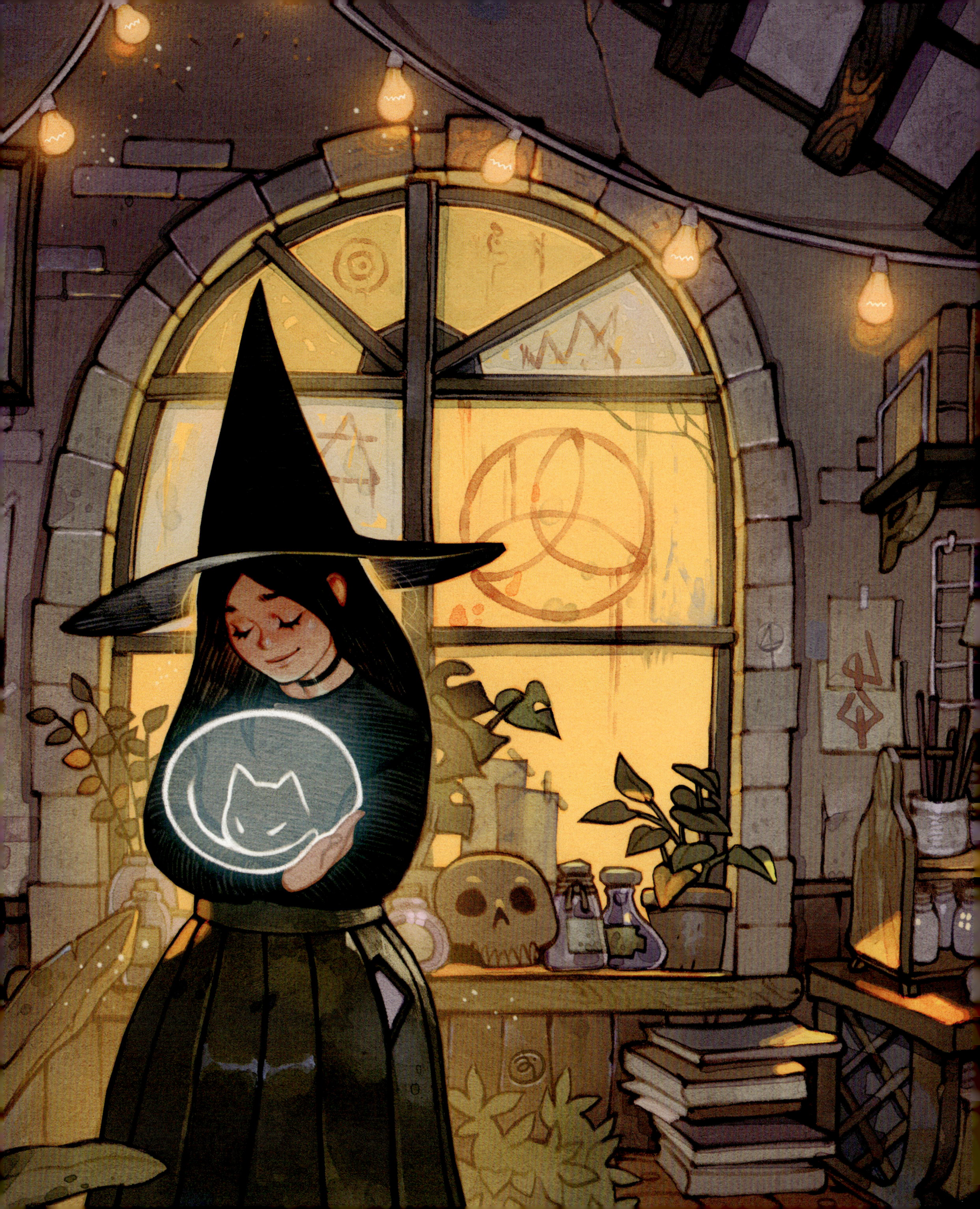

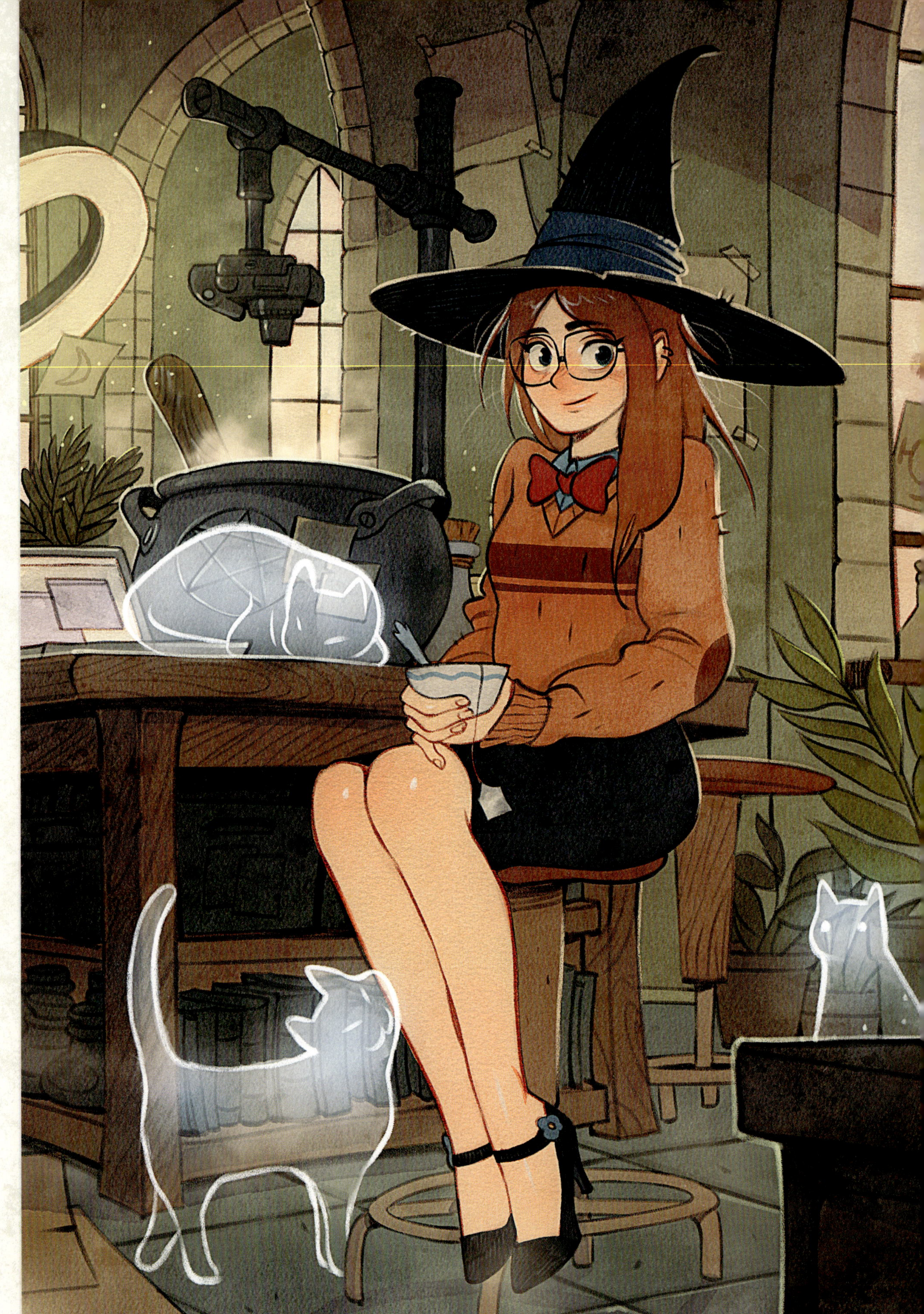

PLANNING AHEAD

In the future, I just want to continue being an illustrator. My goal has always been to draw, and so far, so good! As long as there are people who enjoy what I do, and I get the same joy from working on my illustrations, I'm happy. It's all I could ask for.

A goal of mine for the next few years is to become an author. By continuing my comics, I hope that Ghost Cats and Tea will grow so that I can create something that branches outside the illustrator niche and into projects that involve other content creators. I'm already working on the comic and with a publisher, but who knows! I could segue into animation, or video games … it's all connected to my current project.

In a nutshell, my objective is to create an even bigger project with a larger reach.

THANK YOU

My first and biggest thanks goes to my community who have supported me from the get-go. Without all of you, I would never have made it to where I am today, and you would certainly not be reading this book in your hands.

A big thank you to my parents for supporting and helping me, especially when I really needed it. Although it was hard to initially convince you that art was a viable career, you still believed in me, and you are now my number-one fans.

I would also like to thank my girlfriend for bearing with me through all the days and nights spent drawing.

Finally, thank you to my school for forming me as an artist, even though it wasn't as the specific kind of artist I am today. The most important aspect of my career is not my skills in illustration, but more the creative approach that I learned from the Accademia di Belle Arti di Napoli.

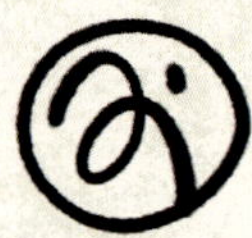

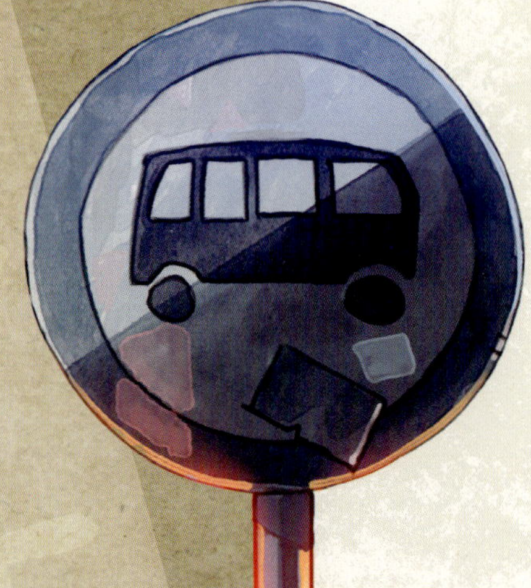

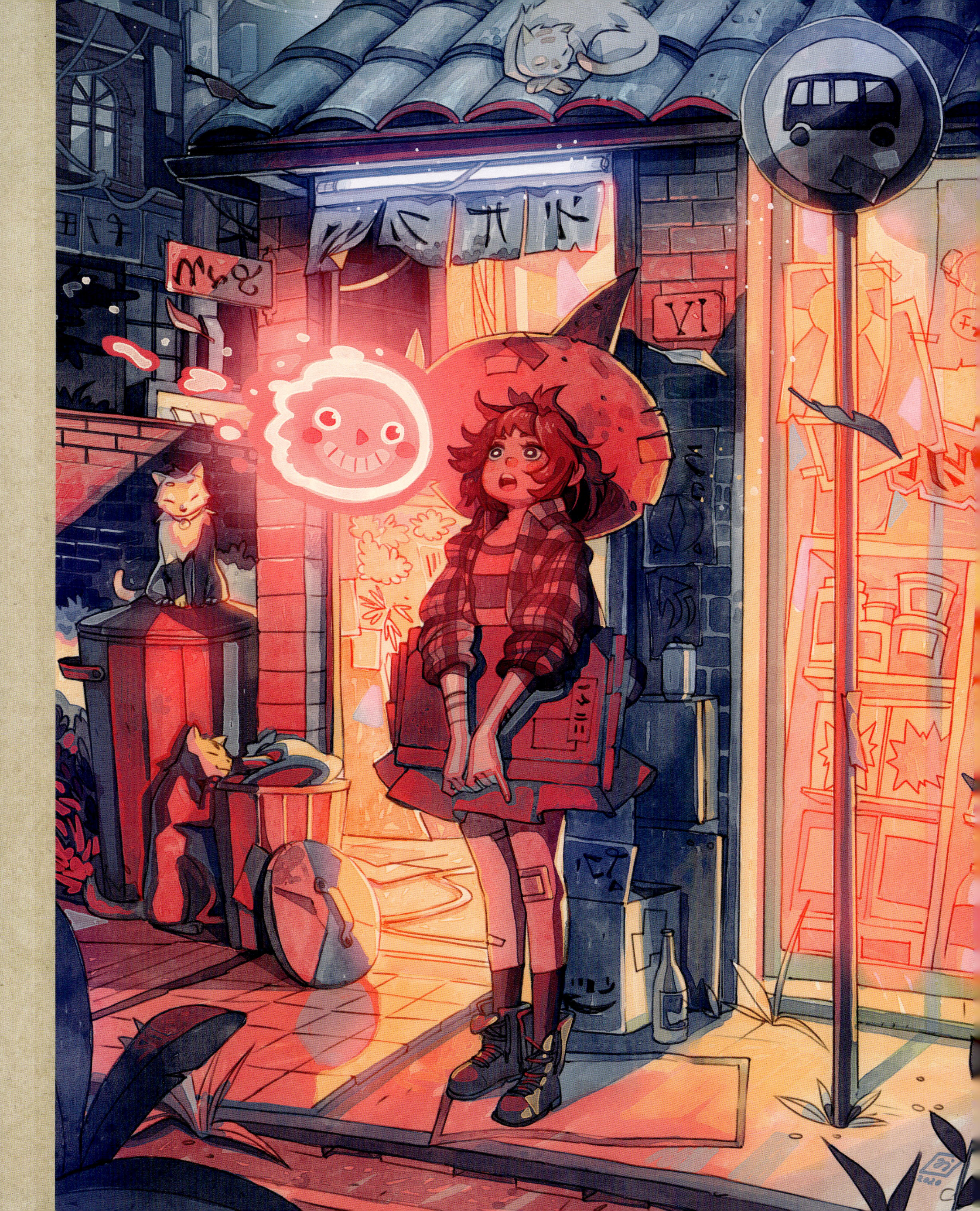

3dtotal Publishing

3dtotal Publishing is a trailblazing, creative publisher specializing in inspirational and educational resources for artists.

Our titles feature top industry professionals from around the globe who share their experience in skillfully written step-by-step tutorials and fascinating, detailed guides. Illustrated throughout with stunning artwork, these best-selling publications offer creative insight, expert advice, and essential motivation. Fans of digital art will enjoy our comprehensive volumes covering Adobe Photoshop, Procreate, and Blender, as well as our superb titles based around character design, including *Fundamentals of Character Design* and *Creating Characters for the Entertainment Industry*. The dedicated, high-quality blend of instruction and inspiration also extends to traditional art. Titles covering a range of techniques, genres, and abilities allow your creativity to flourish while building essential skills.

Well-established within the industry, we now offer over 100 titles and counting, many of which have been translated into multiple languages around the world. With something for every artist, we are proud to say that our books offer the 3dtotal package:

LEARN | CREATE | SHARE

Visit us at 3dtotalpublishing.com

3dtotal Publishing is part of 3dtotal.com, a leading website for CG artists founded by Tom Greenway in 1999.

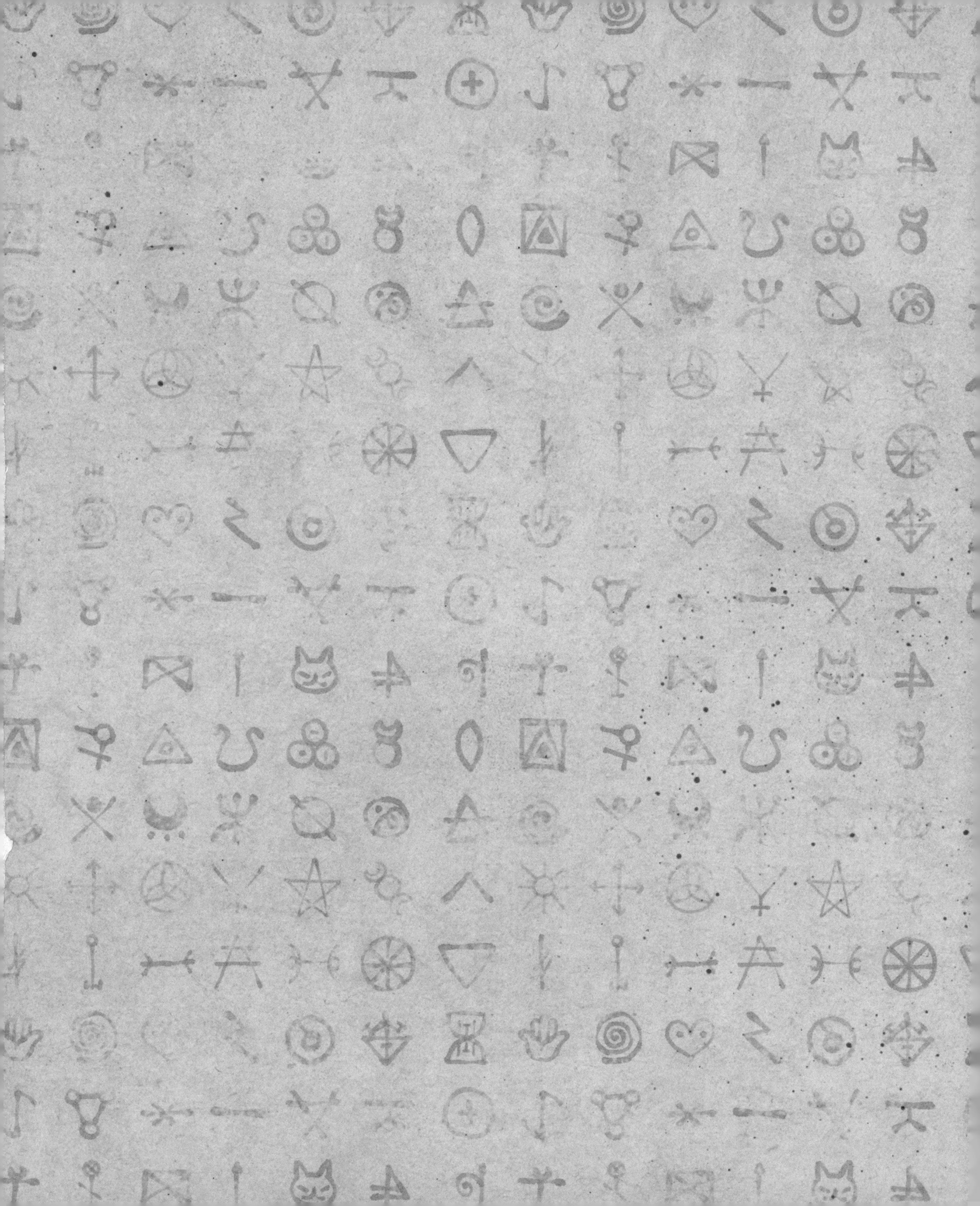